NAMES ARE THICKER THAN BLOOD

Kinship and Ownership amongst the Iatmul

NAMES ARE THICKER THAN BLOOD

Kinship and Ownership amongst the Iatmul

by
Andrew Moutu

A British Academy Postdoctoral Fellowship Monograph

Published for THE BRITISH ACADEMY
by OXFORD UNIVERSITY PRESS

Oxford University Press, Great Clarendon Street, Oxford OX2 6DP

First edition published 2013
Reprinted 2015

British Library Cataloguing in Publication Data
Data available

Library of Congress Cataloging in Publication Data
Data available

Typeset by New Leaf Design, Scarborough, North Yorkshire
Printed in Great Britain
on acid-free paper by
TJ International Ltd, Padstow, Cornwall

978–0–19–726445–4

MIX
Paper from responsible sources
FSC® C013056
FSC www.fsc.org

Contents

Illustrations

Preface and Acknowledgements

Melanesia has been disproportionately influential in the development of anthropological methods and theory. As a Melanesian scholar who comes from a country that has been the subject of much anthropological thinking, the present exercise is an attempt to examine the foundational assumptions of social anthropology. In so far as this anthropology is driven by epistemological assumptions, the present argument seeks to imagine anthropology in reverse, in terms of an ontology. This book is a revised version of my doctoral dissertation (Moutu 2003), and derives its moral and intellectual inspiration principally from the profundity with which Marilyn Strathern has made me think about the nature of relationships in Melanesian societies. Incisive commentaries from my doctoral examiners, Simon Harrison and Stephen Hugh-Jones, have contributed much to the reshaping of this text and I record my gratitude for their interest and stimulation. Tony Crook had an equally incisive input with regard to its present editorial shape, but the limitations of this project remain my own. The Heideggerian imports of James Weiner and the figure–ground reversals of Roy Wagner also have a seminal influence in the theoretical position advanced here. No anthropologist could easily state the influence their ethnographic subjects have upon their thinking, and this is undoubtedly my experience with the people of Kanganamun village who inhabit the middle Sepik area of Papua New Guinea. The nature of kinship and the behaviour concerning ownership among this Iatmul people provide an ethnographic basis to embed the analytical posture articulated here.

Scholars are forever indebted to many institutions and people that provide financial, moral and intellectual support in the course of their careers. This book is written in the course of a postdoctoral fellowship awarded to me by the British Academy. The Academy has since extended its embrace to grant me a book contract from its postdoctoral monograph competition. I am extremely grateful and humbled by both of these awards from the British Academy. My graduate training in social anthropology was in Cambridge, and there I am indebted to several organizations which have provided funding towards my training. The British

Overseas Research Studentship, an Honorary Frazer Studentship and a studentship from the Cambridge Commonwealth Trust allowed me to commence studies between 1998 and 2002. The Wenner Gren Foundation for Anthropological Research was equally generous, providing me with a year's grant from its Developing Countries Training Fellowship, which complemented the funding that I received during the four years of my training in Cambridge. During my fieldwork, the Cambridge Smuts Memorial Fund provided me with a return airfare between London and Papua New Guinea. A grant from the Crowther Beynon Fund allowed me to make a small collection of Iatmul artefacts for the Cambridge Museum of Archaeology and Anthropology. A grant from the Ling Roth Fund, administered by the Department of Social Anthropology, came in good time to help with expenses as I was reaching the final stages of my PhD. I want to record my deepest gratitude to all these organizations and individuals for their financial support towards my training. I am also grateful to the Government of Papua New Guinea, which, through the PNG National Museum and Art Gallery, granted me a secondment in order to undertake graduate training and postdoctoral research. I record my sincere gratitude particularly to Soroi Marepo Eoe.

Many people have shaped my interest in anthropology. In PNG, these include Jacob Simet, Joe Ketan, Vincent Warakai, John Muke, Linus Digim Rina, Bill Sagir, David Lea, William Ferea, Claudia Gross and Steven Winduo, who have all encouraged and stimulated the progress of my scholarship. Mark Busse and Colin Filer showed a personal interest in developing a Papua New Guinean scholar to follow in their footsteps and, without their enthusiasm, my academic progress would have been impossible. Relatives from my native Araphesh village of Wautogik provided a different kind of intellectual inspiration. And of them I thank Bernard and Vergil Narokobi, Joe Gabut and Anthony Yauieb. I am also grateful to the support of Nick Manjina, Philip and James Moutu, Moses Jimgori, Dominic Sengi, Albert Mellam, Joe and Lyna Naguwean, William and Anna Nindim, Tony Naguwean, John Sileng and Mathias Nindim, Andrew Yauieb, Camilus Narokobi, Tony and Toby Gabuogi, Balthasar Ilowen and Michael Yagro. Other friends in PNG, including Paul and Thomas Hukahu, Tone Ute, Mange Matui, Samuel Koyama, Ian Marru, John Numa, Miran Solomon, Freda Bagai and Paraka Pena, provided me with support of various kinds.

In Cambridge, I am forever indebted to Marilyn Strathern, who thought it reciprocal to sponsor a Melanesian to undertake graduate training under her supervision. Her abiding generosity extends to include personal support, while her penetrating insights into Melanesian sociality are compelling. Drawing upon her ideas often makes me feel guilty of cheating with originality. Without her moral support and intellectual guidance, both my training and the current project would have been inconceivable. Anita Herle, of the Cambridge Museum of Archaeology and Anthropology, provided moral and intellectual support and co-curated with me the Iatmul exhibition entitled 'Paired Brothers' in that museum in 2004.

I benefited from the joint Cambridge–Brunel 'Property, Transactions and Creations' research project through many conversations with Marilyn Strathern, Eric Hirsch, Tony Crook, James Leach, Andy Holding, Adam Reed, Karen Sykes and Lawrence Kalinoe. Fellow graduate students and colleagues provided many stimulating conversations. I thank Kyle Rand, Martin Holbraad, Manpreet Janeja, Wenzel Geissler, Dawn Nafus, James Suzman, Fiona Scorgie, June Sato and John Friedman. James Leach and Tony Crook treated me as if I was a kin to them and the generosity of Andy Holding, Fleur Rogers, Emma Sutton, Gilbert and Ariane Lewis was of a similar order. Papua New Guineans in England brought a distant home closer and I thank Paul Laias Kandi, who studied in Cambridge between 2002 and 2003, David Katu in East London, Margaret Chant and her family in Kent and Jean Kekedo with her family in London.

Last but not least, I wish to thank the people of Kanganamun village, who took me in and made me become one of them. There are too many to name, much like their names that attracted me to their village in the first place. Those who have lodged their memories permanently in me include my adopted parents, Yarme Mambingawi and Veronica Marimbunjin, my closest friend and adopted brother, Lewis Yarme, and mentors including David Yaman, Raymond Amisongmeli and James Noru. Others who were of considerable help include Ismael Gramban, Cyril and Jack Kapi, Tobias Wali, Bonnie and Ben Mafa, Timothy Yanu and Freddy Kabrakamei, Alois Mondi, Michael Kanuat, Joseph Saungombi, James Lanjin, Luke Kamangari, Albert Lumutbange, Manuel Sumbakwan, Manuel Yarme, Martin, Mark and Jimmy Karue, Kambonamak and Theo Akanawi, Peter and Otto Truk, Francis Mam, Clement Kandapi, Vincent Yaman, Clement and François Yaman and Job Suat, at the PNG University of Technology.

The Iatmul say that 'all of us come from women'. There are three women who have cast the most lasting influence on me. These are Monica Barismon, my mother, Cecilia Moutu, my sister, and Esther Gaegaming, the love of my life. During my training, my family was absorbed into Esther's natal kin so I can't stop thanking Michael and Shirley Gaegaming and their daughters Margaret, Daisy and Susan, the twins and my Bougainvillean brother, Clement Totavun, who helped in my absence.

This book was written when Esther, Antonia, Michael, Ernst and I were residing together in Cambridge. We are extremely grateful for the memories Girton College has left in us through occupying its Front Lodge. I am also grateful to the Girton College Council for granting me the status of a non-stipendiary research fellow within the duration of my postdoctoral fellowship. Further editorial work on this book was done when I was the Leach/Royal Anthropological Institute Postdoctoral Fellow at the National University of Ireland Maynooth. I thank all these institutions for the opportunities that have made it possible for this monograph to be accomplished. While in Ireland, I came across a Papua New Guinean, Tine Ningal, studying for a PhD in Cartography at University College Dublin. Tine not only drew two of the maps in this book but also provided a constant supply of fresh humour that enlivened the charm and oddities of living in Ireland. As the preparation of this book was drawing close to its completion, Sophie Richmond came in as a thoughtful copy-editor whose help is both considerate to the author and kind to the reader.

The acknowledgements above are populated with names but there is still one significant name that is supremely pre-eminent in all things. Since this book is the first fruit of labour, it is dedicated to the One whose name is above all names . . . (Philippians 2: 9)!

Andrew Moutu
Girton College, Cambridge, January 2007

National Museum and Art Gallery
Port Moresby, 2012

Introduction

Anthropology and its presumption of social relations

The Sepik River Iatmul people, their famous *naven* ritual, and their first ethnographer, Gregory Bateson (1932, 1958), are equally well-known and of enduring importance to anthropology on either side of the Atlantic and in Australasia. Until very recently, anthropology has remained a Western analytical project for understanding and conceptualizing non-Western societies, and was often geared towards the pragmatics of colonial and post-colonial interest. In the spirit of social science, it has invented a rigorous method of research and a specialized language of description and analysis in order to reveal itself as a social science to its audience and practitioners while concealing from its research subjects that it was dealing with their form of social relations. Embedded within its methodological approach and analytical enterprise are metaphysical assumptions about the nature of human society, culture, history, power, knowledge, etc. This book offers a comment on that endeavour, and focuses on the way in which social relations are assumed and prefigured in its methodological approach in data-gathering and in the subsequent theorization. Written from the view-point of a Melanesian scholar who comes from a country that has been the subject of much anthropological thinking, this book examines the founda-tional assumptions of anthropology through an argument that seeks to imagine anthropology in reverse (cf. Kirsch 2006; Wagner 1975).

From a methodological standpoint, anthropologists have to enter into and insert themselves into a world already pregnant with social relations in order to study and make knowledge out of these social relations. Social relations are already assumed. In serving as the foundation of anthropology, social relations model both the subject matter and the method by which such relations are made visible through its specialized language of analysis. This leads to a basic confusion of the mode of elicitation and the object of analysis (Weiner 1993). Weiner observes that: 'because social relations are the pre-figured end-product of anthropological analysis, they model both our subject-matter and our procedures for making them visible . . . we continue to model our procedures and theories on the assumption of relationships . . . We confuse a mode of eliciting with the thing elicited' (2001: 73). Weiner (2001) holds that such confusion arises from a social constructionist attitude of aestheticizing social relations. The aestheticization of social relations is an unexamined analytical assumption that people's social and cultural practice is always about investing their energies in deliberately imbuing their world of experience with meaning and significance. Weiner argues to the contrary, through an argument based on cultural practices of revelation and concealment, which he uses to account for the place of the uncanny and dehiscence in human social life. For Weiner, such a dialectic of revelation and concealment exposes the way in which meaning, relationship and temporality run counter to the direction of human subjectivity and intention.

I discuss this here because the theoretical posture expressed in this book is partly inspired by an ingeniously critical question originally posed by James Weiner (1993). With arresting philosophical import, Weiner observed that if the Heideggerian version of phenomenological hermeneutics is a philosophical quest that seeks to fully resolve the question of Being, and if this question is a central theoretical motif in centuries of Western metaphysical speculation, at least according to Heidegger (1962), anthropology must also submit itself to a similar question about the ontological nature of social relations. In other words, the philosophical question of what is Being for Heidegger (1962) translates into what is social relations for the anthropologist. Weiner is calling for anthropology to examine, excavate, and lay bare the assumptions which are prior to and which inform anthropological method and analysis. However, Weiner (2001) has since developed his argument along a tangent that seeks to highlight the manner in which the dialectic of concealment and revelation imposes itself as a constraint upon human freedom and action. He utilizes the dialectical interplay of revelation and concealment to launch a blazing critique against what he identifies as a social constructionist approach that underlies the presumption of social relations in anthropology. The original question put forward by Weiner (1993) is eclipsed by his concern with concealment and revelation (Weiner 2001). In a sense then, this book attempts to resuscitate this question by arguing that the confusion Weiner identifies emanates not so much from a practice of aestheticizing social relations as from an unexamined epistemological economism that underlies the anthropological presumption of social relations.

One of the ethnographic artefacts that comes under heavy fire from Weiner's critique of social constructionism is the recent proliferation of 'indigenous video and film products', which attempt to represent indigenous subjectivity with a sense of realism and authorial authority that privileges the visual over the discursive (see Weiner 1997). One of the drawbacks of this televisualist project is the failure to 'distinguish between the *representation of relations* and a *relation to representative praxis*' (Weiner 2001: 136, original emphasis). For Weiner this is exemplified in a statement from a Kayapo Indian who observes that the sheer fact of him holding of a camera doesn't mean he is not a Kayapo. Weiner counters this by pointing out that the holding of a camera does not necessarily make a Kayapo Indian a film maker (2001: 136). Here, however, I want to push this question in a different direction. I am asking, not about indigenous video production as such, nor the attendant claims of representational politics, but rather about the question of 'indigenous anthropology' and the presumption of social relations. What kinds of assumptions underlie the anthropological preoccupations with social relations?

Rather than participating in the political rhetoric of indigenous anthropology that aligns itself so ubiquitously with the poetics and politics of representation, this book argues that it is the epistemological presumption of social relations that needs to be scrutinized in order to make an advance in anthropology's own understanding of its subject-matter. An analytical metaphor is therefore needed to ground such an argument. Thus one of the common analytical methods is the use of ethnographic data and theory as reflexive devices, which anthropologists use, much like mirrors, to reflect upon the social and cultural practices, as well as the moral and ideological assumptions, of their own society. This reflexive exercise is made possible through the invention of a specialized language of description and analysis that is inevitably rooted in particular metaphysical assumptions about the nature of social relations. This specialized language of analysis and description conceals a particular set of social relations in order to reveal it as a subject-matter which is of analytical value to anthropologists and their audience.

If the analytical metaphor of the mirror is an apt image of anthropology's reflexive project, then how does one imagine the question of an 'anthropology at home' (Jackson 1986; Peirano 1998), undertaken by the so-called 'indigenous scholars' in their own societies? How does an 'indigenous anthropology' imagine social relations, the fundamental bedrock of anthropology? When non-Western anthropologists study their own societies, does it necessarily follow that such anthropologists, trained in Western theories and method, must assume the same kind of presumptions that underlie metropolitan anthropology? If we still retain our mirror metaphor, it will be obvious to the reader that the image one sees in a mirror is possible only because one is looking into the mirror. But one wonders whether one could see anything from the back of the mirror? If one was looking at anthropology from the back of the mirror as it were, what kind of assumptions might underlie social relations? This string of rhetorical questions underlies the theoretical stance that shapes the thinking about anthropology and social relations that is expressed in this book. To this end, I contrive an analysis that seeks to conceive of relationships in ontological terms. In this vein, the direction of thinking here is indebted principally to the manner in which Marilyn Strathern (1988, 1996, 2001b, 2005) has conceptualized relationships.

In referring to my doctoral dissertation (Moutu 2003), her most recent exposition on the epistemological dimensions of relationships (Strathern 2005: 38, 49, 195) not only foreshadows this book but also provided the most compelling impetus, without which this project would have been delayed. This book may therefore be read as a counterpart to Strathern (2005). The argument is presented through a concern with issues of kinship and ownership. The first three chapters (Chapters 1–3) attempt to provide a basic ethnographic picture of Iatmul people and villages, as it appeared to this ethnographer during the period of fieldwork between June 2000 and October 2001. The three final chapters (Chapters 4–6) resort to the familiar method of anthropological comparison in order to illuminate and help specify the complexity evident in Iatmul understandings of kinship, marriage, and the naming system. The comparison employs ethnographic material from neighbouring societies (Ambonwari, Iatmul, and Manambu) in the Sepik River area and from the Highlands (Daribi and Iqwaye or Yogwoia) of Papua New Guinea. Map 1 locates the societies that are mentioned in this book.

Kinship and ownership among the Iatmul

This is an ethnographic study of the nature of personhood, name, and marriage systems, gender, kinship, and concomitant issues of ownership, all of which provide a vantage point to rethink the anthropological presumption of social relations. This book looks into the modes and behaviour of ownership as it is instantiated through items of cultural heritage, ritual action, and a system of personal names in Kanganamun, an Iatmul-speaking village on the Sepik River in Papua New Guinea (see Bateson 1932, 1958; Houseman and Severi 1998; Laycock 1965; G. Schuster 1990; M. Schuster

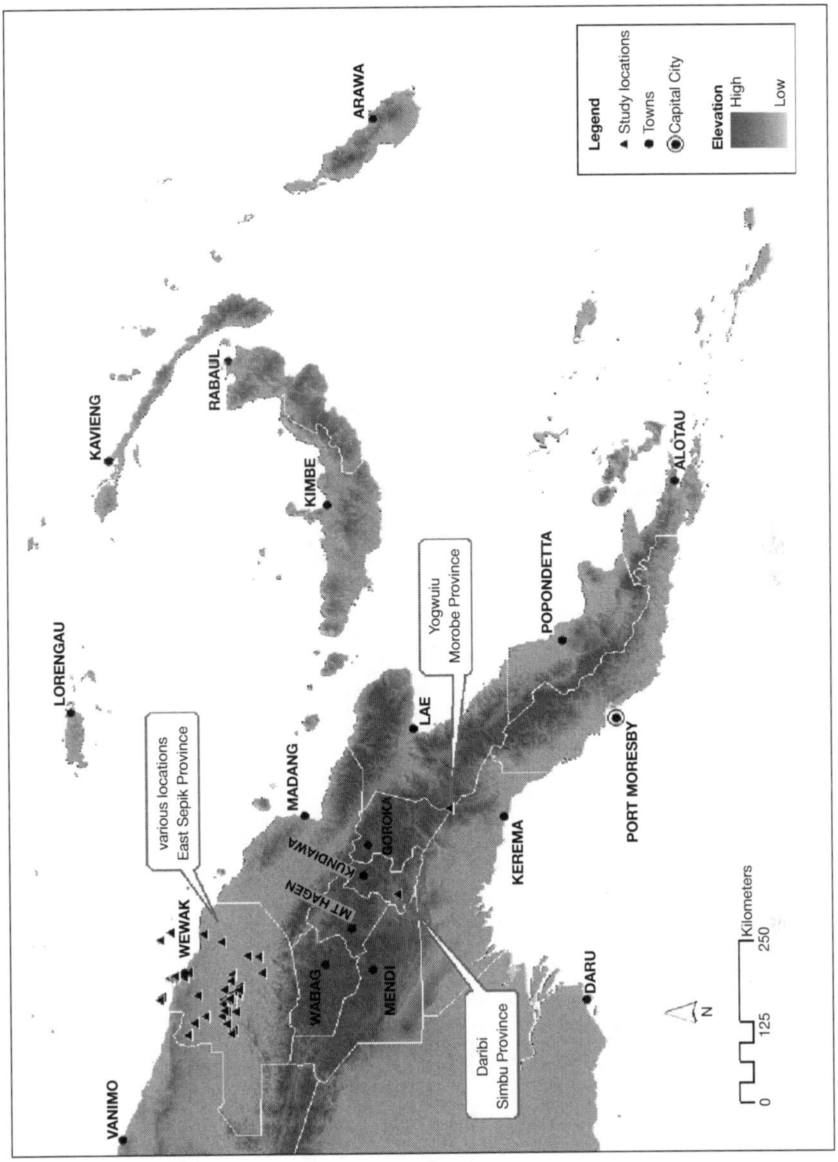

Map 1. Papua New Guinea showing general study locations and towns

1990; Silverman 1996, 2001; Stanek 1990; Wassmann 1990, 1991). Instead of the conventional anthropological style of furnishing ethnographic material to scrutinize ideological assumptions behind models of property relations, this book adopts the concept of ownership and shows how it appears in the context of a particular Melanesian village.

Whilst the book accepts the basic anthropological insight that ownership is a function of relationships (see Hann 1998; Leach 2001), it goes further to argue that ownership exercises itself as a constraint upon the relationships that exist and are enacted between people. Since ownership is also bound up with particular forms of sociality, personhood (Hann 1998; Hirschon 1984; Strathern 1984a), and temporality, the book will provide a description of the Iatmul concept of 'person' and temporality with respect to ownership and relationships. Although a language of personifying idioms is foreign to the Iatmul (or Melanesians in general) the analysis borrows such a language as an analytical strategy to assign both ownership and relationships an ontological character that may be extended beyond the confines of a particular ethnographic setting. Amongst the Iatmul, the concept of 'ownership' is known as *nyait*, the same word that is used in referring to one's 'father' (see also Bateson 1958: 84). Like a father who brings forth his progeny, the term 'father' implies a relationship, and so one could say that ownership is always embedded within a matrix of relationships in the same way an owner is implicated.

Based on an Iatmul style of asserting a claim of ownership, the temporal dimension of ownership will be discussed with a view to showing how time is constitutive of ownership, such that in synthesizing temporal 'moments' (see Gell 1992: 315, 1998: 238–9) 'ownership' asserts its abiding presence as a concern in the present 'now'. As will be shown, this ability of ownership to bring together seemingly disparate temporal moments is akin to the synthetic behaviour of relationships. And, as I will come to argue, it is the synthetic behaviour of relationships that provides us with a clue for thinking about the ontological status of 'relationships'. The language of personifying idioms employed here derives its inspiration from, and is indebted to, the manner in which Strathern (1996, 2001a, 2001b) has conceptualized 'ownership' and 'relationships' with her characteristically phenomenological wit. Ultimately, the book will use the ethnographic case as a particular instance to raise an ontological question about the category of 'relationships' that is employed by anthropologists in general.

At the time of my fieldwork, the Papua New Guinea (PNG) government was almost on the brink of collapsing financially. At that time, the government's purse was funded largely with money derived from the export of oil and mineral reserves in the Highlands of PNG. However, as is the case in many parts of PNG, compensation claims (see Filer 1997) by local landowners brought the process of extraction and export to a standstill for several months and the PNG national economy was almost crippled. Conferences and a dialogue of sorts were held to sort out this situation and the print media in PNG carried reports and reflections about the awesome power that 'ownership' commands and dispenses in a place as turbulent as PNG. Such media reports and commentaries describe 'ownership' as a very powerful phenomenon, with a potency to mobilize persuasive and compelling sentiments. In reminiscing about these events, I seek solace in a Strathernian observation that the world was going to witness 'an explosion of concerns with ownership' (Strathern 1998: 216).

According to Honoré (1961; also cited by Hann 1998: 6 and Reeve 1986: 17–18), 'ownership' is a defining institution of all human societies. Honoré makes a legal distinction between what he calls greater and lesser interests, and conceives of 'ownership' as the greatest possible interest in a thing whose ownership is legally recognized. As can be deduced from Honoré's exegesis, interest is defined in terms of a comparative advantage which is continuous with the ownership of a particular thing. Rights, on other hand, are defined in terms of the liberty, power, or dispositional control one has in making decisions or choices regarding the use and enjoyment of that which is owned. The owner(s) is/are the final arbiter over how and what is to be done to that which is owned (see also Christman 1991: 29).

Honoré (1961: 113–28) describes and enumerates eleven 'incidents' or elements which underlie the essence of ownership in a capitalist economy and these are: (1) the right to possess; (2) the right to use; (3) the right to manage; (4) the right to income; (5) the right to capital; (6) the right to security; (7) the incident of transmissibility; (8) the absence of term; (9) the prohibition of harmful use; (10) liability to execution; (11) the residual

[1] A summary of these 'incidents' is as follows. (1) The *right to possess* refers to the right to be in control and to remain in control over that which is owned, and this control restricts or forbids others to interfere with the owner's rights. (2) The *right to use* refers to the use and enjoyment of the thing owned. (3) The *right to manage* refers to decisions which are made about how and by whom a thing owned is to be used. This right is premised on a cluster of powers such as those of licensing, the power to admit and permit others the use (and enjoyment) of the thing owned, the powers to specify the conditions upon which the thing owned is used etc. (4) The *right to income* is a surrogate for use and refers to the benefit (including financial) or the use, for instance, of a rent-free house. (5) The *right to capital* refers to the power to alienate or modify the whole or part of the thing owned. (6) The *right to*

character.[1] According to Honoré ownership is a universal institution and one or more of the incidents are sufficient to make ownership visible and effective (see Lea 1997: 181–2). Although these 'incidents' are legal in character and relate specifically to the liberal notion of private or individual ownership, Honoré utilized this as a specific instance to provide an exegesis on the concept of ownership as such. We shall see how some of these incidents work in an ethnographic setting such as that of Kanganamun village. Writing with a focus on self-ownership, Christman (1991: 29) classifies these incidents outlined by Honoré into three categories: the primordial, derivative, and adjuncts to these initial two, which include:

> (a) the right to posses, use, manage, alienate, transfer and gain income from property. Derivative from these are (b) right to security in ownership, transmissibility (after death), and absence of term. Adjuncts to these elements are certain structural necessities of any system in the owner's array of powers and rights. These are the prohibition of harmful use, the residuary character and the liability to execution.

Christman's classification stems from a conception of ownership which is defined in terms of rights and powers, and sees liabilities as simply adjuncts, which are not constitutive of ownership. A particular ethnographic case discussed in this book will show that 'power' and 'liability' are necessarily constitutive of ownership depending upon the nature of the thing owned.

Legal notions of ownership, such as the one explicated by Honoré, have also been used in the theorization of Papua New Guinean forms of land tenure (Lea 1997) as well as riparian resources (Kalinoe 1999, 2001). Narokobi (1988) provides a linguistic and legal exposition on the Arapesh

---

security refers to being in control over the thing owned for an indefinite period of time so long as the owner remains solvent. (7) This right is a safeguard against expropriation, and ownership can only be transferred if a consensual agreement has been reached. Although it is related to the right to security, the *incident of transmissibility* makes visible how is 'projected upon the plane of time' (Honoré 1961: 120). This incident refers to an unlimited duration, when ownership is transferred to successive holders *ad infinitum*. (8) The *absence of term* refers to temporal limitations on the thing owned because of determinate and indeterminate factors (such as bankruptcy), which affect the rights of an owner. (9) *Prohibition of harmful use* refers to the careful use of that which is owned so that the use of that which is owned does not cause harm or injury to others. This incident might also be seen as a facility of accountability, which sometimes renders an owner susceptible to liabilities that stem from the use and enjoyment of that which he or she owns. (10) *Liability to execution* refers to the rights of an owner being taken away from him or her as a result of debt or insolvency. (11) *Residual character* refers what Honoré terms as 'corresponding rights', which come into play when ownership terminates. In such a case, there may be interests which are however less than ownership.

concept of ownership through a discussion of how land is acquired and managed through social relations in his Araphesh village of Wautogik (see Bashkow 2000, 2006). This present book is not directly concerned with landownership amongst the Iatmul but with relationships that grant them access to resources such as land and fishing lagoons. The first three chapters provide a general sense of the Iatmul people and their place; they specify the conditions under which the fieldwork was carried out; and outline the nature of social organization found amongst the Iatmul. The fourth chapter focuses on the Iatmul notion of *nyamun shambu*, the elder brother and younger brother, to articulate an Iatmul version of the 'fractal person' (Wagner 1991). This chapter also provides a prelude to the two final chapters that advance a theoretical understanding of Iatmul names. The final chapter reiterates the analysis provided in the book and suggests how an anthropologist might conceptualize relationships in ontological terms.

1

A Sense of People and Place

Canoes are our feet, canoes are our mothers.
(Makamoi, a woman of Kanganamun)

Villages are like canoes fastened to a pole on the banks of the Sepik. Without stories villages go adrift like a canoe set loose on the river.
(Raymond Amisongmeli, a man of Kanganamun)

Missing canoes

'Canoes are our feet. We move around by and with the canoe to find food. Now that my canoe is gone, I am handicapped.' These were the words of Makamoi, wife of Timothy Nganu, an elderly woman in Kanganamun village. On that fateful morning, Makamoi was on her way to the fishing lagoon. However, as she went by where her canoe is usually moored by the banks of the Sepik River, she discovered that it was missing. She checked around the bank where all other canoes were berthed but came to the stubborn conclusion that some ill-intended person had insidiously set loose her canoe in the cover of the night and allowed it to drift down the river. Makamoi returned to her house to discover that her husband had already gone into Wolimbi *ngeko*[1] where a men's meeting was under way. Thus she pursued him there to inform him of the fate that had befallen them. Timothy had made the canoe from a tree taken from his own clan land, for Makamoi to use in fishing, going to market or for the general purpose of movement between different places of her choice. After informing her husband and one of the village *komiti*,[2] she extracted her husband from the meeting and they set off down the river in pursuit of the missing canoe.

[1] *Ngeko* is the Iatmul word for the ceremonial men's house.
[2] *Komiti* is *Tok Pisin* (from the English 'committee') and it refers to an introduced form of leadership, i.e. to an office holder; this leader serves under a village councillor (*kansol*).

They located the canoe in the Eastern Iatmul village of Kamanimbit and had to pay K25 (approx. £6.25) to reclaim it from the man who took custody of it when he saw it drifting aimlessly down the river.

Makamoi later told me that they had to bargain with that man to reduce the price he was charging them to return her canoe. She said villagers downstream are often greedy because they claim 'ownership' of stray canoes too quickly. Timothy explained that the man who took custody of the canoe argued that he could have allowed the canoe to continue its aimless drift, but he took it in for his own purposes and so the canoe was now his. Timothy did not want to argue over it and, because he had recently made that canoe, and because there seemed to be no possibility of getting it back freely, they had to pay for it. Another man who heard about this incident told me of a similar experience that happened to him. However, in his case, he was lucky to get back the vessel without paying anything for its return because the person downstream who picked up his canoe was the son of a classificatory sister of the man's clan in that village. He noted that when stray canoes are found and brought into the custody of persons who are related to the owner of that canoe, the discovery by its owners provides a chance to reaffirm and consolidate kinship ties and commitments. The custodians of such a canoe would say: 'The canoe knows where and who its relatives are and it has gone straight to them, so that by them, it can return to whom and where it belongs.'

Canoes and the riverine economy

These two vignettes provide some leads for the reader to develop a sense of the geography, economic livelihood as well as an example of the sorts of (clan) relationships that prevail in Iatmul villages. Because the area is a riverine environment with seasonal inundation, canoes are the major means of transportation within and between Iatmul villages. Most of the canoes are built during the dry season when men go off, often in pairs, to work (on the canoes) in the bush nearby. Canoes are made from logs taken from trees grown or found on land owned by a man's clan or lineage. Building a canoe is an arduous process; it can take up to four or more weeks for one canoe to be ready before it is used. Men as well as teenagers often help and reciprocate each other's help in working on their canoes.

They share and borrow appropriate tools for work. Often expert canoe makers, especially the older men, are engaged to help young men fix up their canoes. Each house in the village has several canoes, and ideally each person should have a canoe of his or her own. Children within a family often share canoes, while their parents have separate canoes. The man who has more than one wife must have a canoe for each of his wives. Husbands (or fathers) as well as their grown-up sons are expected to make canoes for their wives (or mothers and sisters), daughters and other small children in a family. Under particular circumstances, people share the use of their canoes or borrow canoes from one another. But sometimes, when a canoe is borrowed in order for the borrower to go to a market, for instance, the owner may be given a reward of some sort for the use of his or her canoe. The paddles used with the canoes are produced by neighbouring Sawos villagers, and are then sold to the Iatmul people. The Sawos people are also the producers of sago, the staple starch of the Iatmul. Previously, the Iatmul women used to engage in barter exchange (*wenga*) with their Sawos neighbours through the use of their fish to get sago. This has now changed and money is fast becoming the main medium of exchange for the acquisition of sago, fish, and other comestibles. Such exchanges, as well as the production of fish and sago, are activities undertaken primarily by women in Iatmul and Sawos villages respectively. Occasionally, however, Iatmul men do go fishing and attend markets to acquire sago for their families.

Like the canoes which are made from a man's own clan trees, so do women fish in lagoons which are owned by their husband's clan, and unmarried daughters use the lagoons of their father's clan. Women married into other villages are denied the right to fish in lagoons which are owned by their father's village. If the Iatmul women need their men to make them canoes and houses, then the men require their women to provide them with fish and sago.[3] Canoes allow women to go fishing in their husband's clan waters and to bring such fish as they catch not only for their families to consume but to acquire sago through market exchange. On average, a Kanganamun woman brings home around 7–9 kg of fresh fish each day. Some of these fish are eaten while others are smoked over fire stoves and preserved to be consumed later or sold in markets. The money earned from such sales is used to acquire food such as sago and other household goods such as kerosene, salt, and soap for their families. Weekly markets are sometimes held on Fridays in Kanganamun village, or in a place located on a track connecting the Iatmul village of Yenjan and the Sawos village of Nangusap. A fortnightly market usually takes place in the Sawos village of Marap. When women (as well as men) attend markets held in other villages, they often travel together in pairs in their canoes.

[3] A comparable point is made by Strathern (1998: 227) who observes that Hagen men not only need women to produce pigs for them, 'but that women need pigs to produce men'.

Kanganamun men and women often tell me that if they were given the choice of travelling either by foot or by canoe, the latter would always be preferred. If their bodied feet allow them to walk on land, then canoes are their feet that allow them to walk on water. Canoes are a means of transportation and they also epitomize local idiomatic understandings. Expanding from this immediate instrumental relationship between people and canoes is an idiom that portrays canoes as an extension of the human body. In particular canoes are described as 'feet', while in other contexts canoes are metaphorically associated with the body of mother. The capacity of canoes to 'carry' people and things is analogous to the ability of mothers to bear children and carry other things, such as food items, firewood, and cooking utensils, the appurtenances which are culturally associated with women. The metaphorical association between canoes and mothers is widespread in other Sepik River villages as well (see Barlow and Lipset 1997; Harrison 1982: 152, 1993: 31; Silverman 2001: 77; Telban 1998: 17, 174–5).

At the level of cosmological understandings, canoes feature in a striking imagery of rest and motion. 'A village is like a canoe, stories (*sagi*) are like the erima tree.' This was a statement made to me by two Kanganamun men as they were explaining to me the relationship between a name and a person who is given a particular totemic name. 'Every village is sitting on stories, and stories are big things to us. Just as a canoe is fastened to a pole when it is moored to prevent it from drifting away by the tidal currents, stories are like the erima (*wani*) tree [scientifically known as *octomeles sumatrana*], the pole by which villages are fastened.' In esoteric mythology, the *wani* tree would be a metaphorical referent for primal crocodiles, which are responsible for the establishment of the cosmos. In mythology, the Iatmul region as well as the entire Sepik River basin was once a primal ocean called Maramba, an account which curiously echoes archaeological evidence about an inland sea which existed in the area during the Pleistocene period (see Swadling et al. 1988: 14–15, Swadling 1990: 71–86). After that primal ocean was drained by cosmological heroes, the Sepik River emerged and the ocean shrank in size to become what is now the Chambri Lakes (see Gewertz 1983; Wassmann 1991).

Physical geography

The Sepik River basin in which the Iatmul region is located ranges in altitude between sea level and 300 metres. Tidal patterns of the sea therefore affect the flood level that the Iatmul region experiences in terms of seasonal inundation. In common with other parts of PNG, the Iatmul region goes through wet and dry seasons. The dry season runs between the months of May and October and the wet seasons begins in November and ends in April. Associated with these seasons are different kinds of economic and social activities that people engage in throughout a year. For instance, the wet season is the time when men in particular fell and accumulate logs for building their houses during the dry season. Ideally canoes are made during the dry season, but the sudden onset of the wet season may force men to immediately commence making canoes for their wives and children if they do not have canoes as yet. An advantage of the wet season, which is always remarked upon, is that inundation compresses time and space. Because two points are connected by water, it takes less time to travel between them as compared to the dry season when water is absent. For children, inundation provides new and interesting places called *ndau* for their water games, and they enjoy climbing and jumping off from high tree branches into the water below them. It is also during the wet season that men and young boys go off on hunting expeditions to look for eggs of different species of birds which make their nests in grasses pitched above the reach of water. The dry season provides an opportunity for men to make small gardens to grow particular food crops such as *kaukau* (sweet potatoes), yams, sugar cane, pumpkin, melon, *aibika* greens, and other plant crops which are ready to harvest before the next wet season. Depending on where they are going to, travel during the dry season alternates between walking and canoeing, whereas if the place is completely inundated, people travel only by canoes. If the flood covers the whole village, people may have their bath and even sit for toilet outside their houses. In view of rising flood levels, Iatmul houses are built upon high stilts. The floors of houses are built with enough flexibility to be moved if the flood level reaches up to and encroaches on the floor.[4] It is the task of men to build and maintain their houses, and while an individual man builds his own house, his relatives and close friends also help him from time to time. Work on building the house itself takes

[4] The floors, which are made from the *limbum* palm, are semi-permanent and are easily moved and replaced when necessary. The floors lie on more or less permanent beams, but when the water level reaches the floor during the wet season, particular logs which are light and act as rafters are put on the beams which then lift the floor up. When necessary more such rafters are added until the ceiling is reached, then the people seek temporary refuge in places which are upon higher ground (see also Wassmann 1991: 8). The last time people had to lift the floors in their houses in Kanganamun village was in 1973.

place during the dry season, while the collection and accumulation of building materials is done during the wet season.

Building materials are taken from one's own clan land. In Kanganamun, clans which belong to Wolimbi *ngeko* have their land and forested areas to the east, while those of Minjimbit and Kosimbi have theirs to the west of the village. (This reference to the clanship and the three ceremonial houses will be explained in the Chapter 2.) The vegetation of the region is characterized mainly by pockets of riverine forests interspersed with patches of sago swamps and areas of grassland which are marshy and inundated from time to time. The Iatmul region as a whole is bordered by huge expanses of lowland—swamps and stagnant water areas covered in densely matted grasses. Stands of wild sugar cane (*sacharum robustum*) and the phragmites reed grace the mud banks of the Sepik River (see also Harrison 1990a: 12). Aquatic plants such as the wild sugar cane and even the Sepik River itself are owned as totems by specific clans in Iatmul.

The headwaters of the Sepik River are located on the mountains along the international border between PNG and the Indonesian province of West Papua. About 1,200 km in length and with variations in its width, the Sepik runs tortuously in an easterly direction, like a mysterious serpent stretching and winding its way through alluvial flood plains.[5] As it runs through, it brings and deposits heaps of sediment and other debris along the banks and meanders, before releasing volumes of 'dirty water' into the Bismarck Sea. The tidal current on the river flows at about 5 knots and increases during the wet season. The water on the river appears opaque in colour, resembling coffee mixed with a bit of milk, while in lagoons the colour of the water is terrifyingly dark. Because the Sepik is surrounded by a range of mountains on either side of its banks, such as the Torricelli mountains to the north, strong winds descend from these lofty heights and speed through the basin at several knots often causing the waters on the river to turn rough and choppy. The Iatmul have two totemic names for such winds: Walilakwa, which blows in a southerly direction, is associated with trading, and the Balalakwa, which blows from a northwestly direction, is associated with rain and the wet season. Both of these two winds are also owned as totems. During the evenings, when the sky flickers with sparks of lightning that illuminate distant horizons, I am often told that the electric red and gold colour in the sky portends sunny days ahead, while a dull gold surrounded by silver-coloured clouds suggests the imminent arrival of rain.

[5] This poetic portrayal of the Sepik River as a serpent is based on Iatmul totemic understanding (see also Bateson 1958: 224–5).

The Sepik is not a river of tranquillity, as it is often portrayed in some tourist magazines. Intermittently it changes its course and this erases or inscribes new banks, inundates new or old grassland, or recedes from old grassland. It may create or abandon oxbow lakes and fishing lagoons.

It is said by many in Kanganamun that the Sepik gives and takes away land and fishing lagoons. The power of the river is often utilized to create new fishing lagoons and we will be considering one such lagoon in Kanganamun village. The village itself is already popular in the ethnographic literature. It is the men of Kanganamun who featured prominently as the informants and the ideal types of personalities described in Bateson's (1958) ingenious yet dense ethnographic theorization of the Iatmul *naven* ceremonial. It was also in Kanganamun village that the intellectual exchange that led to the romance between the pioneering anthropologists, Margaret Mead and Gregory Bateson, took place (Lipset 1982). My own decision to undertake research in Kanganamun was motivated by the fact that one of its *ngeko*, namely Wolimbi, was declared in the 1960s to be part of Papua New Guinea's national cultural heritage. I was particularly interested to look at the dynamics of 'ownership' which surround such a cultural monument. In his ethnography, Bateson (1958: Plate VIIA) described Wolimbi *ngeko* as 'the finest ceremonial house in any of the river villages'. Unsurprisingly, it attracted the interest of Papua New Guinea's colonial administrators so that in 1965 it was declared, by legislation, to be part of PNGs cultural heritage (see Busse 2000: 81–95). The current *ngeko* in Kanganamun village is the third one to be built since the one that was so declared collapsed. It is built on the same location and retains the same structural (social) and architectural (physical) configurations as its predecessors. Despite the changes Wolimbi has seen, it is considered to be the same ceremonial house under the terms of the national heritage legislation.

Kanganamun village

Kanganamun village lies along the northern bank of the Sepik River. On a topographic map it is located on the following approximate bearings: 4° 12′ South latitude and 143° 17′ East longitude. It is surrounded by an area of forest, within which are tracks that lead to its fishing lagoons, garden land, as well as to the neighbouring Iatmul and Sawos villages located further inland from the northern bank. Lying on the river in front of the village is a small island which has emerged in the last 40 years as a result of sedimentation and accumulated debris. Due to constant accumulation of debris and sedimentation, the western tip of the island is expressing an inclination to merge with the northern bank of the river, the side on which the village is located. Several Kanganamun people have individual plots where they make small gardens on the island. To the east of the village are three fishing lagoons controlled by clans of Wolimbi *ngeko*, and there is another such lagoon on the other side of the Sepik River near an Iatmul village called Maringe. To the west of Kanganamun is the neighbouring Iatmul village of Yenjan (see Schmidt 1990). Beyond the tall column of trees, which rises at the back of the village, are some kilometres of grassland and swamp that run into the border with the neighbouring Sawos village of Gekorobi (see Schindlebeck 1990).

Kanganamun is surrounded by villages on all sides; it is part of the group of villages which live around the Central Iatmul area, and both the people and the villages are locally known as Parimbe. The Iatmul people think of themselves as belonging to three groups: the Nyaura (Western Iatmul), Parimbe (Central Iatmul), and Woliagwi (Eastern Iatmul). A common myth of origin is that their ancestors emerged from a hole in the ground located near the present-day Sawos village of Gekorobi (see Wassmann 1990, 1991). The Western Iatmul (Nyaura) tend to have historical accounts of their genealogical connections and other relationships with Parimbe villages, more so than with the Eastern Iatmul who are further away from them (see Wassmann 1991: 12), whereas the Central Iatmul people tend to have stories about both the Eastern and Western Iatmul villages. The Iatmul people understand their area to be divided into four main regions. (1) The area to the north and occupied by their Sawos neighbours is called Mivimbit—a term which is often explained in *Tok Pisin* as '*as graun*'—the ground of origin—or the cradle of humanity. The people who inhabit Mivimbit are called Sawos, a term which means the bush people. (2) The area to the south of Kanganamun beyond the Iatmul villages is called Kambrangawi and the people who inhabit these areas are called Kambrangawi *numungi*, meaning people of distant places. (3) The area occupied by Eastern Iatmul villages and beyond is called Woliagwi and the people there are called Woliagwi *numungi*—meaning people of the floating grassland. (4) The area inhabited by the Western Iatmul villages and beyond is called Yambun (see also Bateson 1932: 253; Wassmann 1991: 11), which refers to the upper-course of the Sepik River.

Anecdotal accounts report that Parimbe used to be one big village and all the people who now live in other Central Iatmul (even Eastern and Western villages) lived together in this big village. Through the process of fission arising out of particular disputes, people began to move to other

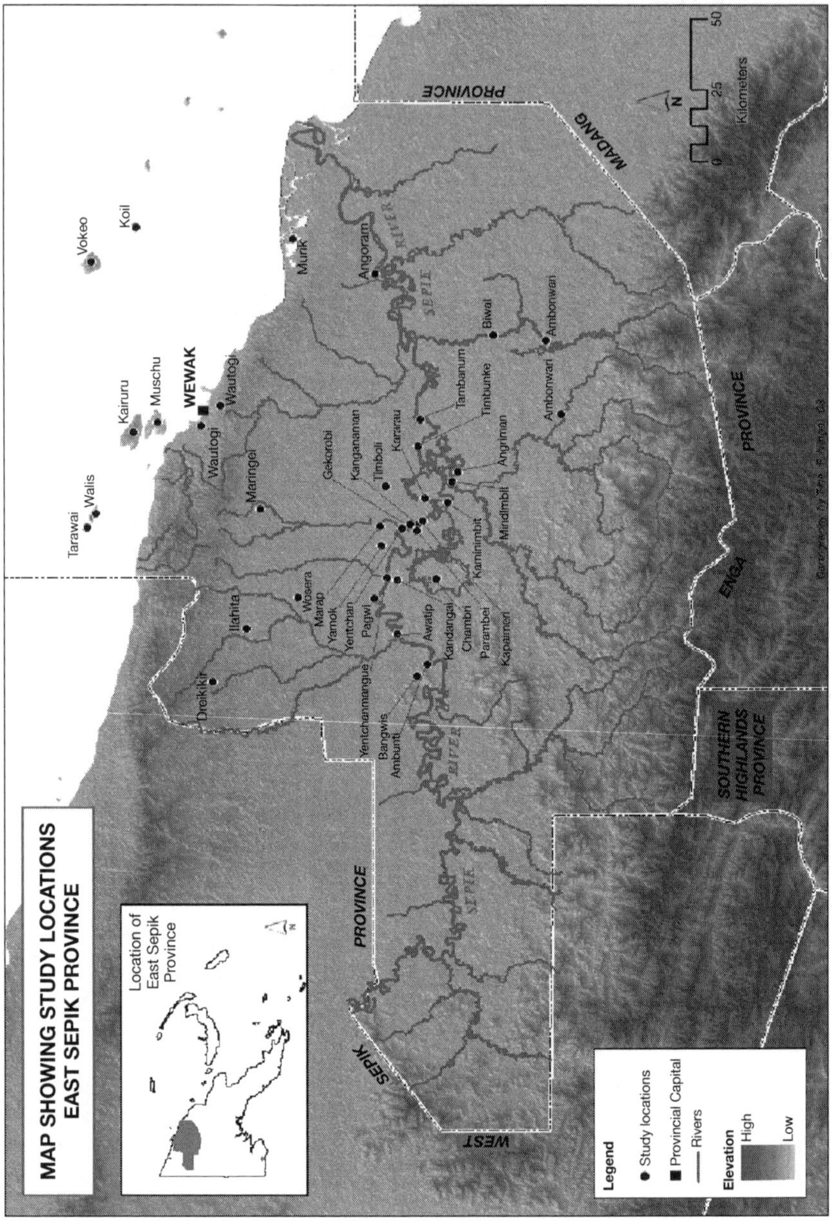

Map 2. Study locations, East Sepik Province

places, and with these movements came villages which sprout and 'proliferate like the rhizomes of the lotus'—to invoke Bateson's metaphoric description (see Bateson 1932: 419, 1958: 94, 236). 'One of the contending groups then leaves the village and founds a colony elsewhere, but with the same sort of norms as the parent community' (Bateson 1958: 107). Kanganamun is considered as the 'elder son' village of Parimbe, followed by Maringe the 'second born', and Yenjan the 'last born'. What are now Sotmeri and Indabu villages are recent offshoots of Maringe and Parimbe villages respectively. The remnants of that big historic village make up what is now Parimbe, the 'root or origin village' of the Central Iatmul people. A conflict stemming from adulterous liaisons with a particular woman in Parimbe forced men of certain clans to move across the Sepik River to start Kanganamun village.

However, there are conflicting claims over which clans actually started the village, and members of some clans would say that they did not come across from Parimbe but from other Sawos villages. Consequently there are two groups of people in clans in Kanganamun which are categorized as '*tepma nimba*' and '*yakua min*'. *Tepma nimba* literally means 'coconut people' and makes reference to the people who originally settled in the village and planted coconut trees as a gesture of their colonial presence within that area. '*Yakua min*' literally means 'come-man' and makes reference to persons who have a recent history of settlement in the village, and by recent I mean in the last 150 years or so. The plots of land which are closest to the village are all owned by clans categorized as the 'coconut people' while the 'come-man' do not own such land and are forced to go and cultivate unnamed land areas, which are often located further away from the village. Apart from land bound up with totemic names, land ownership in Kanganamun is based on historical precedence so that the first person who 'cuts *pitpit*' (wild sugar cane) and makes his or her garden on that parcel of land can claim ownership over it. Land areas which are known by totemic names are owned by the clans which own such names. Not all land areas have personal names, because of the movement of the Sepik River, which gives new and takes away old land areas when it changes its course. Therefore some areas of land, which are newly created by the activities of the river, are not cultivated and therefore are still yet to be owned; however, such land generally comes under the control or sovereignty of a particular village, and it is the inhabitants of that village who are allowed to make gardens in areas which are not yet cultivated. 'What is not owned exists either to be owned as some future resource not yet exploited or else is notionally owned by [the villagers] in general, including the generations to come' (Strathern 2001a:

12). In this context, ownership of unnamed land areas exists as a potential to be realized through the injection of creative work, whereas land that is already named is already owned and cannot be created anew.

The majority of the people of Kanganamun, much like other Iatmul villagers, have emigrated and now squat as settlers in the towns of Wewak, Madang, Bulolo, Rabaul, and the cities of Lae and Port Moresby. Only seldom do such people in towns return to the village. It is mainly the people now living in the village who travel between the village and the urban centres. Families that have relatives living and working in urban centres sometimes remit money to their relatives in the village. At the time of my fieldwork, the population of Kanganamun numbered a total of 238 men, women, and children, scattered in 55 individual residential houses, which are understood as economic units. There were six babies born to different women, and two others died some few weeks after they were born. Although the Iatmul live in a mosquito-infested area, they have developed a remarkable degree of resistance to malarial infection, but other illnesses such as colds, flu, and dysentery are experienced intermittently.

Often people ascribe the outbreak of colds and flu to the seasonal flowering of wild sugar canes, which emit particular viruses responsible for the infections. Skin diseases such as grille (a fungal infection) and scabies are limited to a very few cases. The Catholic Church, operating through its Health Centre in Timbunke, sends its officers to carry out monthly clinic patrols to the village. However, such patrols are intended mainly to provide immunization to newborn babies and to carry out pre- and post-natal checks on mothers. Villagers with serious illnesses are often taken by motorized canoe down the river to Timbunke, which is about three hours downstream. To the outsider, the most serious health hazard facing the villagers is having good and clean drinking water. There are two water tanks established in the village by a Christian mission organization based in Ambunti, the nearest government station on the river located several hours upstream beyond the Manambu region (Harrison 1990a). One of these tanks serves the people of Wolimbi while the other serves those of Minjimbit and Kosimbi. However, during the dry season the tanks become empty and people rely on water taken from the mainstream Sepik River. As happens daily, people use their hands to cup and drink water taken directly from the Sepik.

Kanganamun used to host a reputable Catholic Mission station, which served the whole of middle Sepik by the 1960s. The station, located in an area of land called Kapaimari, used to host a small airstrip, a Church building, and a priest's house, as well as a primary school. Many educated people from the middle-Sepik area who are now employed and living in different parts of PNG received their primary education at Kapaimari. This station has been closed since the early 1990s, however, due to landowner complaints as well as theft and vandalism on Church property. Now the nearest school, established by the government, is about 20 minutes away in canoe-time from Kanganamun. The new school is located on the southern bank across the river from Yenjan village. However, for all sorts of reasons,[6] Kanganamun people have not been sending their children to that new school. Consequently there is an increasing number of children and teenagers who are illiterate in the village.

In terms of government administration, Kanganamun belongs to the constituency called Gawi and this includes Chambri (Errington and Gewertz 1987; Gewertz and Errington 1991; Gewertz 1983) and outlying areas such as Ambonwari (Telban 1998), as well as the Nyaura of Western Iatmul (Wassmann 1990, 1991). This constituency is represented by a person who is a member of the East Sepik Provincial Government. The small government station at Pagwi has also been closed as a result of the decline of government presence—a common phenomenon in many rural areas in PNG. The closest administrative centre is Maprik, or alternatively people have to travel to the provincial town in Wewak, located on the coast further north of the Iatmul region. The Iatmul are also represented by a Member in the National Parliament (MP) of PNG and they share an electorate with the people of Wosera, Abelam-speakers (Forge 1966; Kaberry 1941). At the time of the fieldwork, the MP for Wosera Gawi was Galos Yambui, who hails from the Wosera area of the electorate. During the time of fieldwork, I heard people of Western and Central Iatmul complain about being put in the same electorate as the Abelam, because they have little in common in terms of economic needs and electoral aspirations. They are planning to ask the PNG government to put them in an electorate that shares more in common with people on the Sepik River, so that their needs can be appro-

[6] Three reasons why Kanganamun people have not sent their children to this new school: (1) the school is located in a no-man's land, too far away from any village to take interest in it; (2) the school is operating under the name of Kapaimari Primary School and the subsidies from the government that should have gone towards restoring the school at Kapaimari are being diverted to this new school; (3) since its establishment, it has enrolled several grade six classes, none of whose students have made it to high schools in the province, in contrast to students at Kapaimari school. Parents want their children to go on to high school and some have instead sent their kids to stay with relatives elsewhere to be educated. Some have sent their children to attend the school located further inland in the neighbouring village of Nangusap.

priately addressed by their elected leaders, because they feel they are often neglected.

Some of these views were forcefully expressed by Mr Keman Kaman, a long-time village and political leader of the people of Parimbe villages, in a meeting held in his Yenjan village on the eve of national elections in 2002. Keman is one of the many kinds of leaders amongst the Iatmul but he epitomizes the leader who is knowledgeable in totemic mythology, and in oratory and ceremonial debate. He is very charismatic and kindly, hospitable. Other types of leaders in Iatmul villages would be village court magistrates, councillors (*kansol*), village committees (*komiti*), and leaders of various church organizations in the area. Each village in Central Iatmul has its own *kansol* and *komiti* but only one village court magistrate serves all the villages of Central Iatmul. In Kanganamun however, their *kansol* has left the village and is living in town. The leadership of the village therefore falls to the three village *komiti*, who represent three of the men's houses (*ngeko*) in the village. At the time of my fieldwork these *komiti* were David Yaman (Wolimbi), Cyril Kapi (Minjimbit), and Ismael Gramban (Kosimbi). The next chapter will provide details about the division of the village into totemic moieties and the men's house.

With respect to religion, the Iatmul—much like the rest of modern PNG—profess to be Christians by faith, but indigenous religious ideas and practices prevail and exist concurrently with the belief in the Christian God. There are three (Christian) religious denominations within the village, which include the Catholics, Seventh Day Adventists (SDA), and the Assembly of God (AOG).[7] The impact of the Christian faith cannot be easily gauged but I have heard many men explain that they have decided to forgo some of the ways of magic and sorcery out of fear of the Christian God. One conspicuous but subtle impact of Christianity is its supply of Christian names such as John and Betty to the Iatmul people. I was dumbfounded when I entered and walked through the Wolimbi *ngeko* when I first arrived in the village to conduct my research. When I walked through the corridor of the *ngeko*, meeting and shaking hands with the men who were gathered there, I realized that all of them had introduced themselves to me by their Christian names and not their Iatmul names, which I had intended to study. In my own mind, I thought I had made the wrong decision to be interested in such totemic names, let alone to study them in that

[7] In terms of membership by denomination, the largest in the village is SDA, which has about 45 per cent of the village's population followed by the Catholic Church, which has about 40 per cent, while the AOG has the remaining 15 per cent.

village. But then after some time had elapsed I came to realize that the Iatmul were very comfortable with the Christian names they were using. This is because such Christian names are not capable of being owned, as can the Iatmul ones. Christianity has provided them a common pool of names, which all of them can use freely without worrying about 'stealing other people's names' (Harrison 1990a).

Christianity was introduced into the region by the 1900s and the Catholic missionaries were the first to do so. They were based in Timbunke and then, in the early 1950s, they opened up their station and established the school and the airstrip at Kapaimari. The SDA missionaries did likewise and made their base in Angriman village, just up the river from Timbunke. Missionaries from both of these denominations moved around in different parts of the Sepik River to evangelize and convert the people to Christianity. Meanwhile, many of the people in Central Iatmul villages have become affiliated with the Catholic Church and had their children attending the school in Kapaimari.

One day a man from Parimbe village, who works as a catechist with the Catholic Church, chastised a child who is the son of a man from the Kosimbi *ngeko* in Kanganamun village. Because the local leadership within the Catholic Church was dominated by men who were of the totemic moiety opposed to those of Minjimbit and Kosimbi, the chastising of their child was seen as an attack on their moiety, and this therefore rekindled prevailing tensions within Kanganamun at that time. Thus the men of Minjimbit and Kosimbi approached the missionaries of SDA and brought the SDA denomination into the village. Today, the majority of the people who worship with the SDA Church are mainly from Minjimbit and Kosimbi *ngeko*, while a few of them are from Wolimbi. The Catholic Church, however, is composed predominantly of people from Wolimbi. The AOG Church was introduced in 1986 and most of its members are from Wolimbi *ngeko.* In general, the introduction of Christianity into Kanganamun village followed lines which were already drawn along local totemic enclaves and their contemporary membership perpetuates the prevailing totemic opposition within the village.

Research method and experiences of gathering information

Before concluding this chapter, I need to say something about the nature of research methods and the kinds of problems I encountered in the gathering of ethnographic information. When I began making contacts with people from Kanganamun to help me get into the village, little did I know what the effect of the news of my going there had on some Kanganamun people who were living in Nuigo, a squatter settlement on the periphery of Wewak town. When I was taken to meet my adopted father, who was then living there, allegations emerged that I was someone who would 'steal and take their culture to England and America'. The village councillor rightly argued that under the present reforms in government administration, village leaders had control over activities of researchers. He feared particularly that I would 'take their *kastom* and culture to the place of the white men' with no returns for them. He was therefore against my research in the village. Yarme Mambingawi, a very knowledgeable man in stories and carving, advocated on my behalf. He observed that it was unfair and premature for people to raise arguments against my research, because none of them knew what I was to do in the village, and it was not right for them to say anything unless they knew exactly what I would be doing. I came to know about these complaints through one of Yarme's sons, who was working as a driver for one of the big trading companies in Wewak town. Yarme's son, Emmanuel, told me about the complaints but advised me to forget about them. Despite this complaint, I was encouraged by other Kanganamun men and then I set off for the village in the company of my adopted father.

Three weeks after I had arrived in the village, the village councillor sent a letter to complain about my presence in the village and setting out the legal powers that can be invoked to prohibit my research. The matter was discussed in the *ngeko* and the men who gathered there brushed aside the letter from the councillor. However, soon after this meeting, another man arrived from town and came with the same message from the councillor. Despite these repeated complaints, I persisted in staying in the village at the behest of the villagers themselves. The major problem I had was people's reluctance to give me the chance to record people's names and genealogies. I encountered five men who refused me such information, and I conducted full genealogical studies with only three families in the village. Along with this reluctance was the view held by many that the research was for my own good and had nothing profitable for them. Indeed, becoming adopted into Yarme's family in the village prevented me getting stories from people in other clans. It was feared that I would divulge these stories to my adopted family, who would then use this knowledge against those whose story I had recorded if there were any disputes between them in the future. Furthermore, others felt that I was not entitled to know other people's stories because of the fact that I already belonged to one clan and therefore was not supposed to know other people's stories. Another difficulty arose from my association with the Wolimbi *ngeko.* I had no previous knowledge of the politics of *ngeko* affiliation amongst the Iatmul, or Kanganamun in particular. Owing to their totemic feuds, membership or association with a particular *ngeko* is fraught with highly charged political and emotional sentiments, as we will see in Chapter 2. I had spent a lot of time staying and working with men from the Wolimbi *ngeko* and neglected, by sheer ignorance, the two other *ngeko* in the village. By the time it dawned on me that I was neglecting the other two *ngeko*, it was too late to build and stabilize relationships which would allow me to work with and get information from them. However, late on in my stay, men of Minjimbit and Kosimbi began opening their doors to me, showing an unusual degree of support towards my research. This made the men of Wolimbi complain about me making visits to men of the other two *ngeko* and twice I was asked to reveal the kinds of information I was given. I really was caught up in an ethnographic double-bind,[8] which was at times disconcerting for me given the nature of the politics associated with the opposing totemic moieties. At one stage I was pressed by men of the Wolimbi *ngeko* to reveal things I was told by men of Minjimbit and Kosimbi *ngeko.* However, a man of Minjimbit advised me to tell my interlocutors in Wolimbi to summon him to their *ngeko* so that he could tell them himself what he was telling me instead of forcing me to reveal what I should keep secret. They had solutions to the dilemma of an anthropologist caught between two competing houses of knowledge within a single cosmological universe and ontological plane.

Finally, I would like to say something specific about my experience of being adopted into the family of Yarme Mambingawi in Kanganamun village, an act of kinship that had both advantages and disadvantages. First, it provided me a home away from home and I had a very strong and close relationship with Lewis Waligawa, the last of Yarme's three sons. The kindness of this young man and his consideration for me was unceasing from the day I entered the village till I left. Marimbunjin, Yarme's wife, became my mother and took me in as if I was born of her own womb. When I underwent men's initiation, an experience recited in Chapter 3, she showed her love by providing food to a stranger as I was and did for me what

[8] This 'ethnographic double-bind' refers to how, for instance, an Iatmul man whose parents come from clans of the opposing totemic moieties, knows esoteric information from clans of his mother's side as well as his own. He is caught between these two opposing camps of 'knowledge' as it were.

Iatmul women would do for their sons. Staying with the family allowed me a chance to observe and participate in domestic life and relationships which gave me an insight into the micro-dynamics of Kanganamun families.

A major stress I had was the inability to satisfy all the financial expectations of my family, and particularly that of my mother, who may have thought I denied her relationship with me. Towards the end of September 2001, my adopted father fell ill with dysentery. My mother and Vincent, my brother, alleged that, because of my talking and learning stories from other clans, spirits of those other clans were punishing my father. What was particularly disturbing was their prophetic view that the death of my father was imminent upon my departure from the village. I had given my father some treatment for malaria when he first fell ill, but the persistence of his illnesses indicated to his family that I was contributing to his illness.

After consulting a mentor in the village, I was told that the allegations were baseless and had no substantive merits according to their *kastom*:

> The spirits of other clans will not harm your father because of you engaging in talking about secret things. Even if you are taking such information, it is the man who is divulging secret information who will be punished and it's neither you nor your father. Men from one clan are not supposed to talk about stories from other clans because the spirits of other clans are also listening. When people mention their names, and if they are not related to them, these spirits will then bring harm to the person who is telling the story.

I was advised to clear myself of this allegation by putting a bunch of betel nuts and two coconuts on the cross-beams that run across the middle section of our residential house in order to appease the spirits of the clan, who would then release my father from his illness. After discussing the allegation with the members of my adopted family together, we shared and chewed the betel nuts. I was also advised to raise this matter in the *ngeko* to gauge the view of other men. My father's situation worsened. So I organized a canoe trip to the Timbunke Health Centre and we returned home after a doctor treated him there. Although my father was still a bit sick when I left the village, the men of the village told me that I had done all that was within their *kastom*, and if he passed away, he would be dying for reasons other than the allegation that Vincent raised against me. One young man, Freddy Kabrakamei, summarized the views of the men in the *ngeko* with the following words: 'We will be with you in good and bad times.' Referring to the scars from the initiation which were by then imprinted on my body, he said:

> We have put our mark (*waalumi*) on you and you are now one of us. You can go with clear thoughts, with good feelings in your stomach. The spirits of this *ngeko* are listening and looking at you as I am talking and they will be with you in your endeavours.

Most of my time in the village was spent going around with men in the bush working on canoes, cutting posts for houses, working on gardens, going to fishing lagoons, cleaning waterways, and on Sundays I played for the village men's soccer team. I wasn't able to grasp the Iatmul language fully and many villagers made genuine complaints against me for not being able to speak their language. The information presented in this book is based on what I gathered through the use of Melanesian pidgin, *Tok Pisin*. Although I did not speak their language, what I considered important was for me to try to grasp their pristine episteme by doing my best to live as they do, in all of their complexity. This book reflects an attempt at trying to live and think as if I am from Kanganamun myself and I am grateful for the opportunity to be adopted and given the name, Walindanmeli, the most senior name in the Samiangwat clan throughout Iatmul region. Likewise, my mother's brother's name, Wangipalapan, will return to my adopted mother's Suaru clan after my life has ended, but the names themselves have an immortal life that is thicker than blood! That is, they live beyond the life of the individual person who bears the names. As we shall see, far from serving as an index of classification, Iatmul names are intricately linked to a cosmo-ontological understanding of the 'person'. Because these names survive or live beyond the lifespan of individuals who bear these names, and because these names are also bound up with issues of kinship and ownership, I have found it appropriate to capture this dynamism with the title of the book: *Names are Thicker Than Blood*.

I have used the vignette on missing canoes as a way to enter into a general discussion that conveys a sense of place and the people with whom I stayed for the duration of my fieldwork. I moved from the discussion on how canoes appear in the local geography and economy to providing some brief details about the people—their multifaceted religious associations as well as local political leadership. At several points, reference was made to totemic moieties and the three different *ngeko* in Kanganamun village, so we shall consider how they feature in Iatmul social and cultural life in the following chapter.

2

Two in One: Houses and Moieties

The contrast between the ceremonial and dwelling house is fundamental for the culture and will serve as the best starting point for ethological description.

(Bateson 1958: 123)

There is a series of tales . . . [in which] the elder [brother] . . . was of the discreet type while the younger [brother] was a man of violence.

(Bateson 1958: 162)

This chapter focuses on two distinct architectural forms: *ngeko*—the ceremonial men's house—and *ngeio*—the dwelling or residential house. These two particular types of houses within an Iatmul village such as Kanganamun may best be understood as domains or 'spheres of interaction' (Strathern 1988: 269). By providing a description of the kinds of relationships and activities that revolve around these two types of houses, this chapter not only presents a picture of social life but also makes visible different spheres of ownership which are concomitantly associated with each of these two types of houses. In addition, there is an interesting gender dimension of these two architectural forms and the chapter also aims to bring this into clear relief. We begin with the organizational form of Iatmul moiety systems.

If we borrow a conceptual image from anthropological accounts of segmentary lineage structures (Merlan and Rumsey 1991; A. Strathern 1972), the following observations are in order. There are two kinds of moieties among the Iatmul: one is totemic and the other ritual. As I will come to explain shortly, the ritual moieties cut through the totemic moieties. The totemic moieties are called *nyowi nimba*—the 'sun/father people'—and *nyamei nimba*—the 'mother/earth people'. In totemic mythology, 'sun/father people' are considered the elder brothers to the 'mother/earth people', the 'younger brothers' (cf. Bateson 1958: 242). Beneath the totemic moieties are clan associations, each of which is composed of several clans. The clans are further divided into lineages. Clan associations are grouped into clans which are elder brothers and those which are younger-brother clans. The same process of pairing applies to individual clans, so that in each clan there is a lineage associated with a putative elder-brother ancestor and another that is associated with a younger-brother ancestor.

The ritual moieties are also divided into an elder-brother group known as *nyamun arambandi* and a younger-brother group called *shambu arambandi*. Beneath each of the initiatory moieties are men who belong to a 'father's generation' and a 'son's generation'. All the people in the village belong to one or the other ritual moiety. The junior men's houses (*tigal* and *mbare*) associated with ritual age grades, which Bateson (1958: 136) refers to, have since disappeared and only the senior men's house—*ngeko*—remains today. As we shall come to see, it is in the *ngeko* that the ritual and totemic moieties converge and diverge. A *ngeko* is as much an abode of opposition amongst the clans of opposing totemic moieties as it is of unity and opposition within itself.

Furthermore, since the *ngeko* is the site where ritual moieties converge during the initiation and it is also the place where totemic moieties are separated after the initiation, it effects a perspectival difference in the way the Iatmul conceptualize gender relations. Looking at Iatmul from the perspective of ritual moieties, one could only see the difference between the initiated and the uninitiated. The initiated are male and the uninitiated are female. An uninitiated male is considered a woman (*takwa*) and has to be brought into ritual enclosure (*bandi*) in order to be transformed into a man (*ndu*). Separation is necessary to give effect to such identities. Women do not undergo the initiation ritual and for them perhaps the closest analogue to the initiation ritual is marriage. Marriage is organized along the lines of totemic clans. Thus, looking at an Iatmul clan from the perspective of totemic moieties, one finds that gender is based on an analogy between cross-sex and same-sex siblings who address each other as *nyamun shambu*.

Although the significance of such a relationship may be lost in translation, the terms *nyamun* and *shambu* can easily be translated into English as elder brother and younger brother respectively. The term *nyamun shambu* will be modified in the chapters to come in order to specify its complexity without compromising its analytical purchase. The nature of this siblingship is locked into a generational system that causes women to move in between groups of patrilineal clans (*yaranga*). Internally in their own clans, an analogic gender (Strathern 1988) organizes the nature of siblingship so that cross-sex and same-sex siblings relate to each other as 'brothers'. According to the logic of this kinship, a clan cannot reproduce itself homosexually so it has to recruit women through exogamous marriage. Thus a man's female siblings become women when they are recruited into the other clans during marriage. This view of gender stems from an alternating play of totemic and ritual moieties, which are entangled in a relationship that can aptly be described with the perceptual trope of figure–ground (Wagner 1986, 2001). When relations in one of these moieties are activated the other is eclipsed, thus effecting the kinds of gender understandings the Iatmul otherwise display (Strathern 1988). When Iatmul men say that a female sibling becomes a woman during marriage, this is a statement coming from the perspective of totemic moieties, whereas if they say that an uninitiated male sibling is considered a 'woman' they are talking from the perspective of ritual moieties. Both of these moieties converge upon and diverge from the men's house (*ngeko*) thus giving rise to these gender positions.

Ngeko and the system of moieties

When the men's initiation ritual is carried out in an Iatmul village, the village's totemic moieties are temporarily suspended and the initiated men who belong to opposing totemic moieties come together on the occasion of the ritual to carry out particular roles and responsibilities during the period of the ritual. 'In the ceremonial [men's] house the clans are . . . allotted seats according to the totemic system of groupings: but when initiation ceremonies are to be performed this arrangement is discarded and in its place comes another based upon the crosscutting initiatory moieties and grades' (Bateson 1958: 225). However, as I have mentioned above, the totemic dimension of a ceremonial house is not discarded as Bateson's gloss suggests, but is rather eclipsed and functions as the ground upon which the ritual dimension appears as a figure. After the ritual is finished, the ritual moieties are dissolved and men (as well as women and children) revert back to their clan membership within the system of totemic moieties. While the constitution of totemic moieties divides and separates clans in much of mundane social life, men's initiation ritual temporarily dissolves totemic moieties, with the ritual moiety drawing its membership from clans throughout the village irrespective of their totemic affiliation. Thus both halves of the ritual moiety will contain members from each of the totemic moieties.

The same system of ritual and totemic moieties exists throughout the Iatmul region so that membership of each of the moieties extends beyond the confines of one particular village. With the totemic moiety, what makes people identify each other is the set of personal names they bear, which come from both sides of one's parents. With the personal names, one can easily find relatives of one's clan in another village. People know which village has their kind of men's house and where their totemic clan relatives are located. The personal names function much like a navigational cipher that guides them to totemic clan relatives in other villages. The ritual moieties do not operate with personal names; people are generally born into ritual moieties. They can also be adopted into the opposing ritual moiety, or, in times of disputes within a ritual moiety, some of its members may decide to go and join the other moiety. A man and his wife or wives may or may not belong to the same ritual moiety. Children belong to their father's ritual moiety, but the father may also decide to give one of his sons to the other moiety. When people from one village such as Kanganamun visit other villages, the membership with their ritual moiety extends across to other villages so that, if the initiation ritual is held in the other village, people would want to know at once which moiety is leading the ritual proceedings and which is not, so that they can fit themselves in according to their own affiliation with their ritual moiety.

For example, a day after coming out of the men's house following the initiation ritual in Kanganamun, I was taken across the Sepik River to Maringe and Parimbe[1] villages to observe a similar ritual there. I was in the company of men who belong to both ritual moieties in Kanganamun. The initiation ritual that I underwent in Kanganamun was controlled by men of *shambu arambandi*—the younger-brother group, but when we went across the river the initiation ritual in Maringe was under the control of *nyamun arambandi*—the elder-brother group.[2] Thus men of *nyamun arambandi* in

[1] Both Maringe and Parimbe are younger-brother villages to Kanganamun in local understandings of how villages are formed out of the original Parimbe village. In mythology, Kanganamun is the older brother to Maringe the younger brother, and along with this pairing of villages go their respective ancestral crocodiles, Wani and Kabak as well.

[2] Note that *nyamun arambandi* and *shambu arambandi* are two ritual moieties. Inside each of these moieties are two generations of initiators, those who belong to the 'father's generation' and the 'son's generation'. Those in the father's generation in the *nyamun arambandi* are the 'elder brothers' to those in the father's generation in the *shambu arambandi*. Those who are in the 'father's generation' in the *shambu arambandi* are the 'elder brothers' of those who are of the son's generation in the *nyamun arambandi* who in turn are the 'elder brothers' of those in the 'son's generation' in the *shambu arambandi*.

Kanganamun had to make arrangements with members of their ritual moiety in Maringe so that our entourage could be allowed to enter the men's house in Maringe where their initiates were kept. When we entered the *ngeko*, the initiates were about to have their main meal of the day. Because it was their moiety which was in control, men of the *nyamun arambandi* from Kanganamun asserted the same authority as their counterparts in Maringe did over members of the *shambu arambandi*. Men of the *shambu arambandi* from Kanganamun were made to eat with the initiates during the meal. Though I was a member of the *shambu arambandi*, members of the opposing moiety, *nyamun arambandi*, in Kanganamun cleverly negotiated my way out of the ordeal that goes along with the feeding of initiates, the details of which will not be revealed here. Men of my ritual moiety had to endure the ordeal even long after our entourage left the *ngeko* in Maringe to return to Kanganamun. While the ritual was still going on in Maringe, it had ended in Kanganamun, where social life had returned to a secular mode of existence free from the constraints of ritual restrictions. This vignette is reported not only to show that membership in one ritual or totemic moiety in an Iatmul village extends beyond one's own village, but also to describe how the alternation between totemic affiliation and ritual activities play out. The social life of each Iatmul village alternates episodically between secular existence and ritual observations.[3] While it is tempting to say that secular life is associated with totemic opposition (village divided into totemic moieties) and religious life is connected to ritual unity (village brought together into a *ngeko* during initiation ritual), secular life is equal to the religious, as exemplified in the totemic incantations one encounters during initiation rituals. Thus, while the temporal alternation is the general axis of orientation in social life, when one mode is activated, the other is eclipsed and only invoked from time to time.

Although initiation rituals used to be frequent as an annual or biennial event, it is no longer the same. Sometimes a village may go for several years without holding a men's initiation. In Eastern Iatmul villages, the initiation ritual is no longer practised, but that does not mean that social life and relations are not imbued with religious considerations. All Iatmul villages still maintain their system of personal names derived from their totemic cosmology, and it is through these names that Iatmul are able to invoke and access the powers of their ancestors, tutelary spirits, and cosmological heroes. These totemic names are invoked not only in secular social life but

[3] Harrison (1990b: 352) makes a similar point about the alternation between secular and religious life for the neighbouring Manambu.

also when initiation rituals are carried out. Although men revert to their affiliation with totemic moieties after an initiation ritual is completed, the ritual moieties continue to exist as social categories and do not disappear completely. The same can be said of totemic moieties too. When totemic moieties are suspended during the initiation ritual, they are not discarded altogether. As we shall see in Chapter 3, the onset of an initiation ritual does not dissolve the totemic moieties. The totemic moieties assume a particular legal and moral responsibility during the period of the initiation ritual.

In secular life, one will find men of one ritual moiety often referring to themselves as *arambandi*, which means men of the same ritual moiety. Because of the fact that their membership extends to ritual moieties in other villages, men of Kanganamun often address their colleagues in Yenjan, Parimbe, and Maringe villages as *arambandi* as well. Much like in the totemic moiety, men of the same ritual moiety often define themselves as a unit in opposition to the initiated men of the opposing ritual moiety. At times when men of both ritual moieties combine to work on communal activities such as cutting the grass on the road into the village, men of one *arambandi* would collect themselves as a team to mock and ridicule those of the opposing ritual moiety. The jokes and laughter are kept alive by the men as they work. However, when they are mocking or ridiculing the other moiety, they do not recall the political tensions that are created during initiation rituals. They avoid this not only because of the fear of revealing ritually orchestrated dynamics to uninitiated males who are in their midst, but also because such political tensions belong properly to the context of rituals, and when the initiation ritual comes to an end, such tensions must also be submerged. The only time these tensions are reignited is when the next initiation ritual is staged in the village. The political tensions between the ritual moieties are repressed in secular life until the next initiation, which then provides the context for such tensions to be rekindled or for moieties to settle or reciprocate debts incurred in the previous initiation ritual.

The nature of political relations within totemic moieties is different from that found within ritual moieties. This difference stems from the fact that, in totemic moieties, tensions arise from competing claims in totemic beliefs (or esoteric knowledge), ownership of names and stories, and access to resources such as waterways and lagoons. The politics of ritual moieties ensues from the observation of ritual protocols and prerogatives, and the enforcement of penalties during the initiation ritual. However, in both ritual and mundane social life, when social and political relationships turn into litigious encounters, people seek recourse in precedents, historically prior debts and obligations that have been established in the past and which continue to maintain their hold and relevance for the present for respective moieties, groups, and individuals to assert the claims and positions. Let me illustrate this with the following examples, taken from the context of an initiation ritual.

During the time of the initiation ritual that I participated in, there were two incidents which nearly brought the men of opposing ritual moieties to fight against each other. In one instance, a young man named Sumbakwan, who belongs to the elder-brother group, came and told me to give instructions to an initiated man, namely Wariang, who is from my ritual moiety (*shambu arambandi*). The instruction was for Wariang to go and chop down a tree that was standing at the eastern edge of the ceremonial ground (*wombuno*) of the Wolimbi *ngeko.* The tree had to be chopped because its branches were intruding into the ceremonial ground. Instructions given by initiates are normally issued to initiated men who are of the same totemic moiety and clan as the initiate. This is where the totemic moieties come into view during initiation rituals. The initiate and the initiated belong to the same totemic post in the *ngeko*. In this case, Wariang and I belong to the Samiangwat clan and our ceremonial post is called Wobasui, which stands at the back part (*ngumbu ngeko*) of the Wolimbi *ngeko*. Since initiates are accorded such a pride of place during the ritual, the instructions issued by initiates are executed immediately and the tree was felled in no time. Then an enquiry began: my own ritual moiety was in control of the proceedings of the initiation ritual then, but how was it that I gave instructions to a man of my own moiety to fell down the tree? The enquiry soon found that the instruction I issued was flawed because it did not follow appropriate ritual protocols. Wariang was of the 'fathers' generation and I was of the 'sons' generation in our ritual moiety (*shambu arambandi*), and it is improper that a son should instruct a father as I did to Wariang, who was also a classificatory brother of my adopted father, Yarme. The enquiry forced me to tell my own ritual moiety who it was amongst my 'ritual mothers' that planted the idea of instructing Wariang. A tense dynamic evolved and I was caught in another instance of a double-bind.

Sumbakwan and my other 'ritual mothers' (members of the opposing ritual moiety, which in this case are men of *nyamun arambandi*) who initiated me, impressed upon me the need to deny and conceal the identity of the man who gave me the idea to instruct Wariang by insistently telling my 'ritual fathers' that the idea was my own. On the other hand, my 'ritual fathers' (members of my own ritual moiety *shambu arambandi*) probed me to tell them who actually told me so. I was torn inside since part of me wanted to be true and honest to my ritual fathers and the other part of me developed a sense of betraying my 'ritual mothers'. My ritual fathers insisted that 'babies cannot talk while they are inside their mother's belly. Babies do not talk, they only eat and sleep'. It was obvious that one of my 'ritual mothers' had planted the idea and it was pointless for me to deny this to my 'ritual fathers'.

Eventually I had to reveal that Sumbakwan had made me issue the instructions to Wariang. It was wrong for me to have given an order to Wariang. Despite the fact that we belong to same clan, and therefore the same ceremonial post called Wobasui located at the back of Wolimbi *ngeko*, Wariang was of the 'father's generation' and I was of the 'son's generation' within our ritual moiety. Recognizing this breach of procedure, men of the leading ritual moiety (*shambu arambandi*) then charged Sumbakwan, who belongs to the opposing ritual moiety (*nyamun arambandi*). Although Sumbakwan belongs to a different clan (Masam), we all (i.e. Wariang, Sumbakwan, and myself) belong to the same clan association and therefore gather around the same ceremonial post Wobasui. Although Wariang's mother and Sumbakwan's mothers are sisters, their two sons belong to opposing ritual moieties and the responsibility therefore fell upon Wariang to prosecute a charge against his cousin brother Sumbakwan. The discussion of this particular offence led to a heated exchange of words. During the exchange, a leading figure in the son's generation in *nyamun arambandi* raised a point that embarrassed and humiliated his counterparts in the moiety that was leading the ritual. In harsh and provocative terms, the men of *shambu arambandi* were asked whether any of his counterparts had ever killed a pig and given it to the men's house during their initiation. This young ritual leader observed that his father had to provide pigs to the men's house when he (the speaker) was initiated. This set him apart from his peers and he therefore used this as a privilege to shame his peers in the opposing moiety. He argued that his peers were just K50 *bandi* (novices), which meant that they were initiated cheaply by just paying K50 to the men's house during their initiation, whereas his initiation was paid for with a pig, an item of considerable wealth and prestige. This sort of shame and ridicule is very much part of the language and the tenor of relationships that come into play during initiation rituals. When one moiety was getting too powerful, the other would respond with shaming and ridicule.[4]

[4] Here one might recall Bateson's model of schismogenesis, for instance the *wau* (mother's brother) who resorted to a *ngarik,* a kind of sexual salute in which the *wau* slides his buttocks down his nephew's *(laua)* shin to reprove his nephew's boasting (Bateson 1958: 13; cf. Plate XIIIA).

A short time after this, a bloody fight could have erupted between the moieties again. A man of the leading ritual moiety and his wife had cooked a meal and invited me to eat at their house that evening. That ritual leader belongs to the same moiety as me, but he is of the father's generation and was therefore considered as one of my ritual fathers (*nyait*). Since I was nursed as a *bandi* by ritual mothers in the 'crocodile's nest', one of them had to escort me to the man's place and the responsibility fell upon one of my ritual mothers (*nyamei*). This ritual mother came to the upper chambers of the men's house, informed some men of the leading moiety and, together with another of my ritual mothers, escorted me out for dinner that evening.

There were only two of us who were initiated during that time when the ritual enclosure (*bandi*) was built in January 2001. Since my fellow novice (*bandi*)[5] had yet to return to the men's house from his evening meal, it was not appropriate for me to leave, so my going was delayed. But when the 'metaphoric birds'[6] stopped singing in the *ngeko*, a case was presented to my ritual fathers, who allowed me to leave for the dinner. Because it was they who erected the enclosure at the request of my fellow *bandi*, the men of my ritual moiety owned the ritual enclosure, the nest in which 'young crocodiles' were being nursed, and so their permission had to be given before going away for the evening. However, when we returned to the *ngeko*, we found that one of my ritual mothers had been accused and charged for putting an abrupt end to the 'birds' that were singing in the *ngeko*. The *ngeko* had drawn into an unusual silence (since birds normally sing every night in the *ngeko* during the initiation ritual). The beautiful flute music that graced the early hours of that evening, the humour and the laughter that characterizes the charm and pride of the *ngeko*, were all suspended for the night.

Most of the men in both ritual moieties had withdrawn to their residential houses and a few who remained in both sides of the men's house—*ndama ngeko* (front) and *ngumbu ngeko* (back)—conversed in soft voices as they shared tobacco and pondered over the ritual offence (*kuchal*) that allegedly had just been committed. While the dark interior of the *ngeko* receives a dim greeting of light from the sporadic flickers emitted from the

[5] *Bandi* is the term for the ritual enclosure as well as for a novice.

[6] In local idioms metaphoric birds are flutes. I retain the local metaphor to highlight the fact that the flutes are secret ritual instruments handled only by initiated men. Although they are played in the secret recesses of the men's house, women and the uninitiated also compose part of the audience that listen in to the music.

embers and logs in the fire place, an uncanny mood of vengeance and resistance had set into the minds of the men in the two respective moieties. Some had gone home to sleep on it and others who remained in the *ngeko* were drawn into moments of contemplative silence which were interrupted by occasional whispers and clearing of throats, followed by talk in low and soft voices. Men of both moieties were weighing out the charge, recalling precedents, and mulling over the points of arguments they were to debate the following day, to prosecute or evade the alleged offence. When they finally retreated for the night, it was the wild fowls and roosters that made their routine calls in the night, the village as a whole slept the night in silence.

When the following morning came, the secret 'crocodile sound' (*waal*) was not heard and the initiates were led to the river for their baths without the accompaniment of crocodile sounds. Because of the alleged offence, men took time to gather in the *ngeko* one after the other. When members of both moieties were gathered, a member of the leading moiety pressed charges against Vincent, my ritual mother, and his ritual moiety. The man who charged Vincent belongs to the same ceremonial post (Wobasui) and is of the same ritual generation (sons) as Vincent.[7] It was alleged that Vincent breached a ritual procedure by forcing the birds in the men's house to stop singing when he took me out of the ritual enclosure to Wali's place. For his part, Wali, who belongs to the leading moiety that was charging Vincent, confirmed that he had invited me to his house that evening and had organized with Vincent to bring me along, but assumed that Vincent would follow the appropriate ritual procedures and protocol when doing so. He was surprised to hear of the allegation in the night, however, and, because it was his moiety that was charging Vincent, Wali remained quiet and just observed the ensuing debate.

The offence allegedly committed by Vincent was not entirely clear, and Vincent and his moiety resisted the charge. Vincent argued that he was aware of the fact that to stop birds from singing in the men's house during initiation rituals is a serious offence, and he was careful to notify and seek permission from some of my ritual fathers, who were with me in the upper chambers of the *ngeko*, before taking me to Wali's place. Vincent argued that his accusers in the opposing moiety were only trying to fault him so that they could enjoy a charge that he and his moiety will pay them. Men of the leading moiety then accused Vincent of sneaking into the 'crocodile's

[7] This is another instance in which totemic clan association comes into play during initiation rituals.

nest' (see Allen 1987). They argued that Vincent acted like a thief in the night and went in silently up the ladder of the *ngeko* into the crocodile's nest and took the 'baby crocodile' away. Although Vincent was entitled to the 'baby crocodile' as its ritual mother, they argued that it was not his moiety's *bandi* (ritual enclosure) and he could not simply make a casual entrance into the crocodile's nest at his own discretion. Entry into the crocodile's nest is a prerogative of the leading ritual moiety and, in this particular instance, it was the *shambu arambandi*.

Members of the *shambu arambandi* argued that the 'baby crocodile' does not talk nor does it walk on its own. Vincent, who was acting as my ritual mother, should have informed them before entering the upper chambers of the men's house to take the baby crocodile out of its nest. Vincent persisted with his defence. However, the accusations of theft and of stopping the birds from singing went hand in hand with other kinds of insults and abuses, which is typical of the rivalry between ritual moieties. Men of opposing moieties, who are entitled to speak before the ceremonial stool, took turns in presenting their case in either prosecuting or defending themselves from the alleged offence. The ceremonial stool is located in the centre of the *ngeko* and it will have a secret name that belongs to the clan that owns that name. Different *ngeko* will have different names for the ceremonial stool. Only fathers, and in their absence, first-born (and initiated) sons are allowed to speak on the ceremonial chair. Each speaker would walk up to the chair, pick up some leaves that are on the chair, make his tally of points, and then smash the leaves on the chair after all his points are completed. After he makes his final blow, those who agree with what the speaker has said will make a strong inhaling sound and then call out 'woo oooh'. 'The style of the oratory varies a great deal from speaker to speaker and that of the more admired performers may tend towards the display of erudition or towards violence or to a mixture of these attitudes' (Bateson 1958: 126).[8] In the case under discussion here, the exchange of words became so heated that it transformed into a bout of fisticuffs, with some men of the leading moiety taking up spears and threatening to use them against their opponents in the other moiety. Two men from the opposing moieties exchanged blows and another two took up position to do likewise. Swear words and insulting abuse were thrown at each other. Women and children in the houses nearby crept to positions around the mounds near the *ngeko* and the novices in the upper chambers of the *ngeko* tiptoed

[8] Men who exhibit admirable skill in debate and erudition are those who have committed themselves to the learning of stories and secret names.

to crevices in the ritual enclosure to spy on the violent drama that was being enacted as a spectacle below. Luckily, no spears were used and the fight subsided when the men of Vincent's moiety withdrew from the *ngeko*, although they returned the next day after collecting themselves. I have recounted these two disputes to exemplify the kinds of political relations and emotional dynamics that come to the fore when initiation rituals are carried out in an Iatmul village such as Kanganamun.

Outside of the mode of ritual observation, mundane social life goes on at its own pace within the constraints of totemic affiliation as well as with the general sanctions of moral conventions. The *ngeko* is a public space (Bateson 1958: 125) as it is a ritually exclusive sphere of interaction amongst the initiated men. That is, when rituals are being held, the men's house becomes exclusively an initiated man's place, to the exclusion of uninitiated men, women, and children. Although the *ngeko* is deemed to be a public arena, women and children are seldom allowed to enter its precincts. Much of the social life of initiated (and nowadays uninitiated) men revolves around the *ngeko*, whereas women's and children's lives revolve around the residential house.

Initiated men who belong to a particular men's house are expected to meet in their *ngeko* on a daily basis, from dawn till late in the night. Unlike the men's (spirit) houses of Abelam and Araphesh societies, the Iatmul *ngeko* is a seat of lively social interaction amongst the men of the village or a particular totemic moiety. While a *ngeko* is associated with a particular totemic moiety, members of the opposing totemic moiety may make visits to their friends or relatives in the other *ngeko*. There is a strict protocol regarding how men, women, and children should comport themselves towards a *ngeko* (see also Bateson 1958: 123). Many of these protocols are learnt from others and it is expected that an initiated man should exercise these protocols as a matter of habit.

It is expected that, when an initiated man goes into the *ngeko*, he must light a fire and sit around the fireplace in his own clan's area within the *ngeko*. The first man who enters the *ngeko* in the morning is expected to sweep off the ashes left from the previous night in his fireplace before making a new fire. In the night, when a man wants to leave the *ngeko*, he can take fire and set it alight on dry coconut leaves when he goes back to his *ngeio*. He may never do this (bring fire) in this way if he is entering the *ngeko* at night. For bringing fire into the *ngeko* suggest one of two things: either one is trying to torch the building or that one is bringing to the *ngeko* a successful kill of a game, such as a pig or a crocodile. A serious penalty is held against the man who does this and it is also believed that if he were to torch the *ngeko* its guardian spirits will strike him dead.

When in the *ngeko*, a man cannot call another man who is at the other end of the *ngeko* or the ceremonial ground. Neither can one call out to persons who are outside the *ngeko*. Instead, if a man in the *ngeko* is wanted by a woman or a child, who may be asking for him from outside the ceremonial ground, a message is sent into the *ngeko* via another man, or if that particular man is seen, he can be called using hand signals. When that specific man gets his message, he exits silently and makes his way slowly to the person who has asked for him. A man leaving or entering the *ngeko* is never in a rush but always gentle. Once he is inside the *ngeko* he can talk and laugh as loud as he chooses. Once in a while, when something funny comes up in the *ngeko*, you find the *ngeko* coming alive with laughter, and often it is a place of socializing, discussion, and debate.

Issues of public concern and interest are discussed and debated in the *ngeko* frequently. When a pressing concern requires the participation of women as well, women and children will gather on the ceremonial ground outside the *ngeko* and sit there while the matter is being discussed before a decision is taken. Women will raise their concerns while men listen attentively and contribute to the discussion, depending on the matter being discussed. If an allegation of some sort is being deliberated, one or two of the village *komiti* will preside over the conduct of the discussion, allowing equal opportunities for the concerned parties to state their positions. In ceremonial debates (*pabu*) over the ownership of totemic names, I am told, women sit outside on the ceremonial ground while the debate goes on inside the *ngeko* (cf. Harrison 1990a: 154–67).

On other occasions, the men enjoy themselves with loud applause and peals of laughter while they are inside the *ngeko*, while women do so in their residential houses or when they meet on pathways in the village. Women, however, are not allowed to laugh and chatter loudly when they are anywhere close to the *ngeko*. When women's laughter and chatter outside the *ngeko* becomes too loud and disturbing, men inside the *ngeko* will immediately quell the noise outside, either by scolding the women or by blowing one of the secret trumpets; once the trumpet sounds, the laughter recedes. Although there is no restriction on the level of noise that emanates from the *ngeko*, it is usually moderate. On some occasions one could hear the melodious antiphonal of flute music which reverberates throughout the village in the night. Except for the occasional treat of flute music and during ceremonial occasions, no singing or whistling are ever allowed in the *ngeko*.

Men are not allowed to wear caps or listen to radios, play guitars or any kind of card games or chess in the *ngeko*. When a man is entering the *ngeko* from his residential house or returning from his place of work with his knife and axe, he should not keep the tools on his shoulders but at his sides. Failure to do this might mean that he is intent on striking the *ngeko*. A man should never walk from one end through to the other end of the *ngeko*, nor should a man walk in front of platforms where other men are sitting. If a man (say Luke) wants to talk with another man (say Ben) who is sitting at the end of the *ngeko*, Luke should not walk through the corridor of the *ngeko*; he must leave by the exit near his sitting platform and enter where Ben is sitting. Neither Luke nor Ben should call out to each other for this is considered disrespectful to other men, even to the *ngeko* itself, for it is not their residential house where they could conduct themselves in such a manner (see also Bateson 1958: 123).

I have specified the manner in which people relate to the *ngeko* in order to convey the fact that it is held in such a degree of veneration. Yet it is also a social club, a seat of village authority, as well as an abode of powerful clan spirits. Within every Iatmul *ngeko* each post, beam, sitting platform, ladder, mask, flute, trumpet, slit-gong, and other paraphernalia connected to the *ngeko* has a personal name and is owned by individual clans who are part of the group of clans which compose that particular *ngeko*. Sometimes, however, clans from one *ngeko* may keep important paraphernalia such as flutes in another men's house not their own so that they can be used regularly. For instance, I have come across two female flutes with the names Numbukmaringawa that are owned by the Wengwandu clan but are kept and played often by men who belong to the opposing totemic moiety in the Wolimbi *ngeko*. Wengwandu is a clan of the other totemic moiety and its own *ngeko*, Kosimbi, has fallen down. The owner of the flutes, Ismael Gramban, has sought permission from the men of the Wolimbi to keep his flutes there. The music which is produced from these two particular flutes is aesthetically graceful, and Wolimbi men enjoy playing them from time to time. Sometimes these flutes are used to entertain visiting tourists who stay overnight in the village. Two other female flutes with the name Mangran are owned by the Suaru clan and are played only at the time when an initiation ritual is to be concluded. It is the men of Suaru clan who clean and decorate these two flutes and prepare them to be used. The Suaru clan belongs to the same totemic moiety (*nyamei nimba*) as Wengwandu but it has become part of Wolimbi which belongs to the other totemic moiety called *nyowi nimba*. Some members of the Suaru clan who are now part of the clans in the Wolimbi manage these two flutes.

So far I have portrayed the men's house as primarily a sphere of male interaction and residential houses as the abode of female interaction. However, they are not exclusively separate spheres. Initiated men in particular move to and fro between the *ngeko* and *ngeio*, and participate actively in chores that take place in both of these spheres. Women, however, do not enter the *ngeko* in the same way as men do with residential houses.[9] For the most part women provide men with food and bear them children, while men build houses and make canoes for women. While the procuring of food and rearing of children are a daily preoccupation of women, it is only once in a while that men build houses. The activities of men and women are held to complement each other in the production of things and perpetuation of values that sustain family and communal life. It might be helpful to point out that totemic moieties provide a general basis of residence, with each clan having its own residential area (*yaranga*). Female and male members of this clan are separated at marriage. So if totemism creates a condition for separation, ritual moieties, on the other hand, provide a general condition for unity, as we shall see in the next chapter.

It is believed that each residential house has a guardian spirit that looks after the house and the well-being of its inhabitants. These particular spirits are closely identified with individual clans, and in most cases the people actually know the name of such spirits and have particular kinds of relations with this guardian spirit. Each *ngeko* has a particular guardian spirit associated with the 'elder-brother group of clans' in that *ngeko*. The village as a whole may have other guardian spirits and such spirits may be closely associated with a particular clan, clan association, or *ngeko*.

All Iatmul *ngeko* have feminine names and an intriguing female symbol dominates certain parts of the *ngeko*, such as the finial masks that adorn the top of the *ngeko*. Another feminine symbol is found on the pole that leads up to the finial mask at the top of the *ngeko*. This pole stems from a carved female figure squatting with her legs stretched wide. Men go under this female figure when they enter the upper chambers of the *ngeko*. The debating stool which stands on the ground in the middle of the *ngeko* also has the incision of a vulva, and it serves to warn and remind men that those who have just engaged in sexual intercourse must not touch the stool or take part in debates going on at that time. There is a particular sitting platform in each *ngeko* that is considered to be the *karu*, or the looped net bag

[9] See also Wassmann (1991: 42–3); Errington and Gewertz (1987: 64–5) and Mead (1935: 239) for a comparable description of the contrast between the *ngeko* and *ngeio* and the segregation of the sexes in Iatmul and Chambri societies.

in which an infant child is normally kept. In the Wolimbi *ngeko* this particular *karu* is the sitting platform called Bangrajambi, and its associated *karu* is called Meimbeinjawakaru, which is owned by the Miembei clan. *Miembei* is the name of the clan while *njawa* is the feminine suffix of that name and *karu* is the looped bag. This particular platform is symbolically associated with peace and immunity. The symbolism is drawn from the imagery of an infant child resting peacefully in comfort and security inside its mother. As a platform, the name Bangrajambi derives its etymology from *bangra*, the word for areca nuts, which serve as a token of peace and dialogue. Whenever there is conflict that brings about strife and tension in the village the afflicted person may go and sit on that platform. This means that that person is now immune from further attacks. If the contrary happens, this will provoke the wrath of the *ngeko* and, as a matter of principle, the entire village or members of that particular *ngeko* would take vengeance on the assailant(s).

When someone or a group of people seek comfort and protection from that particular platform in a time of conflict, they are granted immediate immunity. This establishes a period of truce and a process of dialogue gets under way to resolve the conflict. The particular *ngeko* which contains the platform has a responsibility to try and meet the requests of the afflicted. Because it is located in the *ngeko*, the platform is used by men on a daily basis, but only in the context of duress does it involve immunity and protection from further violence. The counterpart of this particular platform in the men's house is the residential house of the senior lineage of the Miembei clan. Under the same conditions of conflict as described here, one may also go and seek refuge in the residential house of this particular family instead of going into the *ngeko*. The same rules and obligations apply to this particular residential house as well.

When I enquired into why Iatmul men's houses have feminine names, I was told that, at an abstract level, all houses are like women who contain in them other persons (see also Silverman 2001: 64–80). It was explained to me that:

> Everyone comes from women. You and I are born of women. And like a woman, this *ngeko* is peopled with different sorts of persons. [Pointing at me, he said] Look at me and what you see immediately is my body which is made up of flesh and blood. Flesh and blood come from the mother whereas the bones which are concealed and lie beneath the flesh come from the father. Likewise, what you see of the *ngeko* at first sight is its outward physical structure which is like our skin and flesh. The outward physical structure

> of the *ngeko* conceals the king posts inside. What holds the *ngeko* together are these five king posts which are like the bones in our bodies.

The interlocutor was careful to observe that 'all of us come from women' and used an analogy employed from the idiom of kinship to explain the gendered composition of the *ngeko*. His explanation rests on an interconnection between human bodies and houses. In its personification, the *ngeko* appears 'as an extension of the person; like an extra skin, carapace or second layer of clothes, it serves as much to reveal and display as it does to hide and protect' (Carsten and Hugh-Jones 1995: 2). Thus, if we recall our discussions above, we can now see how the men's house and the residential house are not only spheres of social interaction but they also serve to hide and protect people. The contrasts between revelation and concealment, as well as 'outside and inside', are structural forms that appear in different permutations in many other societies in Melanesia (see for instance Mosko 1985; Strathern 2000: 54–57).

Iatmul descent is of a patrilineal cast but the affiliation with one's mother's side is very strong. Clans are exogamous and formally the residence after marriage is virilocal. The source of an Iatmul clan lies outside it in other clans (or more specifically lineages), where women are taken in during marriage. However, a *ngeko* is not just composed of male and female substances; like a human person it is riddled with a cluster of male and female appurtenances and its gender status shifts from male to female; at times it takes on an explicitly androgynous composition. What is also conveyed in the observation above is the connection between the 'outside', which is associated with one's mother's side, and the 'inside', which is associated with one's father's side. This logic is also extended into the naming system. As we shall see in Chapter 5, each pair of parents contributes particular body substances in procreation and the names given to a person derive from both sides of one's parents. While matrinames connected through the mother's blood are associated with the fleshy exteriority of one's body and the external appearance of the men's house, patrinames are connected with the father's semen and are associated with bones and various posts inside the *ngeko*. The bones which lie in the interior of people's bodies are analogous to the main posts, which carry the frame of the *ngeko*.

In addition, like persons who have particular character traits and dispositions, Iatmul also think that their men's houses have personality types. Each Iatmul men's house is connected to a particular conception of personality type (cf. Bateson 1958: 160–70). I will incorporate Bateson's description of Iatmul personality types in Chapter 4, when we consider the Iatmul idea of a 'person'. In the meantime, the discussion below will make clear the connection between men's houses and totemic moieties.

Ngeko, totemic moieties, and personality types

All Iatmul villages have two distinct architectural styles that inspire the external appearance of the *ngeko*. Each of these styles corresponds to distinct conceptions of personalities associated with the particular *ngeko*. Each *ngeko* is intimately connected to a particular totemic moiety, but the clan membership within that particular *ngeko* may not be exclusively from one totemic moiety. One kind of *ngeko* has a personality type that is called Kisameli and is associated with the *nyowi nimba* or the 'father/sun' moiety. The other kind of *ngeko* is called Kimbianmeli and is associated with *nyamei nimba* or the 'mother/earth' moiety. Figures 2.1 and 2.2 are diagrammatic representations of these two kinds of *ngeko*.

Figure 2.1 The Kisameli style of *ngeko*

Figure 2.2 The Kimbianmeli style of *ngeko*

Although they are built out of the same architectural elements, Kisameli stands upright with a protruding finial mask, its face looking straight on, and its roof drops down from a steep gradient. While Kimbianmeli also has a protruding finial mask, its face is cast downwards and its roof declines with a slanted gradient. There are mythological explanations that lie behind the styles of these two kinds of men's houses, but it would be an extremely serious breach of secrecy on my part if the esoteric significance of these architectural styles were to be revealed. If I were to be faithful to public talk about these two architectural forms, one might say that Kisameli is the elder-brother and Kimbianmeli is the younger-brother house. At the surface level of esoteric mythology, the two types of houses have feminine names because there is a mother–child relationship between them.

The clans that constitute the core of each particular *ngeko* belong to one particular totemic moiety, and they would define themselves in oppositional terms to the other totemic moiety. In Central Iatmul, the only village that has all its members belonging to one totemic moiety is Yenjan. This is because the clans which make up Yenjan village were an association of clans that compose the front part of the Paimbit men's house in the neighbouring Parimbe village. However, when these clans moved across the Sepik River they reconfigured themselves into several clans which now compose the men's house in Yenjan village called Nyangrambi. Table 2.1

lists the names of each *ngeko* and the contrasting personality types associated with each of these *ngeko* in Central Iatmul villages.[10]

In theory there are three *ngeko* in Kanganamun village. Two of them—Minjimbit and Kosimbi—belong to the totemic moiety called *nyamei nimba* or the 'mother/earth people'. *Nyamei* is the word for 'mother' and *nimba* means 'people'. The other *ngeko* is called Wolimbi and it belongs to the other totemic moiety called *nyowi nimba* or the 'father/sun people'. *Nyowi* is the word for sun. The earth and sun are the polarized physical extremes of this totemic cosmology. The totemic moieties do not regulate marriage so that, in this particular context, the terms 'father/mother people' should not be taken as referring to an exogamous moiety system. In Kanganamun, Wolimbi is the only fully fledged *ngeko* in the village today, whereas Kosimbi *ngeko* has collapsed and has not been replaced; a small building, which is more like a club house, serves the purposes of a *ngeko* for Minjimbit. The men's houses Minjimbit and Kosimbi have fallen down and whilst there are no plans yet to rebuild Kosimbi, the men of Minjimbit have been talking about their plans to rebuild their *ngeko*.

Discussions about the Iatmul characterization of personalities were held with two of the village *komiti*, each of them from opposing totemic moieties in the village. The two men explained the concept of 'personality' with the Tok Pisin word *pasin*. In my understanding of Iatmul inflections,

Table 2.1 Villages and the personality type of their *ngeko*

Village	*Name of ngeko*	*Totemic moiety*	*Personality type*
Kanganamun	Minjimbit	Mother/Earth	Kimbianmeli
	Kosimbi	Mother/Earth	Kimbianmeli
	Wolimbi	Father/Sun	Kisameli
Maringe	Mindimbit	Mother/Earth	Kimbianmeli
	Mangembit	Father/Sun	Kisameli
Parimbe	Paiambit	Mother/Earth	Kimbianmeli
	Andimbit	Father/Sun	Kisameli
	Nambaraman	Father/Sun	Kisameli
Yenjan	Nyangrambi	Mother/Earth	Kimbianmeli

[10] See Coiffier (1990: 491–500) for an ethnographic account of Iatmul architecture, although he does not mention anything about the connection between the *ngeko* and personality type. Hauser-Schäublin (1990: 460–79) discusses the connection between settlement patterns and the architectural structure of houses amongst some Sepik societies including the Iatmul. Bowden (1983, 1990: 480–90) discusses the connection between Kwoma art forms and *haus boi* associated with men's initiation rituals, but an immediate difference is that Kwoma men's houses are 'male' whereas Iatmul's are 'female'.

pasin may be taken to mean an enduring set of mental and behavioural dispositions or impulses that characterize a particular individual or group, and is articulated in the manner in which such persons comport themselves towards others during the emergence of particular contingencies. One of the *komiti* told me that Kimbianmeli is the 'younger brother' and Kisameli is the 'elder brother' (cf. Bateson 1958: 242n).

According to the two *komiti*, Kimbianmeli is assertive, short-tempered, and has a tendency to react instantaneously when an event such as a fight or a collective work is under way. Thus, in a dispute for instance, men of Kimbianmeli are often quick to pick a fight with their opponents. They are single-minded and their actions are decisive and fast. When they have resolved to undertake a particular kind of work, they mobilize themselves in the manner of work bees and set to, so that the work is done in no time. The manner of conduct of Kimbianmeli differs markedly from that of the men of Kisameli. The Kisameli type are slow to mobilize themselves in getting up to work. But when they get going, they too, like those of Kisameli, are careful to finish what needs to be finished. One of the *komiti* notes, 'Although we are different, when we fight other people, we would want to finish our enemies properly.' The other said:

> You have heard of our recent fight in the village. It's not a new thing. It's always been like this. Although we fight against ourselves in the village, we stand together and fight others from outside of our village. Although it is based on a long history of confrontations between the men of our two men's houses [by which he meant the two totemic moieties], the recent fight is really like another practice session for our young men.

The fight to which this *komiti* refers took place in April 2001, and it involved a combined team of men from Minjimbit and Kosimbi who fought against the men of Wolimbi. That fight grew from an agonizing tension that emerged from a bird-killing competition held amongst small boys and male teenagers who belong to the two totemic moieties in the village. This particular form of competition has been practised throughout many generations and no one told me precise details of how it started. But if this competition led to conflict then it would be fair to say that the tense opposition that exists among the totemic moieties is something that is inculcated into the lives of the young boys at a very young age. And as they grow up they do so with a conscious knowledge of themselves as belonging separately to different totemic moieties and men's houses. Nowadays soccer matches are also organized amongst young boys. Such soccer matches were a particular spectacle for me each morning during the dry season, when the small boys played each other in opposing teams and would invite me to go and watch their matches.

In the months of January and February 2001, a men's initiation ritual was held in the village, during which time the small boys and teenagers were isolated and kept away from the vicinity of the men's house. While the initiated men temporarily suspended their totemic affiliation to carry out the initiation ritual, the young boys and teenagers upheld their totemic allegiances by organizing themselves into two teams based on their totemic moieties and they went about in the bush in search of birds to kill with their catapults. The initiated men of different totemic moieties came together in the Wolimbi *ngeko* for the purpose of initiating novices, whereas the boys and teenagers, who are excluded from the ritual, kept themselves separate by maintaining their totemic differences. The boys of Minjimbit and Kosimbi were in one team while those of Wolimbi made the other team. The competition involved killing birds during the months of January till April. Besides the fact that every bird is worth a point, the size of the bird also matters so that a bird such as a parrot or an eagle is worth more points than smaller birds. The counting of birds killed provides the opportunity for the leading team to put down the name of the other team.

Three months into the competition, it became obvious that the team from Wolimbi was in a clear lead, with a margin far beyond the reach of the opposing team from Minjimbit/Kosimbi. The Minjimbit/Kosimbi team then presented a case to mitigate their poor performance, arguing that it was not really a lack of talent that had caused them to trail behind their opponents but rather their minimal access to forested areas. They observed that the land under the control of the clans of the Wolimbi gave its team the advantage in the competition. Its land, with a bigger forested area, provided a good habitat for a variety of birds which made easy game for the Wolimbi team. The opposing team did not have access to forested areas of any equivalence to that of Wolimbi. Several requests were made to the Wolimbi team that the boys from Minjimbit/Kosimbi should be allowed to hunt birds in the forests owned by Wolimbi clans. The requests were denied and the opposing team was refused access to the forest.

This refusal notwithstanding, some boys from the Minjimbit/Kosimbi team started going off to look for birds in forest areas owned by Wolimbi clans. They were noticed several times and were warned against hunting there again. Three separate warnings were issued but were not complied with. On the fourth occasion, a teenager named Bill of Wolimbi came across four small boys of Minjimbit/Kosimbi and chased them out of the forest, with a threat to chastise them. The small boys reported their encounter with Bill to one of their teenagers, namely Jacob. In the afternoon, when the two teams gathered to account for the day's kill, Jacob angrily confronted Bill and suddenly a fight erupted between the two of them. The news of their fight spread through the village so that it grew to absorb the energies of adult men who represented opposing teams. The fight lasted for about an hour or so, with each side wielding fists and yelling abuse at each other. Along with the abuse threats of further violence were issued. After the fight ended, there was no public or official effort to seek reconciliation between the two opposing factions and the entire episode was taken as very much a momentary bursting out of perpetual tensions that characterize the historical life of the village as imagined through the politics of totemic affiliation. Although there was no public ceremony of reconciliation, individual men and teenagers met and shook hands and looked each other in the face again. It was obvious that to discuss the matter further would reinvigorate and heighten prevailing tensions, which might then become polarized and explode into unintended consequences.

Different men told me that this conflict between the totemic moieties is really a perpetual conflict that underlies the psychological tenor of relations between the totemic moieties in the village. The slightest problem amongst members of opposing moieties has the incidental effect of triggering and recapitulating on the memories of previous encounters, which then balloon and burst into an episodic moment of furious violence before it subsides into the apparent tranquillity of peaceful assimilation. Various people in the village said that this has been going on intermittently throughout the life of the village, and this totemic feud or schismogenic tension (Bateson 1958) is very much at the core of the political and psychological tenor of the Iatmul totemic system.

Two of the men from Wolimbi who were involved in the fight told me that the conflict would never be resolved. One of them said: 'This is a thing that our forefathers have been doing and we the children will still follow. I don't know how and when it will end. Maybe it will stop when this world comes to an end.' He expressed all the pessimism that can be expressed about this feud and he in fact, as I have come to know him, would resist any attempt to resolve this dispute. The other expressed a similar view, but what he said resonates closely with the views of one of the village *komiti* mentioned earlier. He explained that members of the current totemic moieties are descendants of putative ancestral spirits which also had a feud and the prevailing tensions are an enduring legacy that continues on from this totemic feud. Below is an account of a common myth held by the two totemic moieties, reproduced here to exemplify the contrasting sorts of interpretations members of the two moieties have of common myths such as this. Often, when a particular myth is held by several clans or different moieties, the esoteric significance of such myths is not known publicly and interpretations of them vary or even differ markedly.

The clans of Minjimbit/Kosimbi are considered to be descendants of a very powerful group of female spirits called Nduma and Ndangan. These spirits had fire coming out of their vulvas (see also Silverman 2001: 35; Wassmann 1991: 41) and, in other mythological accounts, men of Minjimbit/Kosimbi were able to utilize the fire-power of these female spirits to cut down huge trees to make canoes and slit-gongs. But outside of their own totemic moiety, these women were indifferent to anything male. The spirit women would lie naked under a particular tree with their vulva exposed and the wind would blow the leaves from the tree down. If a leaf landed and touched the vulva of a woman she would become pregnant. If such a woman then gave birth to a male child, the women would kill and eat the child, whereas if a female child was born, they would preserve the child and raise her up as one of their own members. One day a woman gave birth to a male child but instead of killing the child, she decided to keep him. That woman and her daughter raised the child secretly in their house and as he grew up he became the envy of his sister. The mother, however, became fearful that her son might become too powerful and would kill her and other women, so she made a plan to have her son killed. However, her daughter overheard the plans and revealed their mother's malicious intentions to her brother. The brother and sister pair then worked out a counter-attack plan.

The brother and sister secretly made a canoe and several spears. It was planned that the women would hold a big feast after killing the woman's son. These spirit women had gone out and brought in other food items in anticipation of their feast. On the evening of that appointed day, the mother would prepare sago pancake for her son and, when he came and took the sago from her, she would grab him by the hand and other women would also spring upon him and tear him to death. But since the man knew about his ambush already, he kept some spears with him inside their house. Thus, when his mother called him to take his sago, she grabbed his hand but he quickly evaded the grasp of his mother and started killing the women including his mother. Other women came to help but he escaped in the canoe built with the help of his sister. The man was later killed in fierce battle against the women. This version of the myth is held by clans of Minjimbit/Kosimbi or the 'mother/earth' moiety.

Men of clans which belong to the 'father/sun' moiety, however, told me that it was not the intention of the spirit men to be born of women. I was told that the name of this man was Meimban and his sister was called Ponmbi. Ponmbi's story is now held by the Graken clan, while her brother Meimban is a tutelary spirit of the Samiangwat clan and is also considered as the guardian spirit of Kanganamun village. Meimban makes occasional visits to the village as a bird and announces his presence with a high-pitched sound when he flies over the village in the night. My adopted father, Yarme Mambingawi, acknowledged that while clans of the opposing moiety do have a story about the spirit women and their becoming impregnated by the leaves of the tree, it was Meimban himself who caused the leaves from the tree to fall down and touch the vulva of the spirit women. It was Meimban who was causing the women to be pregnant and not the tree leaves as such. After his mother was pregnant, Meimban inclined her will to preserve rather than to kill him. As he grew into a man, he posed a threat to the women and so his mother attempted to eradicate him leading to the fight described above. Although Meimban and his mother died eventually, some Iatmul believe that the fight continues today in the form of conflicts that arise between the two totemic moieties in the village.

Ngeko and the dynamics of ownership amongst the totemic moieties

If we recall the fight amongst the teenagers described above then we might expect that issues of ownership provide reason enough for the explosion of litigious and conflicting claims. The requests and claims to have access to forested areas or fishing lagoons provide an economic rationale by which this mythical charter of totemic feud comes to be expressed as a matter of contemporary concern articulated in the language of ownership. Apart from the fight described above, another of the use-rights that cause friction amongst the totemic moieties concerns the Takasep lagoon. The lagoon is located to the east of the village within a land area whose personal name is owned by clans which belong to Wolimbi. This particular lagoon was created in the 1960s through diverting the course of the Sepik River. This long winding bend is located along the northern bank of the river and clans from Wolimbi took charge in digging a trench. They used digging-sticks and spades to dig while those who knew the appropriate magic summoned ancestral crocodiles to help with the arduous task.

The creation of this lagoon took place under the leadership of a man called Gonduan, who at that time presided as the *kansol* of the village. Gonduan belongs to the Wanigo clan of Wolimbi (father/sun moiety) but was married to a woman from the Lenga clan of Minjimbit (mother/earth moiety). Minjimbit and Kosimbi do not have fishing lagoons located within the vicinity of the village, and the only one that they have rights to use and control is the Limbambi lagoon, located further to the east near the Eastern Iatmul village of Kararau and the Sawos village of Timboli. Gonduan thought of his in-laws and was sorry, for he was moved with emotion for their lack of fishing lagoons. He therefore conspired with his in-laws strategically and devised a plan to divert the men of the village on alternating days to work on the lagoon. Thus while Gonduan made the men of Wolimbi cut grass on the ceremonial ground around their *ngeko,* the men of Minjimbit/Kosimbi went off in the early hours of the morning to work on creating the lagoon. Gonduan reasoned that if his in-laws contributed towards digging the trench, they would then be able to lay a claim to have use-rights to the fishing lagoon once it was created.

However, when it came to the knowledge of the men of Wolimbi that their counterparts from Minjimbit/Kosimbi had been working on the trench, they told them to stop working there and only the men from Wolimbi continued to work until the lagoon was created. Today, however, men of Minjimbit/Kosimbi insist that their fathers also contributed towards digging the trench but their counterparts in Wolimbi are too greedy and selfish to allow them the benefit of getting fish from the Takasep lagoon. Guraki, an old man from Kosimbi, told me that in the past, Kanganamun used to have ten war canoes when the village went out on military raids. The village defended and claimed its territory as a unit and it is fitting that the resources such as fishing lagoons and waterways should be enjoyed by all clan groups. He believes strongly that there should be not any discrimination along the lines of totemic affiliation.

While the men from Wolimbi agree that Kanganamun used to fight together in the past with the use of ten war canoes (six from Wolimbi and four from Minjimbit/Kosimbi), they argue that the fighting was more to do with the heroic culture of masculine pride (see Bateson 1958: 99; Harrison 1993: 80–94) than with anything to do with territorial rights of the village as a whole. Warfare provided an opportunity for warriors to kill and bring back heads as trophies after which they adorned and exhibited themselves with a particular kind of black paint and ornaments which expressed their heroic deeds.[11]

The point of reciting these accounts is to highlight how opposing totemic moieties have different versions of particular narratives, which they use to assert or seek to gain access to or legitimacy regarding the use of particular resources such as forested areas and fishing lagoons. The story of Takasep lagoon has two competing versions of history relating to its creation. Whilst one group is using historical narratives and relationships to seek access to the lagoon, the other is using almost the same kind of information to preserve its hold and deny the other from using it. There is an analytical purchase to be gained from this simple account of the competing claims, for it reveals a critical dialectic that informs the trajectories in which land ownership comes into existence amongst the Iatmul. One of these trajectories is illustrated by Guraki's claim of his father's work in helping to create the lagoon. Because his fathers helped to create the lagoon, they should be allowed to use the lagoon. By the logic of this reasoning, ownership emerges as result of creative energy. A common phrase often heard is that if you were the first one to cut the grass in this place, you then earn the right to use the land, and ultimately have rights of ownership over it. The men of Wolimbi, on the other hand, argue that the efforts of the men from Minjimbit/Kosimbi are derailed on the grounds that they were seeking to create what is already owned by another. And the logic of their claim is that prior ownership exercises a constraint upon creative work.[12] One can only create upon what one owns.

So far I have used the affiliation with men's houses in order to paint a picture of the dialectical tensions that prevail in an Iatmul village. Conflicting claims of ownership often provide a good reason for tensions to become inflated and burst into episodes of violent tussles before subsiding again. The totemic system of the Iatmul clans divides and discriminates between those who have rights and those who do not, and this illuminates the behaviour of ownership itself. Perhaps the most significant behaviour of ownership is its penchant to discriminate between those who control access to and use of that which is owned, and those who do not (see Honoré 1961: 113–61). Furthermore, as one can see from the cases discussed above, ownership behaves in a subtle or insidious way to seize and

[11] See Bateson (1958: Plate XXIVA) for the photographic record of one such attack.

[12] Further elaboration of this dialectical relationship between creativity and ownership is delayed for a separate project.

exploit the intermittent claims to use resources such as lagoons in order to assert itself as a conductor of relations between persons. In this light, ownership is not simply a function of relationships but one that gives form and imposes a constraint upon social relations, including the relations of creative endeavours.

So far the account has been presented as if it were an aerial glimpse from the perspective of someone affiliated with a particular *ngeko* in Iatmul. It also describes the kinds of tensions and issues of ownership that are part of the politics of men's houses in an Iatmul village. I hope to descend from this lofty view and provide a view from the ground, as it were, through the movement of social relations in and out of the contrast between the *ngeko* and *ngeio*. Such a description is also intended to show how ownership appears as an institution that has both a collective and individual dimension, just like an individual Iatmul person, who has personal possessions but also belongs to collective such as a totemic moiety, clan, and lineage.

Ngeko and *ngeio*: men's house and the residential house

The immediate contrast between a *ngeko* and *ngeio* is inscribed through their membership and the nature of relationships and different spheres of ownership that are concomitant with these two distinct architectural forms (see Bateson 1958: 123–51). The *ngeko* is normally a long and tall building overlooking the residential houses.[13] A *ngeio* must never be taller than a *ngeko*, in order to prevent women and children peeping into it. When there are men's initiation rituals going on in the village, women, children, and uninitiated men are required to avert their eyes from the *ngeko* and those who are found to be looking towards the *ngeko* are scolded.

The *ngeko* in other Central Iatmul villages have palm-leaf walls that run from the roof to the ground and act as a screen that prevents people from looking into the *ngeko* from the outside.[14] In Kanganamun, however, the Wolimbi men's house does not have any walls on its sides and what goes on in there can easily be seen from outside it; that is why the uninitiated are not supposed to look into it when initiation rituals are carried out. There are several gates or roads (*yembi*) that allow men to enter and leave

[13] Residential houses in Central Iatmul do not take the symbolic elaboration that they do in Eastern Iatmul (Silverman 2001: 64–80).

[14] The *ngeko* in other Iatmul villages that have walls touching the ground also have windows in their upper chambers that allow for light and ventilation.

the house, and they are expected to use the gates that are nearest to their own sitting platform (*jambi*). Secret implements such as flutes, trumpets, and bullroarers are kept in the upper-chambers of the *ngeko*. Within a *ngeko* may be kept displays of war trophies, totemic posts, slit-gongs, ceremonial stools, fire-places, storage places, and nowadays it is a common sight to find carvings (owned by individual men) displayed to be sold to tourists and art dealers who visit. Women do not display their artefacts in the *ngeko* but they do come onto the ceremonial ground during meetings, ceremonial occasions, and when tourists and art dealers visit the village. Some men make carvings and give them to their wives, children, and sisters to sell and get money for their own purposes.

Boys under the age of four are sometimes brought into the *ngeko* by their fathers, but that happens only when the father is sure that men who are in the *ngeko* at the time will not complain about the small boy's short visit. Nowadays, uninitiated men are allowed entry into the *ngeko* when there are no initiation rituals, but they would be asked to leave at short notice if an issue relating to men's initiation sacra is discussed. Uninitiated men provide additional help to cut grass on the ceremonial ground and are also expected to work on other parts of the *ngeko* from time to time. When uninitiated men help, secret objects are carefully hidden before they are allowed entry and these objects are kept concealed until the uninitiated men leave the *ngeko* again.

Throughout the year, from dawn till night-time, men spend a lot of their time in the *ngeko*. Men from other *ngeko* are allowed in and, when visiting the *ngeko* of the opposing moiety, care should be taken to observe all the necessary protocols. Young initiated men and male teenagers often play mini soccer games on the ceremonial ground in front of the *ngeko*, although these games were never permitted in the past. When men gather in the *ngeko*, they talk about all kinds of things, ranging from mythological narratives to news about national politics, or lament the decline of government services. Gossip about flirtatious and adulterous liaisons abounds, but it is expected that issues of interpersonal relations discussed inside the *ngeko* are not revealed outside.

Many a time I have seen men of Wolimbi lie on their bellies on platforms in the *ngeko* and stare out into the village, watching for mothers and wives to return from the fishing lagoons. The women depart early in the morning, about 6 a.m., and go together in groups or in pairs. Each woman keeps her fishing net in a string bag suspended from her head as she makes her way to the lagoon. During the wet season the women go to the lagoons in their canoes. Ideally each woman should have her own canoe. At the onset of the wet season, some places become inundated with water, giving rise to an army of ferocious mosquitoes. Women who undertake fishing trips often have a fire going on the small stove at the back of their canoes and the fire helps to ward off mosquitoes as well as to provide warmth.

When they arrive at the lagoon, they prepare themselves and then anchor their nets in shallow parts of the lagoon. There is no quarrel over the particular fishing spots on the lagoon but some women prefer to stick to places which they find favourable to their nets. After the nets are set in the lagoon, they return and wait in a small house (*sai*), or they retreat into the cover of trees to protect them from the sun. Some take this time to look for firewood and others tend their small gardens in the bush nearby. Intermittently they check on the fishing nets in the waters. After a sufficient quantity of fish is caught, they go ashore to remove the scales and gut the fish. Some women have their baths in the lagoon before they return home for the evening. After they return, mothers set to prepare meals for their families. It is the task of women to gather firewood for their cooking but some men sometimes help. In the forest nearby, women take firewood only from wood found on their husband's land. At times there are disputes among women over where they get their firewood. I am told that married couples, who are often surrounded at home by their children and relatives, may find collecting firewood in the bush an opportune moment for them to have sexual intercourse.

The main staple of the Iatmul people is sago (*nau*) and fish (*kami*). Meals are normally taken in the company of other family members. During the early hours of the evening till late at night, a very distinctive aroma of freshly smoked fish pervades the atmosphere in the village with a characteristic smell of a fishing community. Some of the fish are kept in storage cabinets, which hang over fireplaces, and due to the passage of time such cabinets have become tainted with a patina and are scented with the smell of fish. Baked sago pancakes are kept either with fish in the storage cabinets or in baskets suspended from the ceiling or crossbeams somewhere in the house. Each member of the family will have a basket in which their sago pancakes are kept. Sago is acquired either by monetary exchange or barter exchange with fish. After a market, each mother takes home an appropriate amount of sago which she will keep in a sago pot in the house and is later used by the family for at least a week before her supplies are replenished the following week.

During the onset of the wet season, when mosquitoes abound in the village, fires may be made on the ground under the (residential) house to help chase away mosquitoes that 'fall from the air' as the evening sets in.

Although the mosquitoes are a real pestilence, the villagers have grown accustomed to them and have a remarkably patient response to the irritation caused by the constant attacks of these mosquitoes. The seasonal preponderance of mosquitoes enlists itself as a subject of social commentary amongst the villagers, similar to the commentaries about weather that occupy daily conversations in England. But the Iatmul do not own the weather, except the mosquitoes which are a totems of a particular (Suaru) clan in the village. It is often rumoured that those who know the stories and secret names of mosquitoes are able to control the influx of mosquitoes into the village. When mosquitoes become an unbearable nuisance, people would take slit-gongs under their houses and, as they beat the gongs, they will call out '*kivia . . . kivia . . . kivia*'. And if it was true that the totemic owners of the mosquitoes have caused their increase, they might be kind enough to make the mosquitoes decline in numbers.

A few families have slit-gongs inside or under their houses, and the gongs are used for sending messages to particular persons. Every Sunday, the catechist of the Catholics and the pastor of the AOG followers within the village would beat their gongs with distinctive rhythms to summon their respective congregations for their Sunday worship. The SDA pastor and his congregation, however, use a metal bell that acts in the place of slit-gongs. Slit-gongs kept inside a *ngeio* are usually smaller in size than those in the *ngeko*. The ones in the *ngeko* are often passed on as heirlooms within a lineage or a clan. Larger slit-gongs kept in the *ngeko* are owned by individual clans and are known by their personal names owned by the clan in question. Although individual clans own gongs in the *ngeko*, other initiated men in the village often use them on particular occasions. However, only men who know the appropriate rhythms for different occasions are allowed to beat the gongs, and the knowledge of these rhythms is learnt from other knowledgeable men within the *ngeko*. Ownership of such gongs does not restrict their use to their owners only, but the owners are responsible for their general up-keep.

Each initiated man has a personal named rhythm that is owned by his clan or clan association. Each of these personal rhythms is analogous to a code or a 'phone number' as it was explained to me. There is an important relationship of hierarchy observed between the slit-gongs and the *ngeko*, and this relationship is also concomitant with the contrast between *ngeko* and *ngeio*. The relationships organized around the *ngeko* and amongst the initiated men are different from those enacted in and around the *ngeio*. Each *ngeko*, each clan association within a *ngeko*, and each initiated man, has a personal rhythm that belongs to his clan association in the *ngeko*. Rhythms that are beaten and sent off from a slit-gong in the *ngeko* cannot be responded to by using the slit-gong kept in a *ngeio.* One could only reply to a rhythm that is sent from one *ngeko* to another *ngeko* and from one *ngeio* to another *ngeio.* The person who makes a reply by beating the slit-gong in his or her house is guilty of an offence. Such an offence is subjected to appropriate penalties, which are enforced by members of the 'elder-brother' group of clans located in the front part of the *ngeko.* The significance given to a *ngeio* is weighted differently to the *ngeko.*[15]

Slit-gong rhythms are analogous to telephones in their instrumental function. The rhythms also connect two men who are related to each other by virtue of their initiation. When a matter concerns the *ngeko*, a slit-gong rhythm may bring together members of opposing totemic moieties who belong to different *ngeko.* When a matter concerns the general public or the interaction between initiated men and the uninitiated, a slit-gong kept in a *ngeio* is used, and this may for instance bring together church-goers on a Sunday morning. At other times, particular rhythms may also be beaten on slit-gongs kept under residential houses to inform and invite men, women, and children in the village to gamble in a game of lucky cards (*laki kat*).

This form of gambling is an occasional pastime for many people in the village. These games are held in a residential area. Much like the fight that started off with small boys and teenagers described earlier, gambling also begins with children playing against each other to win broomsticks made from coconut fronds. But as it gains momentum it captures the indulgence of mature girls and women, and in time it widens to enlist the participation of male teenagers and adult men. When adults have enthralled themselves in these games, what started as a simple competition amongst the children finally evolves into gambling for money. The gambling could go on for several hours each day, starting about the time women have returned from their fishing trips. Small amounts of money are initially used, and then bigger sums of money are thrown down when the game intensifies with higher stakes at risk. The wife of one of my adopted 'mothers' (*mbora*) walked off one time with a hefty K375 after she successfully made other players succumb to her invincibility over a period of three consecutive days.

[15] In political parlance, the *ngeko* is best seen as a seat of government. Accordingly one might think, for instance, of how Canberra (Australia's seat of government) alone can communicate with Waigani (PNG's seat of government). A village such as Kanganamun is like a residential house and Canberra cannot deal with such a village but only with Waigani in matters concerning the two governments.

These *laki* games sometimes include the participation of people from the surrounding Iatmul and Sawos villages, and at times people from Kanganamun go other villages to play. On Sundays when soccer (for men) and volleyball (for women) matches are held in the neighbouring Sawos village of Nangusap, gambling matches go on concurrently in a secluded corner in the vicinity of the games. Men, women, and teenagers participate in these games and there is no restriction on age. The gambling matches provide opportunities for men and women to seek out dating, courtship, and flirtatious, even adulterous, relationships, and some marriages were formed out of such encounters. One of my adopted mother's brothers (*wau*) often boasted to me about how he managed to consolidate the marriage with his second wife through gambling. And when the game continues on in the village, he would jokingly say to me, '*Laua* (nephew), I am going in there now. Don't be surprised if I get you a new aunty (*mbora*).'

Such games are held on Fridays, after people have gone to market, or soon after tourists and art dealers have visited the village and left them with some money from the sale of artefacts. While gambling makes a small contribution to a winner's moderate income, gambling is intended more as a social than an economic event. With respect to such games, some men often remark that: 'Whenever there are women so too there will be men. Women provide a presence that fuels the energies of men.' Women are consciously aware of this and enjoy the attention from men. Playing *laki* is also risky and I have heard rumours of women resorting to sexual exchanges for financial favours from men who sponsor women in games. Along with such rumours are fears of people using magic (*supu*) to influence and maintain their winning, but when such fears abound, counter-magic is made to dilute and dispel the magic. Whether or not magic or counter-magic are used or are effective is hard to tell, except that these are the kinds of talk that emerge from such events of social interaction in the village.

Gambling or other card games are not allowed in the *ngeko.* Men interact with women, children, and teenagers in residential areas, whereas they interact among themselves in the *ngeko*. The distinction between *ngeko* and *ngeio* is based on a gender understanding as revealed through the nature of ritual and totemic moieties in the village. The ritual moieties create a contrast between the initiated and the uninitiated such that all the initiated are 'male' and the uninitiated are 'female'. Through their initiation, males are allowed to move in between the *ngeko* and *ngeio*, whereas females move only between residential houses. From the perspective of totemic moieties, each *ngeio* has a totemic affiliation with a *ngeko*. In so far as a *ngeko* is connected to a totemic clan, all cross-sex and same-sex siblings are regarded as 'brothers'. Because within a clan (defined from the perspective of a *ngeio*) all siblings are of the same 'sex' by kinship understanding, female members of the clan or family are differentitated from their male relatives when they leave their residential houses or clans and get married into other clans. From the perspective of ritual moieties, the uninitiated males are considered as women and have to undergo initiation in order to become 'men'. From the perspective of totemic moieties, women are internally regarded as 'brothers' and they have to be married into other clans in order to become 'women', hence the popular saying, 'women move in between residential houses'.

Residential houses are located on land owned by individual clans (*yaranga*). Each residential compound, which is also called *yaranga*, is separated by mounds which may be as much as a metre high. Each *yaranga* is organizationally divided and is conceptualized as being occupied by an elder- and younger-brother pair of lineages—reminiscent of the elder- and younger-brother clan associations which occupy the front and back parts of the men's house. The front part of the *yaranga* is called *tungungeipa* and is occupied by a lineage identified with a putative elder-brother ancestor, while the back part of the *yaranga* is called *kandingeipa* and is occupied by a lineage associated with a putative younger-brother ancestor. In the bush at the back end of each *yaranga* are places where individual families build their own toilets. Sometimes a pathway (*yembi*) runs through the middle or the back of the *yaranga*.

Yaranga and *ngeio*: clans and residential houses

Each *yaranga* has its houses built facing their *ngeko* and there is an opening (*tuvui yembi*) in between ceremonial mounds on the side of the *ngeko* that faces the village. This opening provides a gate which allows men of each clan to go in and out of the *ngeko* and their *ngeio*. When moving in between the *ngeio* and the *ngeko*, initiated men are expected to use their own clan's pathway and are also responsible for cutting grass, harvesting, and replacing old coconut trees on their ceremonial mound. Coconuts and other food plants which are grown on the mounds (*tuvui*) separating clans are owned by clans which own the mound, and the use and enjoyment of such food plants are controlled by the lineages. There is much sharing of such food plants within a clan.

Within a *yaranga*, a close relationship is observed amongst the members of a particular clan. This relationship is made visible through the sharing of food, and co-participation in heavy menial tasks such as house and canoe building. This close relationship is also manifested in the studious involvement of a clan's men and women in learning clan myths (*sagi*) and secrets (*wan sukundi*). Women learn such totemic stories from their fathers and at events such as initiation rituals, or on the death of a clan member, or during *naven* ceremonials, when their totemic songs are chanted. In the event that lineages of a particular clan are absent in the village, it is incumbent upon the remaining lineage(s) to take charge in exercising custodial care over such things as are owned by other lineages within the clan. Some clans may have no members of their clan living in the village, so clans within the same clan association would take care of, and even use, their residential area or other resources. Sometimes it becomes necessary for clan members of another clan to use another clan's residential area, especially if the residential areas of such clans are adjacent to each other.

Lewis Waligawa, for instance, belongs to the Samiangwat clan and his *yaranga* is adjacent to that of the Sui clan. The Sui clan has no members present in the village. Because of the grass that has overtaken Sui's *yaranga*, Lewis, who is particularly keen on the tidiness of the village, has sought permission from members of the Sui clan living in town to build his house on their *yaranga* in order to help keep their *yaranga* clean and free from grass. Another residential area owned by the Mariambu clan is now taken over with a small plantation of banana and guava trees planted by men of Suaru and Saun clans in Minjimbit in order to keep the area free from grass. Map 3 shows the houses and distribution of clans into totemic and ritual moieties at the time of my fieldwork. The river that runs past the village into the Sepik River can serve as a basic geographical marker between the two totemic moieties. The totemic moieties can be identified with the two men's houses, which are shown in the map as quadripartite structures that stand facing each other.

As noted above, each *yaranga* is organizationally divided into two: each of the pair of brother lineages occupies opposite ends of their *yaranga*. A man, his wife, and children live together in their residential house. The house is often large and is not partitioned into rooms except that it is organizationally divided within it. Normally the man with his wife and children will take up the front of the house, and if the man has a younger brother who is also married, the younger brother and his family will take the back part of the house. A man's elder son who is married with children may stay at his father's house, although a man is expected to live with his

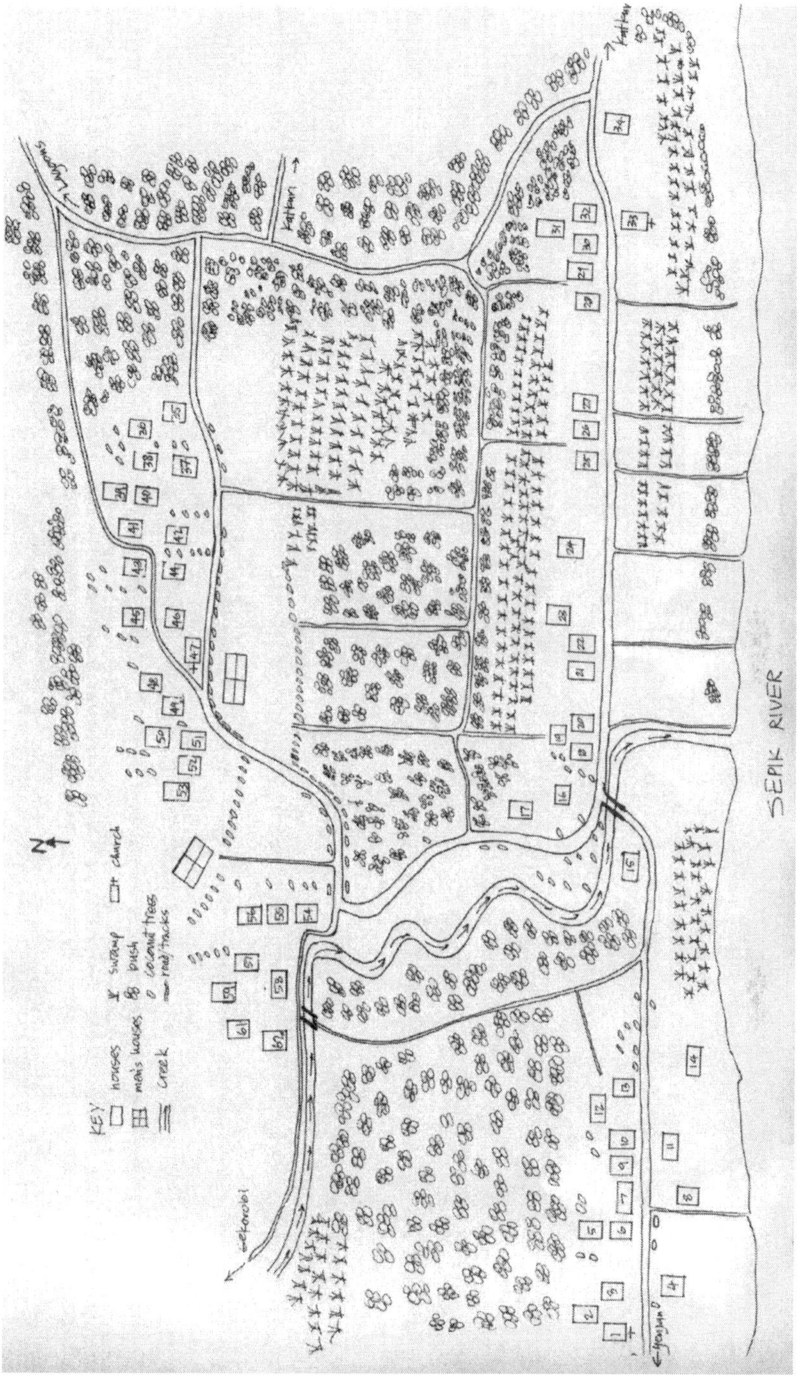

Map 3. Kanganamun village

own family separately. If a young married man and his family are living together in the same house as the man's parents, the two men are conscious of their places, which are more like moral and social spaces within the house. The young man keeps to the back of the house and the man can go to interact with his parents in their part of the house. A father's sitting stool may never be used by any of his sons, and it is particularly forbidden for the eldest son to do so. A father has his own sitting stool, which is often nearer to the window in the front of his house. It is believed that if the father is someone who engages in magic or divination practices, it is when he sits on his stool that particular spirits give him good thoughts so that he may see appropriate dreams when he sleeps in the night. A man's eldest son is also the next to inherit the leadership within the family and it is appropriate that he should not usurp authority while his father is still alive and active.

A man's wife and her daughter-in-law jealously guard their sections of their houses with a sense of ownership that sometimes erupts into domestic arguments between the two of them over the use of cooking utensils, firewood, tools, canoes, and the raising of children. Each person (including children) has their own sleeping place within the house; these are demarcated by mosquito nets and personal bags, in which they keep their clothes and other personal possessions including money, comb, mirror, and so forth. The raising of children is very much a female activity but men do help mind children when their wives attend to other pressing household chores. The relationship between a mother and daughter-in-law maybe one of mutual friendship and close collaboration in the sharing of food, daily chores, and whatever little money they may each have, but at other times these two women may also be formidable foes.

If a man and his adult or married sons are living together in the same house, each one of them (and their wives) should have a bush knife. Men also share tools such as spades, buckets, files, saws, hammer, axes, and other tools, which they use in making their carvings. Grown-up children are expected to take care of their own clothes. What little money that comes into the family through the mother's efforts in markets or the father's sale of carvings or crocodile skin is often used to purchase essential items for the family, and it is the women who are seen to be spending such money, in consultation with their husbands. Essential items include things such as sago, salt, soap for washing clothes, kerosene for lamps, clothes, and men may require razor blades to shave. Other comestibles such as areca nuts and lime, tobacco, cigarette papers, and batteries for torches and radios are also purchased in markets and stores. There is also a lot of sharing of areca nuts and tobacco, and at night people often borrow torches from one another. From time to time a woman will find it necessary to replace her fishing nets and will have to save up some money for this; her husband helps in this regard as well.

As we have seen in the previous chapter, the canoe is one of the most important possessions all adult men and women must have. The person who is without one will find him/herself immobilized and will have to borrow other people's canoes for short trips. Canoes can also be made and sold for money, and some young men do earn some money from the sale either of the canoes they make or from the tree from which a canoe can be made. In my adopted family, my adopted brother sold a canoe to his mother. This was unusual, that a mother should buy a canoe from her son, and many commented about how ironic it was that the canoe was then used to bring fish that fed my brother again. It was later discovered that my adopted brother did this at the behest of his wife, who had a strained relationship with her mother-in-law. Personal possessions within a residential house are often borrowed and shared. Such possessions are kept next to the sleeping bed and mosquito nets of the appropriate owner. It is the manner of its use that makes the contrast between personal possessions and those which are owned by the family as a whole. Often the money that is earned by one's parents is used for the interest of the family, whereas young girls may spend the money they earn from markets as they please.

Within a house, particular heirlooms may be kept as part of the clan's esoteric mythology. In a survey carried out, I found that there were only four families within the village which still keep such heirlooms. These included sacred flutes that are owned by the Lenga clan but are kept under the care of man married to a Lenga woman; a *mwai* mask which is owned by the Prindu clan is kept by a Prindu man; a spear-thrower owned by the Nawa Masam clan association is under the care of a Samiangwat clan man; and a trumpet owned by the Wanigo clan which is kept by a Wanigo man. The spear-thrower kept by the Samiangwat man is actually owned by several clans, including Samiangwat, Nawa, and Masam. I am also told that Iatmul clans may have such heirlooms which are owned as totems for the entire clan throughout the region. One such example is a *mwai* mask owned by the Samiangwat clan which is now kept by a man of the Samiangwat clan who lives upstream in Sotmeri village. All such heirlooms are protected, and their export outside of PNG is regulated by heritage legislation.

Once during my fieldwork I came across a situation that involved members of a particular clan who are now living the squatter settlement in

Wewak town. A particular European art dealer dubiously organized the purchase of an hour-glass drum. This particular hour-glass drum is associated with a mythical account of how an ancient Iatmul village was drowned by a huge flood (see also Silverman 2001: 86; Wassmann 1991: 146–8). This village is believed to be under water in what is now the Yapisat lagoon, located within 30 minutes' walk to the east of Kanganamun village. This particular hour-glass drum, with the name of Kwarum, was saved by a man from the Nawa clan who escaped that particular flood. Another drum like the Kwarum, which was owned by the Graken clan, was sold to European art dealers in the 1970s.

Kwarum is owned by the Nawa clan and was the under the care of a Nawa man who lived in Nuigo settlement in Wewak. A European art dealer knew about that drum and made arrangements to have it shipped to his address in Germany. However, other clan members came to know about the transaction and alerted me, complaining that it was wrong for the drum to have been sold. Acting as an officer from the PNG National Museum, I was able to prevent the drum from being exported. The drum is now retained in Nuigo and I am hoping that the art dealer will be brave enough to challenge this decision in court. This is a situation I allowed to go this way in order to see how the law on national heritage legislation might be interpreted in court and, if ever such a case arises, there might be an interesting tussle of ownership by competing claimants including the state, clan members, and the art dealer. It has not gone to court so far.

The case above highlights the way in which a historical or cultural object owned by a particular Iatmul clan can find itself being tossed into a complex sphere of ownership which extends from the village into the national and international arenas. The Iatmul region as a whole has a total of 37 cultural objects that have been declared by provisions of the national heritage legislation as part of Papua New Guinea's cultural heritage. Some of these objects are still located in the villages while others are kept at the PNG National Museum in Port Moresby. A certain number of such objects have also been stolen from the villagers and sold to international art dealers. The Wolimbi men's house itself in Kanganamun village is an architectural monument that has been declared as a national cultural heritage as well. Before dealing with this men's house, some details about the connection between a *ngeko* and the organization of a clan (*yaranga*) are provided.

Ngeko and *yaranga*: men's house and clan organization

Analytically one may conceptualize a *ngeko* as a microcosmic image of the clans which constitute its membership. Within a *ngeko*, clans are organized into clan associations and these associations occupy one or the other end of the *ngeko*. There are also clans and clan associations in the middle of the men's house (*indi ngeko*) but the clans which compose the middle section are divided organizationally and some of them are aligned with clans in the front part (*ndama ngeko*) and the back part (*ngumbu ngeko*) of the men's house. Clans cohere around main ceremonial or totemic posts in the *ngeko*. Let me spell this out for the three men's houses in Kanganamun.

Although there is no men's house in Kosimbi currently, there used to be one main ceremonial post in the Kosimbi *ngeko* called Womblimeli. Kosimbi was organizationally divided into a side that faces the Sepik River and the other that looks to the bush. The clan association that faces the river is called Kwainguapan while the association that faces the bush is called Meindumba. The Kwainguapan association is the 'elder-brother' group of clans and occupies the front part of Kosimbi while Meindumba is the 'younger-brother' group that occupied the back part of the *ngeko*. The clans which compose Kosimbi are Mbandei, Sangamat, Suaru, and Wengwandu. Mbandei and Sangamat make up the Kwainguapan association, while Suaru and Weingwandu make up the Meindumba association. There were, however, no male members of the Sangamat clan in Kosimbi at the time of fieldwork. Some Suaru members belong to Minjimbit and others have been incorporated into Wolimbi *ngeko*.

Clans which make up the Minjimbit *ngeko* include Mariambu, Yamandanai, Uriap, Saun (Suaru), and Lenga. There are two major ceremonial posts in Minjimbit which are called Walindambui and Kambaimbange. The clans which make up the 'elder-brother group' in Minjimbit are Uriap and Mairambu and they gather around the post called Kambaimbange. Saun (Suaru), Lenga, and Yamandanai clans assemble around the post called Walindambui and are identified as the 'younger-brother' group within Minjimbit. A clan which belongs to both the back and front part of Minjimbit is Mbowi Simal. This particular clan is also a member of the Wolimbi *ngeko* in the other totemic moiety. One of the most prominent past members of this clan is called Malikindjin, who was popularly known for his notoriously heroic deeds, plus magic and sorcery. Malikindjin featured prominently in Bateson's ethnographic account (1958: 160–72) of the Iatmul ideal of personality types. Malikindjin's clan has sitting platforms in both the Minjimbit and Wolimbi men's houses.

The clan associations that make up the Wolimbi *ngeko* are Walgem, Sui, and Nawa Masam. Walgem association is composed of five clans including Mbei, Kembiam, Yabu, Wanigo, and Miembei. Mbei and Kembiam do not have surviving members of their clan and, although their place in the *ngeko* and *yaranga*, and their stock of personal names and body of myths remain, these are now mostly assumed by their 'elder-brother' clans, notably Miembei and Yabu clans. The Walgem association is the 'elder-brother' group and assembles around the major ceremonial post called Kanawimeli, which is located in the front part (*ndama ngeko*) of the Wolimbi men's house. The Sui association, which is in the middle section (*indi ngeko*) of the men's house is made of Sui, Prindu, Mbowi Simal, and Graken clans and their ceremonial post is called Tuatmeli. At the back (*ngumbu ngeko*) of the men's house is the Nawa Masam association, which constitutes the 'younger brother' of clans in Wolimbi. The Nawa Masam association includes the clans of Nawa, Masam, Samiangwat, and Suaru. The Sui association is divided so that the clans of Graken and Mbowi Simal align themselves with the 'elder-brother' group at the front of men's house while Sui and Prindu are aligned with the 'younger-brother' group at the back of the *ngeko*.

The clans are organized into associations for several reasons. Clan associations are active in matters regarding the menial tasks of maintaining the *ngeko*, such as replacing posts or maintaining the roof, cutting grass on the ceremonial ground, and for purposes of the initiation ritual and ceremonial debates. In carrying out menial tasks, men from both sides of the *ngeko* often help each other in their work, but if such help is given, the host association is required to provide food and other comestibles. Clan associations also hold in common particular names and stories which are distinctive to their clan or totemic moiety. Thus, when the last surviving member of a particular clan passes away, one of the brother clans within the association will assume the right to use their names and other resources connected to the ownership of their personal names. Clans are paired as brothers so that one of these paired clans will assume ownership of the names and stories of its brother clan should one becomes extinct.[16] Each clan within the *ngeko* owns particular posts, sitting platforms, slit-gongs, masks, ladders, storage space, and some clans have secret musical instruments which are kept hidden in the upper chambers of the *ngeko*. Although musical instruments are owned by individual clans, they are often used by other initiated men on ceremonial occasions. Personal names owned by individual clans

[16] The pair of brother clans (see also Stanek 1990: 268) compare closely to the pair of names which are also considered as paired siblings.

are bestowed on posts, beams, platforms, ladder, slit-gongs, and other musical instruments inside the *ngeko*. The clan that owns a particular item in the *ngeko* is responsible for its maintenance. Finally, to illustrate the descriptions provide here, we shall focus on the Wolimibi *ngeko* in Kanganamun village. Wolimbi is also a national cultural monument and here we shall encounter some of the ways in which issues of 'ownership' expand beyond the local social context into the national arena.

Wolimbi *ngeko*: a national cultural heritage

Wolimbi *ngeko* stands tall, with a proud height of approximately 25 metres; it is 15 metres in width and 40 metres in length (see Figure 2.3 overleaf).[17] Each successive Wolimbi *ngeko* has always been built on the same location where the present one is located. The process of building the current one began in 1987, after an earthquake demolished the previous one in 1981. The one pictured by Bateson (1958: Plate VIIA) was declared as part of the national heritage of PNG in 1965, together with all of its contents (including slit-gongs, flutes, war trophies, and old ceremonial posts). The current building is the third one to be built since Bateson and, although it is different from the one that was there in 1965, it is still regarded legally as part of PNG's heritage, which is regulated by legislation enforced by the PNG National Museum.[18] Some of the posts and beams (and musical accoutrements) of the previous house are retained and used again. When it has had the financial resources, the Museum has sent its officers to undertake field trips in the area. Since the process of rebuilding began in 1987, the National Museum has donated K4,000 to help towards the reconstruction. This has made the other totemic moiety within Kanganamun and other neighbouring villages desire their *ngeko* to be declared part of the national heritage, so that they too could benefit from government funding for the protection and promotion of their 'culture'.

While people of Wolimbi are aware of the national status of their *ngeko*, they also know that they own it and therefore assume the responsibility of maintaining it. The location of the *ngeko* in Kanganamun village means that it retains its link to the social and cultural context of its people. We have seen that it is in full operational use and how villagers relate to it (as

[17] Taken in the 1970s, this photo of Wolimbi is from Duly (1979).

[18] See Busse (2000) for a discussion of PNG's national heritage legislation; and Eoe (1990) for comments on the legislation with respect to the artistic heritage of the Sepik area.

Figure 2.3 Wolimbi *ngeko*

described above). The schematic representation below shows the floor plan Wolimbi adopted, but modified, from the work of a pioneer researcher in PNG's vernacular architecture, Ruff (1981; Ruff and Ruff 1990). There are three distinct sizes of posts in the Wolimbi *ngeko*. These three kinds of posts are known as *king*, *poro* and *nana*. *King* posts are the major ceremonial posts around which clans cohere and they are also the tallest, reaching up to the ridge to support the central ridge pole that runs the length of the *ngeko*. *Poro* posts hold up the cross-beams, which lie across the width of the *ngeko* and these beams carry the floor of the upper chambers of the *ngeko*. *Nana* posts, which are shorter than the *king* posts, reach up to the roof as well but are located on the sides and they carry the other poles, which run along the lower end of the roof. The *king* and *nana* posts provide support for the roof while the *poro* posts carry the floor of the upper-chambers (see Coiffier 1990). All posts, cross-beams, ladders, and finial masks have personal names and are owned by individual clans. The floor plan of Wolimbi is shown in Figure 2.4, and the reader may consult the Appendix for the names of individual posts.

Wolimbi is divided into three parts: the front called *ndama ngeko*, the middle section (*indi ngeko*), and the back known as *ngumbu ngeko*. These three parts are composed of clans which make up associations. While there are three clan associations in Wolimbi (Walgem, Sui, and Nawa Masam), the Sui association is divided and one half of it joins the front part of the *ngeko* while the other half joins the group of clans at the back. The major ceremonial posts in the centre of Wolimbi also have the organizational effect of dividing the *ngeko* into a side with clans that face the Sepik River (*kingindanangi*) and clans that face the village (*kungiankunangi*). This division of clans is latitudinally organized and, in the past, it served primarily a military function. Thus when the village is attacked, men of clans which are facing the river would attack enemies approaching from the river while men of clans facing the bush would take on enemies attacking from the bush side. The division of the *ngeko* into a bush (*kingindanangi*) and river (*kungiankunangi*) side parallels the arrangements in the residential compound (*yaranga*). The bush side is occupied by the lineage which is associated with the 'younger brother' and is called *kandingeipa*, while the river side occupied by the 'elder brother' is called *tungungeipa*. The axial positions (of front and back), and the lateral positions (of left and right) within the *ngeko* and the *ngeio* are circumscribed by the relational matrix of an elder brother and younger brother, and this is carried over into the naming system as well. The pairing of brother clans in the *ngeko* takes on a function of ownership with respect to the sorts of names members of different clans and lineages within a clan use.

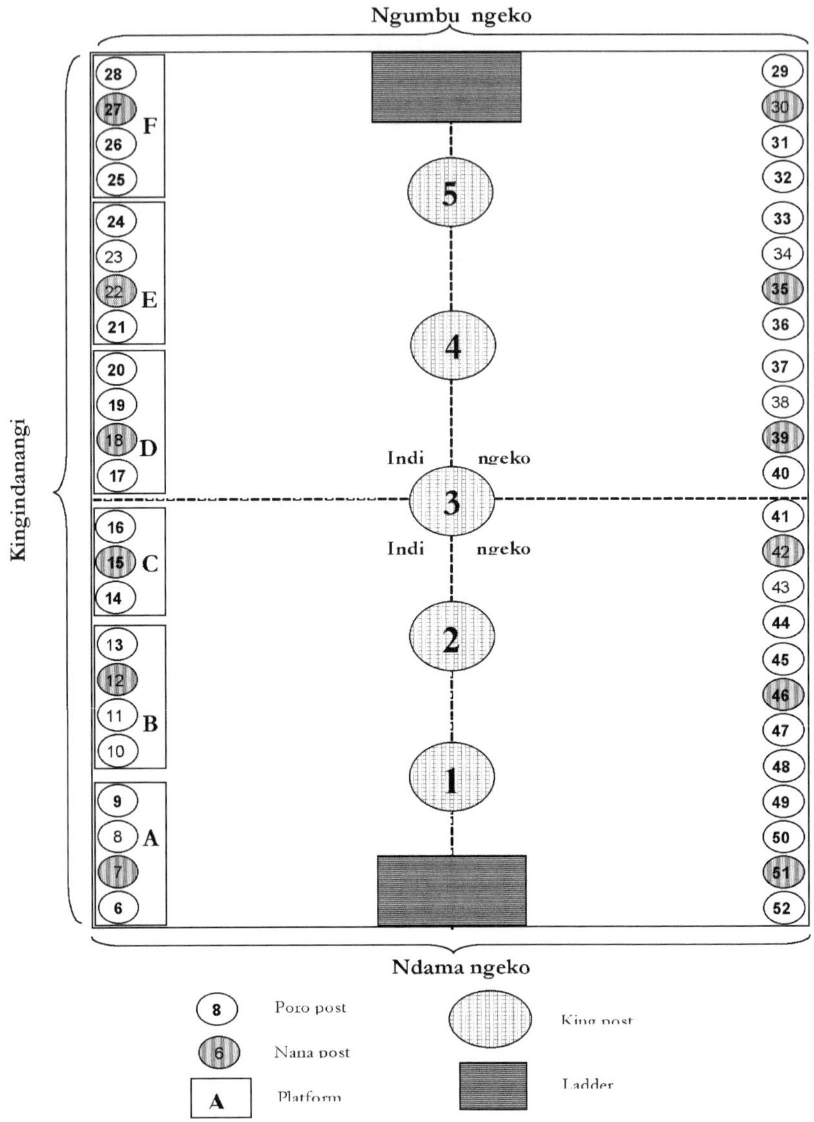

Figure 2.4 Wolimbi floor plan

Finally, since Wolimbi is not only a men's house owned by particular clan groups but is also national cultural heritage, I would like to report on two experiences concerning the *ngeko* which highlight some pertinent issues that relate to the nature of ownership. One day I was part of a team of men who went to collect cane vines from the bush to be used in making intricate designs in the interior part of the roof inside the *ngeko*. The vines were collected in a forested area owned by various clans of Wolimbi. While we were collecting the vines, a man of the Wanigo clan almost slashed himself with his bush knife. Because of my presence as Museum curator living and working with them as a student of anthropology, the incident aggravated him. After collecting himself, he looked at me and asked a very pointed question: 'If the knife had cut me, who would straighten this heavy? Will the Museum pay me for injuring myself when I am working on the *ngeko*? If a man gets hurt while working on the *ngeko*, will the Museum compensate him for such damages?' I was taken aback with these questions but answered that as far as Museum policy is concerned, it is the people themselves who must be responsible for any injuries they may sustain while working for the *ngeko*.

Some months later, an earthquake rocked and shook the village. Consequently a post in the *ngeko*, which had suffered decay, broke and tumbled to the ground, and the crossbeam it supported also collapsed with it. Owned by the Samiangwat clan, the post is called Kusumanapan and is located at the back of the *ngeko*. If and when such a situation arises, the clan which owns the post ought to replace it. Thus a man of the Samiangwat clan took the initiative of organizing its replacement. A tree that was planted by his clansmen was identified and all the men of the Nawa Masam association went off to bring the new post. Two men from the Walgem association also helped. While they were cutting the tree, a man of the Suaru clan within the Nawa Masam association almost cut himself with his axe. After the tree was felled, the man was chopping away its upper branches. Suddenly one of the branches he was standing on cracked and rocked viciously, causing him to fly off the tree. Fortunately he threw his axe away and was not hurt. I was horrified and a sense of guilt consumed me as my thoughts ran back to the previous encounter with the man of Wanigo clan. Other men were pleased that the accident wasn't fatal. I mastered courage to break the silence generated by this incident by apologizing. While the apology was appreciated, the man replied saying: '*Laua* [nephew], it's not a big deal. That's the way life is in the village. We can be injured with our axes and knives, illness and diseases visit us, but that's the way our life is.' Other men smiled at the ease at which the man replied but I probed: 'Don't you think the Museum should assume responsibilities over such fatalities. Why should we call Wolimbi national cultural heritage when it's people like you who will bear the pain of such fatalities?'

I wanted to use that occasion to see how they would respond. Then one of the village *komiti*, who belongs to the front part of the *ngeko* and had come to help the men of Nawa Masam said: 'It's a bit funny, it's not straight for you to talk like this. Who is the Museum? You are the Museum and how can you talk like this? You are already one of us as much as the Museum is a part of us. We don't go anywhere in trying to impose blame on people.' Some village people saw me as a conduit of some sort with connections to the Museum and my research there has inserted me into a definite niche of their own purposes *vis-à-vis* the Wolimbi *ngeko*. Although Wolimbi has been declared legislatively as part of the cultural heritage of PNG, its ownership is still retained at the level of clans which constitute its membership. The clans of Wolimbi continue to maintain and have daily access to its use and enjoyment. On the other hand, the declaration of Wolimbi as a national heritage augments its standing in the local community. The declaration does not undermine but consolidates its local sovereignty as an icon of cultural creativity and seat of traditional village government.

Introducing ownership

The discussion in this chapter has moved in and out of the *ngeko* and *ngeio* in order to emulate the movement of social relations one finds in Iatmul given the organizing presence of these two types of houses. Anchored within and revolving around these two types of houses are different spheres of social relationships with their concomitant spheres of ownership. The fight in the village and attempts to gain or prevent access to the fishing lagoon exemplify one sphere of ownership that can be found between the totemic moieties. Another such sphere exists at the level of clans, which take responsibility in replacing a post in the *ngeko*. Yet another sphere appears to exist within clans, with respect to the kinds of personal names and stories they own. Within a family unit found inside a *ngeio*, we see yet another kind of sphere which illustrates the individual and collective dimensions of ownership, when members of a household share tools, money and food, etc.

The story about the Takasep lagoon reveals three important things to which I wish to alert the reader, about the manner in which ownership is described here in the language of personifying idioms. First, people constantly create cultivable land out of clearing and cutting away wild grass on land that becomes available through the shifting directions of the Sepik River, which then gives or subtracts land from their hold. Thus people own the land that they create through initial cultivation. However, the land that already has personal names attached to it requires the appropriate owners to use it. It is already owned and you cannot create it anew. This account reveals a striking dialectic that appears to be lurking between creativity and ownership. This dialectic gives us two kinds of trajectories which inform and legitimize the claims of land ownership in Iatmul. One of these trajectories is based on cosmological understandings and genealogical precedence, and the other routes itself through arduous physical work.

Second, in view of Honoré's notion of 'incidents' that characterize ownership as a bundle of rights, we find that elements such as possession, use, and management all appear in the different contexts of this chapter. One particular incident that concerns the 'prohibition of harmful use' appears in the form of liabilities that the clans which own Wolimbi have to endure. Contrary to Christman (1991: 29), who thinks of liabilities as a structural adjunct of ownership, I would argue that liabilities are intrinsically constitutive of ownership for, if it were not so, why would the village *komiti* and his band of clansmen in Kanganamun accept it as such? Ownership can appear as a friend who embraces and endows the owner with the power or liberty to use and enjoy that which is owned and, at other times, it can be a foe who places liabilities on the house of an owner, inviting its custodians to exercise responsibility, as indeed it does for the clans of Kanganamun who own Wolimbi. If Christman's conception of ownership relegated and undermined liabilities as simply a structural feature of ownership, then we might find ourselves living in a runaway world of owners who have no sense of responsibility.

Third, ownership claims are negotiated through a historically prior set of actions and relationships. All ownership claims are based on a prior set of historical circumstances and it is in such histories that ownership finds its dwelling place. Ownership therefore appears to reside in history, much like an Iatmul person who resides in particular houses. As much as the Iatmul people conduct and mobilize themselves through the two contrasting types of houses so does ownership reside in and conduct itself in the house of history, and emerges in the dawn of freighted moments of litigious concerns. If ownership resides in the house of history then one might say that relationships are the ground upon which such a house is built. Much like Guraki, who sought to use genealogical connections and productive relations to seek access to the Takasep lagoon, ownership also thrives on relationships and history for its moral persuasion and legitimacy, and in so doing it momentarily appropriates and enacts its own history and relationships, which are entwined in the biography of its claimants, as we shall see in Chapter 6.

3

From Tourism to *Bandi* and *Naven* Rituals

No account of life in the ceremonial house would be complete without some reference to the ethos of initiation.

(Bateson 1958: 130)

Culture and tourism in Kanganamun

This chapter comes in three parts. The first section provides some detail about the kinds of interaction between people in Kanganamun, tourists, and tour operators, then an account of a mock ritual display enacted as a spectacle for tourists is discussed. The description of this mock ritual provides a context not only to engage with Harrison's most influential essay on 'ritual as intellectual property' (Harrison 1992) but also serves as a prelude to a description of men's initiation (*bandi*) and ritual moieties in Central Iatmul. In anticipation of discussions about Iatmul ontological assumptions bound up with ideas of kinship and gender, the chapter finally ends with a comparison of *naven* and *bandi* rituals and engages with the notion of 'ritual condensation' proposed by Houseman and Severi (1998).

The Iatmul's riverine environment is periodically overwhelmed with seasonal inundation; this prevents people from engaging in the production of cash crops such as cocoa, copra, coffee, and vanilla that is found in other parts of East Sepik Province. Given the limited economic opportunities that are available as a result of such an environmental predicament, their only enduring source of income comes from the sale of fish taken from the river and fishing lagoons. Apart from income gained from the sale of fish and other food items at the local market, the sale of various art and craft products to tourists, art dealers, and museum collectors provides the major external source of income for the villagers, even if such money is earned only sporadically. The money earned from the sale of carvings and other handicrafts totalled an estimated K10,000 during the year I was in the village. This estimate covers the villages of Parimbe, Yenjan, and Kanganamun[1] and excludes the money earned by people who take their carvings and other handicrafts to markets in Wewak and other urban centres in PNG.

It is a familiar scene when the news of visiting tourists and art dealers spreads through the village. In time women and children would gather in a straight line along the side of mounds (*tuvui*) and lay their artefacts on the ceremonial ground in front of the *ngeko* with the hope that some of what they are displaying will be bought by the visitors. Items such as grass skirts, net bags, armbands, and headdresses are made by women while men make various kinds of carvings. The majority of men display their carvings inside the *ngeko*, which is itself a peculiar attraction to the tourists. Tourists who speak English are able to converse with some of the young men in the *ngeko*. The majority of the villagers assume that English is spoken by all the 'white people' and therefore they are often surprised about Europeans who do not speak English but sympathize with Japanese tourists who are not able to do so. Thus the interaction with the tourists provides the people with a small window for them to learn a little about people in other parts of the world who come through the village. Tourists who are intrigued with the *ngeko* soon come to discover its connection with the initiation rituals and would ask all kinds of questions about the ritual, such as the pain experienced in scarification and the methods by which the wounds are healed. I have seen several initiated men shrugging their shoulders and smiling in reticence when tourists ask questions about the initiation ritual, and some men sometimes pose for photographs to be taken of the scars lacerated on their bodies during the initiation.

Tourists and art dealers who are intent upon buying artefacts take their time to look closely at the pieces that are on offer and often negotiate the prices of the artefacts with the village people. Both men and women would initially put a higher price on the piece they are selling because tourists (and art dealers) often bargain for a second or a third price offer on the same piece. While tourists would settle for a price that the carver is happy with, people sometimes complain that they themselves do not ask for a second or a third price when they go to a store. Because of the irregular visits of tourists and art dealers, people often take the opportunity to sell their items. They feel that it is much better for them to sell the carvings

[1] Gewertz and Errington (1991: 48) mentioned a similar estimate of K10,000 earned by the Chambri over the year although the currency has since devalued. At the time of fieldwork, K1 was approximately £0.25 in pounds sterling.

rather than to risk losing such an opportunity in the hope that they would fetch a higher price in the future.

The sizes and styles of carvings and other artefacts vary from village to village. Many tourists prefer to buy artefacts which are small in size and can fit easily into their luggage whereas transporting bigger carvings is complicated. In Parimbe village, many of their carvings are decorated with brightly coloured paint, whereas such painting is either limited or absent from the carvings one finds in Kanganamun village. The skill in adorning a carving, *bilum* (string bags), or a bracelet with shells, feathers, and painting is a quality only a few men and women have. Often carvers from different totemic clans, and even totemic moieties, cooperate in making or decorating a carving. They also share and borrow tools which they use in making carvings. Shells and birds' feathers, dog's teeth and pig tusks, which are incorporated into carvings such as the *mwai* mask, headdresses, and necklaces are obtained from either local markets or from the market in Wewak town. The price of *mwai* shell and other related accessories in markets is quite high, and when art objects such as *mwai* masks are elaborately decorated with such ornaments, their price also increases.

One of the gifted carvers in the village, James Lanjin, told me that just before tourists come to the village, he often gets twitches on the palm of his hands which portend the likelihood of him selling a carving to a tourist or art dealer. Village leaders, particularly a *kansol* (councillor), often go out to Wewak town and make attempts to bring in tourists and art dealers to their villages; in so doing they are seen to be bringing an economic service to their people, thus legitimizing and consolidating their status as leaders in the village.[2] The carvings and other handicrafts and men's houses are often the kinds of attractions that such leaders talk about to market their villages as attractive tourist destinations.

Kambonamak, an elderly woman in Kanganamun village, once commented that the bulk of the carvings which are sold to tourists and art dealers are pieces made by men. Such pieces also cost a lot more in comparison to the things that women make and sell to tourists and art dealers. She observed that tourists (and art dealers) seem to be more attracted to the kind of things that are made by men. In addition, when visitors arrive in the village, their guides normally take them to the *ngeko*, where they spend

[2] Gewertz and Errington (1991: 25–100) describe a similar situation, in which the charismatic village leader, Maliwan of Chambri, was instrumental not only in building the Walindimi men's house in his village, but also for the staging of initiation rituals for his sons as a spectacle to entertain tourists.

a lot of time, whereas women stay outside on the ceremonial ground in front of the *ngeko*. However, she notes:

> It is the *ngeko* that is attracting the tourists to the village and therefore it is appropriate that the tourists visit, take pictures, and carry with them memories of our *ngeko* so that they can make and lift the name of our village [to] grow up big. And when our name grows big, more and more people will come here.

The picture of the interaction and the mutual extractive agendas of tourists and villagers painted so far is one that seems amicable. However, there are times when local opportunists prey upon visiting tourists. In 1995, a gang of men went aboard a tourist boat called the *Sepik Spirit*, which was berthed on the waters near the banks close to Kanganamun village, and robbed the tourists on board. Initially it was suspected that Kanganamun men were responsible for that crime but later it emerged that the gang came from villages further downstream who had followed the boat with the intention of robbing the tourists and taking money and beer from the boat. As a result of this, the *Sepik Spirit* stopped delivering tourists to the Central Iatmul villages for a long while and only the cruise ship, *Melanesian Discoverer*, continued to bring in tourists. Below is a description of a dispute between the people of Kanganamun village and the operators of the luxury cruise ship, *Melanesian Discoverer*, owned by Sir Peter Barter, a prominent politician and entrepreneur who has invested his lifetime in building tourism in Papua New Guinea.

The dispute with Melanesian Tourist Services and the mock ritual

In late December 2000, 40 American tourists came into Kanganamun village to look at the Wolimbi men's house. It was the first time in many months that such a large number of tourists had visited the village. The tourists came aboard the luxury cruise ship. The previous day, Sir Peter came ahead of the tourists to inform the people of their visit and asked whether the village people could put on a 'cultural entertainment' for the tourists. Sir Peter was also in the village to discuss and settle a dispute that has risen between the villagers and his tourist company, Melanesian Tourist Services (MTS). A month earlier, Kanganamun men tried to forcefully grab and bring into their custody a tugboat owned by MTS that was berthed upstream in Yenjan village (see Schmidt 1990). MTS uses two such boats to ferry people between the cruise ship and the river banks along which villages are located.

For one reason or another, MTS had been bringing tourists to the villages of Parimbe and Yenjan only, and had been neglecting Kanganamun for some while. Kanganamun people made several attempts to get the company to bring the tourists to the village but without success. Thus Kanganamun men thought that forcefully taking one of the company's tugboats would make the owner of the ship, Sir Peter, take note of their pleas of wanting tourists to visit their village. On that particular occasion, tourists, MTS employees, and Lady Barter, the wife of Sir Peter, were visiting Yenjan village when the men of Kanganamun went up in two canoes and tried to seize control of one of the tugboats. A commotion ensued between an MTS employee and two men of Kanganamun. All of this took place in front of tourists, who were outside the *ngeko* in Yenjan village. In fright and humiliation, Lady Barter escaped with some tourists to the cruise ship.[3] After some negotiation with one of the MTS employees, the men of Kanganamun were given a sum of K200 for what they perceived as the failure of MTS to deliver tourists to the village. But the aggressive confrontation that the Kanganamun men staged against MTS provoked an angry response from men in the villages of Yenjan and Parimbe. A gang of men from Yenjan and Parimbe mobilized to fight against the men from Kanganamun. However, leaders of Yenjan village intervened and prevented the fight, and instead sent word of a meeting to resolve this matter. A meeting was then held in the Wolimbi *ngeko* in Kanganamun village with men from all three villages attending. During the meeting, Kanganamun men explained their frustrations with MTS and with what they considered the arrogance of Lady Barter, who refused to hear their repeated pleas to bring tourists to their village. While the men from Yenjan and Parimbe sympathized with them, they argued that the men from Kanganamun insulted the strength and sovereignty of Yenjan village by harassing MTS employees in their village. Kanganamun men objected to this accusation and explained that they waited till all the traditional songs and dances had ended before they confronted Lady Barter, and were careful to not do so on the ceremonial ground in Yenjan, for that could have been

[3] In comparison to their Chambri neighbours, who hazed and intimidated tourists who were observing a phase in the men's initiation at Chambri (Gewertz and Errington 1991: 77–87), the Kanganamun men did not want to humiliate the tourists but to send a strong message to the Barters, the owner and operator of the MTS.

seen as an attack on Yenjan village. Kanganamun men apologized to their neighbouring villagers and agreed to solve the matter with MTS.

This was the point at which I was asked to write a letter that expressed the views of Kanganamun people. The letter was sent to Sir Peter and Lady Barter, expressing disgust and disappointment over the way in which MTS had not allowed tourists to visit their village. Hence Sir Peter's visit to the village was in response to that letter, in order to resolve the tensions. Much like their Chambri neighbours (Gewertz and Errington 1991: 54–6), the Kanganamun people must have seen Sir Peter through his company as an exchange partner in a way reminiscent of their Sawos partners, who supply them sago within a long-term relationship. In this vein, one could say that in delivering tourists to them, Sir Peter's company is comparable to the trading relationships between the Iatmul and the Sawos, who exchange fish for sago respectively on a regular basis. The people in Kanganamun told me that they had once put on a form of *naven* ceremonial and given a *mwai* mask to congratulate Sir Peter when he brought his first luxury cruise ship, the *Melanesian Explorer*, onto the waters of the Sepik River. A *naven* ceremonial is a kinship-based ritual held to congratulate the first time achievements of particular kin members, and it is the father's sister (*iau*) and the mother's brother (*wau*) who are the main protagonists in this ceremonial ritual that celebrates the achievements of their nieces and nephews (Bateson 1958; Houseman and Severi 1998; Silverman 2001). Since Sir Peter's company grew partly from his tour operations along the Sepik River, the people have come to see him as a trading partner of a kind, who supplies them with a constant stream of tourists while they make available their men's houses, exhibit their prolific art industry, and open up aspects of their secret world of men's initiation ritual for tourists to see. When MTS was denying them scores of tourists, the men of Kanganamun took action in order to restore, as it were, the trading relationship they think that they have with Sir Peter through his company.

After the discussion, Sir Peter informed the Kanganamun men of the impending visit of some tourists who were arriving the next day on his ship. He requested the villagers to put on a cultural performance for the tourists. The following day, Sir Peter flew in with his helicopter while the tourists on his ship came in by boat. Women and children assembled on the ceremonial ground in front of the *ngeko* with their artefacts displayed for sale to the tourists. Men of Wolimbi displayed their carvings inside the Wolimbi *ngeko* while those from Minjimbit and Kosimbi had theirs displayed on the road leading to the Wolimbi *ngeko*. Some tourists purchased carvings and other handicrafts that were on sale, others talked with women and children in the village, and others gathered in the *ngeko* and talked with the men there. Tourists are not always from abroad; some are wealthy Papua New Guineans and expatriates who work in different parts of the country and visit when they are on holiday. On that particular visit, one of the tourists was someone who worked with a Kanganamun man employed as an electrical engineer in Port Moresby. That tourist sent word to see the engineer's mother, Kambonamak, one of the elderly women whose views on tourist visits were cited above. Kambonamak came into the *ngeko* and talked with this visitor. After a little while, a man who was sitting in the upper chamber of the Wolimbi *ngeko* jumped on the floor above, landing with a loud bang, and immediately a chorus of trumpets and bullroarers started up. At that point during my fieldwork, I did not understand the significance of the sound of these musical instruments and, as they began, I could see the rushing and scattering of women and children who had gathered on the ceremonial ground in front of the *ngeko*. Uninitiated men who were in the *ngeko* had to leave. I didn't know what was going on. Kambonamak, who was in the *ngeko*, apologized to her tourist friend and made her way out; as she went by, she explained to me that the men were trying to show *kastom* to the tourists. Kambonamak was using the word *kastom* as a short-hand for things connected to the men's initiation sacra.

As the music went on, two men came in from the bush nearby, carrying an old canoe into the men's house. The canoe was upturned and laid on the ground in the men's house. Another three men joined in and they all started to enact a pantomime based on the manner in which novices are lacerated during initiation rituals. Despite its caricature, it was a captivating performance which showed some of the ritual postures and conveyed in some way the pain and derision that initiates undergo during their initiation. Imbued with playfulness and with equal seriousness, the ritual pantomime held the interest of the spectators for its duration. The tourists watched with awe and admiration the pantomime that was enacted as a theatrical spectacle. Sir Peter himself was taken with the performance and commented that in his 30–year career as a tourist operator along the Sepik River, he had never seen anything as spectacular as that ritual pantomime enacted by the five men. Moved by the performance, Sir Peter offered K200 as a reward for putting on the show.

The money was given to one of the five men who enacted the ritual pantomime. That man shared the money among the men who took part in it. This then provoked a complaint about the sharing of this money. The complaint grew big and engaged the attention of all the initiated men in the village. A meeting was organized and the issue was debated in the

Wolimbi men's house. Some of the initiated men who did not participate in the mock ritual complained that they too should have been given a share of the K200. These men argued that they could not have participated in the mock ritual because the performance required only about five men to do it. They argued that anyone of them could have put on the performance. However, because the play required only five of them, others didn't participate and their lack of participation did not mean they should not be given a bit of that money.

The debate went on until two men from opposing ritual moieties raised two important points that brought it to an end. Alois Kuanuat, the oldest and most senior man in the Wolimbi men's house and of his ritual moiety—*nyamun arambandi*, the 'elder brother group'—made a point about the evident breach of procedure in the distribution of the money. According to the *kastom* of the *ngeko*, the man who distributed the money, Vincent Yarme, was already wrong to have done so. He explained that Vincent belongs to a clan which is located at the back part of the men's house (*ngumbu ngeko*) and by decree of *kastom*, the right to share and distribute such a money is a prerogative of men who belong to the clans which are in the front of the men's house (*ndama ngeko*).

> *Ndama ngeko* is the head of the crocodile and *ngumbu ngeko* is the tail of the crocodile. The crocodile does not think with its tail, it is the head that gets the crocodile to move. *Ndama ngeko* is the government and they are the people that should have broken this money. *Ngumbu ngeko* is like the opposition arm of government in the parliament. It does not make decisions about the budget of the country.

Alois employs the analogy between the men's house and the country's national parliament in order to highlight the procedural error that has been committed in the distribution of the money.

The other man, Tobias Wali, was formerly the village councillor and is also a senior member of the other ritual moiety—*shambu arambandi*—the 'younger-brother group'. Tobias made the following observations:

> What you have showed is the inside of us men. It is my picture and story as much as it is yours. We all own these actions that you have showed to the tourists. Thus if there be any payments gained from such a show, it is straight that all of us should benefit from such a payment and not just a few of you who put on the show. It is good that a mistake has also been committed and so you young men can be reminded of our *kastom*. Since all the money has now been recouped from the hands that it has gone into, we must now share this money together. However, we must thank those who put on the show and maybe they could be given some extra *toea* for their efforts.

Despite the fact that the mock ritual derives from an improvisation based on the initiation ritual, the series of actions that were displayed during the mock ritual are already owned by the collectivity of all initiated men in the village and it cannot be regarded as something that is created just for the performers to entertain the tourists. The observations made by Tobias Wali and Alois Kanuat brought the debate to a close and the men from the front part of the *ngeko* took charge of redistributing the money amongst the initiated men. The issue of the ownership of ritual action will be taken up again in the next part of this chapter. In the meantime, however, the description of the mock ritual and the tussle over ownership claims provide a bridge to move into a discussion about ritual moieties and the male initiatory cult of the Iatmul. Explicit details of this ritual are withheld in order to avoid compromising the secrecy involved in the ritual. Because initiation rituals are always held at the request of one ritual moiety, which then prompts its complementary half to initiate its novices, the description that follows involves a young man of Kanganamun village and myself when we were initiated. This description focuses on Iatmul initiation rituals and explains Bateson's remark (1958: 130) that any account of the ceremonial house (*ngeko*) is incomplete without reference to the initiation ritual.

Ngeko, *bandi*, and *waalumi*: crocodile's nest, initiate, and the crocodile's teeth

Peter Walindambui is a man in his late fifties who has only one son, named Harry. For about twelve years, Harry has been away from the village, being educated in a high school in Madang town. Weary of his waning ill-health, and of his own place in the *ngeko*, Walindambui wanted to have his son initiated so that Harry could take over his place before anything as catastrophic as death happened to him. An initiation is important because it confers the right to participate in ceremonial affairs in the *ngeko*. Without initiation, a man cannot take up his place in the *ngeko*. With all this in mind, Walindambui undertook a trip to Madang where he visited his eldest daughter with whom his son Harry was also staying. In Madang, Walindambui discovered that his son had befriended a girl who was living with him as a wife. Harry's mother also comes from Madang and Walindambui thought his son was following in his footsteps by taking a Madang woman too. After some discussions with his son, Walindambui sent word back to the village about his desire to have his son initiated into a 'man'.

In the company of his son and daughter-in-law, Walindambui arrived in the village in July 2000. June to October is a perfect time for initiation rituals to be held because it is the dry season and there will be no mosquitoes around. However, for some reason, Walindambui procrastinated over the move to initiate his son. It was not until January 2001, when the wet season was setting in, that Walindambui moved to 'put a bunch of betel nuts in the Wolimbi *ngeko*'. In Iatmul understandings, when betel nut is put in the men's house, such a gesture is take to mean that someone is seeking to be 'eaten or devoured by the crocodiles'. The betel nut is normally left hanging on a hook suspended inside the *ngeko*. The act of putting a bunch of betel nut in the *ngeko* is a gesture that symbolically transforms the *ngeko* into the sanctuary of the *waal wanjimaut*, the spirit crocodile. The presence of the betel nut is considered as summoning or provoking the crocodile. In metaphoric terms, the conventional understanding of a betel nut as a comestible is suspended and undergoes a symbolic transformation whereby the betel nut is seen as a spear that is shoved down into the dwelling place of a crocodile. The act of thrusting the spear provokes the crocodile to take revenge on the person who has provoked it. In transforming the *ngeko* into a crocodile's place, it also brings into play the function of ritual moieties.

Walindambui and his son Harry belong to the ritual moiety called *nyamun arambandi* or the 'elder-brother group'. When betel nuts are put in the *ngeko* as a symbolic request for an initiation ritual, it is given specifically to an initiated man who belongs to the same clan association as the initiated man who is making the request, but both of these two men must belong to opposing ritual moieties. Walindambui's clan is called Prindu, his clan association is called Sui, and this association gathers around the ceremonial post called Tuatmeli in the Wolimbi *ngeko*.[4] Men who belong to the same clan association but of the opposing ritual moiety will accept the request and present it to the rest of the initiated men within the *ngeko* (or the village). In this case, the onus fell upon Tobias Wali, who belongs to the Graken clan, which is of the same clan association as Walindambui. Tobias belongs to the opposing ritual moiety called *shambu arambandi* or the 'younger-brother group'. When betel nut is 'put inside the *ngeko*', it is men such as Tobias who take charge not only in distributing the betel nut (accompanied with its condiment) amongst all the initiated men in the village, but also preside over the discussions and act as an advocate of the request for the initiation of novices such as Walindambui's son.

[4] Figure 2.4, the floor-plan diagram in the previous chapter, gives the location of this post in the Wolimbi *ngeko*.

The act of 'putting betel nut inside the *ngeko*' has several outcomes. Apart from transforming the *ngeko* into the sanctuary of the spirit crocodile, it also has a momentary effect of eclipsing the totemic constitution of a particular *ngeko* in the village such as Wolimbi. That is, it suspends for the duration of the initiation ritual the totemic dimension of the clans of each *ngeko*. In its stead it brings to the fore the ritual moieties in the village. In drawing members from each of the totemic moieties, the ritual moieties cut across the totemic moieties, reminiscent of the way in which the avunculate cuts across patrilineal clans. As mentioned already, when initiation rituals are carried out, the totemic aspect of clan membership within the village is temporarily suspended. In its place, a ritually constituted 'government' (*gavman*) is installed. The Iatmul use the *Tok Pisin* term *gavman* to talk about the exercise and enforcement of powers, obligations, rights, and duties that come into force during the initiation ritual. This 'ritual government' is divided into the form of a leading moiety and an opposing moiety. It is appropriate to see that this ritually constituted government is in fact a 'metaphorical crocodile'. The moiety that leads that particular initiation ritual is the 'head' and the opposing moiety is the 'tail' of the crocodile. Recall that Walindambui belongs to the ritual moiety called *nyamun arambandi* or the 'elder-brother group'. However, when he 'puts the betel nut in the *ngeko*', Walindambui is giving Harry away in order for Harry to be initiated by men of the opposing ritual moiety. This therefore makes his opposing ritual moiety—*shambu arambandi*, the 'younger-brother group'—become the 'ritual government' that assumes the prerogative to lead the proceedings of the ritual throughout its duration. In giving his son to be initiated, his ritual moiety loses a sense of ownership over their son for the duration of the ritual. The leading moiety decides and gives direction as to when and what an initiate will undergo during the course of the ritual till the seclusion period expires. During this time, the initiate is owned or controlled solely by his 'ritual mothers', who are the men of the opposing ritual moiety to that of the initiate.

Apart from the metaphoric transformation it inaugurates, the 'putting of betel nut in the *ngeko*' also has the effect of constraining behaviour, such as forbidding uninitiated men, women and children to go anywhere within the vicinity of the *ngeko*. Debate and discussion follow the request for an initiation. When Walindambui did so, several issues were raised. Some men complained that Harry had been away from the village for a long time, and the men feared that he was coming back to the village just for the initiation and would not stay in the village. They felt that they did not want to work for Harry's initiation only to see him return to town again. Others complained that since there was only one child from Walindambui's moiety who would be initiated, there would not be enough money and food to be shared amongst the 'mothers' who would initiate and look after Harry.

This matter was discussed over two days and some members of the leading moiety, *shambu arambandi*, insisted that the other moiety, *nyamun arambandi* should provide another one of their sons to be initiated as well. The name of a small boy of 11 years old who belongs to that moiety was also mooted. Some men of *nyamun arambandi* secretly proposed to me that I should convince my adopted father to give me over to their moiety so that there could be two initiates from the *nyamun arambandi* who would be initiated together. My adopted father dismissed the idea when one of his initiated sons raised this with him. Since he had already given away one of his sons to the opposing moiety, he was not inclined to allow me to follow suit[5] and preferred me to remain in his moiety.

Other men complained that it was not an appropriate time for the ritual to be staged in the village because the wet season had just set in. This means that the bush where they would collect firewood for the initiates would be wet and damp. And, to make matters worse, there is an increase in the presence of mosquitoes which causes discomfort and irritation for everyone. Some men complained particularly against Walindambui, who was too ill to attend the discussions in the *ngeko*. One man from the leading moiety said:

> Why must Walindambui request for the initiation of his son while he remains in his house craving for sex with his wife? He really has been going after prostitutes in Madang and now look, he is sick. He has spoilt himself by having sex with prostitutes. Why should he be allowed to stay and have sex with his wife in their house while all of us are here talking about the initiation of his son?

I include this here to highlight the kinds of talk that prevail when ritual moieties encounter each in other in heated discussions.

[5] For example, my adopted father, Yarme Mambingawi, gave one of his sons to the opposing ritual moiety—*nyamun arambandi*—while he and his two other sons remain as members of the *shambu arambandi*. In the past, tensions between ritual moieties during initiation rituals can lead to violent confrontations between men of opposing moieties. Some fathers who desire amicable relations sometimes decide to give one of their sons to the opposing moiety, so that if a conflict arises amongst them during initiation rituals, the father or the son will consider each other's interest and avoid pushing for drastic measures to be imposed against their opposing ritual moiety.

After two days of prolonged discussion, Tobias Wali, who had received the betel nut from Walindambui, moved the motion that the initiation ritual should be staged immediately. Tobias met me after the discussions and said:

> Since you came here to study and take our *kastom*, this is our *kastom* that you will now see. All of our men go through it and so you should now be prepared to go into the *ngeko*. You must go and tell your adopted mother and see if she is willing to provide food while you are in the *ngeko*. If not, then my wife and I will take charge of your food and we'll organize other women in the village to help along.

The task of feeding and caring for an initiate is burdensome and so, being mindful of this, Tobias wanted me to find out if my adopted mother was willing to endure this responsibility throughout the period of the initiation ritual. While Tobias coerced me to be inducted into the men's initiatory cult, the only other instruction he gave was to look for some money, a rooster, and a bunch of betel nuts and its accompanying condiments. He advised me that I should have all these things ready when Harry, the other initiate, went into the *ngeko* the following morning.

As I discovered later from talking with Harry, he too was given the same kind of information, apart from the need to avoid having sexual intercourse on the eve of the seclusion and to eat as much as one can on the morning before entering the ritual enclosure (*bandi*). It is believed that having sexual intercourse on the eve of the initiation would weaken the body and the initiate would suffer much pain during the process of scarification. Because scarification unleashes a lot of blood and weakens the body, it is also believed that by eating a lot of food on that morning, the initiate may be strong enough to endure the experience. Apart from these instructions, very little information is given to the would-be initiate about what is in store inside the ritual enclosure. Other information about what the initiate is to go through is withheld.

On the eve of the appointed day, the leading moiety erects a ritual enclosure (*bandi*) at the *saii*, a ritually secluded area at the fringe of the village which always remains as a preserve for initiated men only. After his meal in the morning, the initiate who first requested initiation and in whose name the enclosure is erected makes his way into the *ngeko*. Other novices would then follow after, but they go in individually and are received by a man who belongs to their clan association but is from their opposing moiety. When they enter the *ngeko*, they must bring with them a rooster and bunch of betel nuts and give them to the man who meets them.

Thus Harry was met by John Meingra, a younger brother of Tobias Wali, and in my case, Vincent Andingawi met me. Vincent belongs to the Masam clan and is of the same clan association, Nawa Masam, as I was, but he belongs to the opposing ritual moiety. In instances when offences are committed either by initiates, initiated men, or their wives and children in the village during the time when the ritual is held, the person who prosecutes and penalizes the offender will be an initiated man who is of the same ceremonial post (clan association) but belongs to the opposing ritual moiety to the offender. Thus, in the case of this particular initiation, it would be Tobias Wali and Andingawi who would prosecute Harry and me respectively if one of us committed an offence. Men who belong to opposing ritual moieties and are of the same clan association not only make pleas and advocate each other's ritual interest, they also prosecute charges against each other when such a situation arises.

The initiate should keep in mind the offences he commits and the charges he has been given, so that when the initiation ritual is held again in future, he can take the opportunity to reciprocate the charges on those who now charge him if they are in the opposing moiety. Clan associations take up both the moral and legal function of advocacy, as well as the adversarial job of prosecution, during the initiation ritual. Because of the functions clan associations take up in the initiation ritual, it is appropriate to say that the totemic dimension of a *ngeko* is only suspended and lurks in the background in the form of clan associations and the ceremonial posts whose names are invoked during the ritual. Thus, for instance, my ritual mothers in the *ngeko* always warned me that if I 'ever committed an offence, they would dig up Wobasui [my ceremonial post in Wolimbi] and take it down to Kopar, the mouth of the Sepik River'. By this they meant that if I ever committed an offence, they would impose a very tough penalty on my moiety, so that it would take a long while for the men of my moiety to settle it, just as it would take a long while to bring the Wobasui post back up from the mouth of the Sepik River where the Murik (see Barlow 1990; Lipset 1990, 1997) people live.

On the morning when would-be initiates enter the *ngeko*, they walk along the main footpath in the village outside the ceremonial ground (*wombuno*) by the *ngeko*. Dressed only in short pants, they enter the *ngeko* from its front entrance, where each of them is received on the ceremonial ground by a man who then takes their roosters and betel nuts and takes them into the *ngeko*. When I entered, I was instructed to press onto Vincent Andingawi's shoulder the rooster and betel nuts that I had with me. Vincent's face had been painted with black charcoal and he had a black cassowary headdress fixed on his forehead. In that context, the black paint and headdress symbolized anger and rage, emotions that are characteristic of the ritual and which also indicate that the 'crocodile' is now poised to avenge those who have provoked it. When I looked into Vincent's eyes, I saw nothing of the warmth and charm of his admirable character that I knew previously on secular occasions. He stared boldly into my eyes and said: 'Kid, what are you looking for from me and why did you come here? Don't you ever consider yourself as anyone big and strong, just wait, and you will get what you are looking for.' He was referring to the pain and the intimidating derision that lie in wait for the initiate to go through.

When the would-be initiate makes his way into the *ngeko*, before he is detached and secluded from the public, his young relatives, possibly girlfriends and some of his male peers who have gathered along the path outside the ceremonial ground, will bid him farewell. This separation inserts a striking emotional contrast between the uninitiated persons outside and the initiated men inside the *ngeko.* Male peers who cannot afford to be initiated often find it emotionally difficult to stand the sight of their friend entering the *ngeko* to be initiated, because they also want to be in there to be initiated as well. Silence and seriousness set in as soon as the initiate (*bandi*) is inside the *ngeko* and a series of ritual protocols begin. Women, children, and uninitiated men who may be observing the entry of the initiate are no longer allowed to look in the direction of the *ngeko*. From that moment onwards until the ritual ends, those who are found to be looking into the *ngeko* will either be scolded or, if they are repeatedly seen looking into the *ngeko*, they may be prosecuted and charged with an offence.

Within the *ngeko*, the friendship that one previously enjoyed with initiated men in secular life is now suspended and the *bandi* is subjected to an unfriendly and contemptible reception. Upon entering the *ngeko*, the *bandi* is gradually exposed to secret ritual objects, such as the bullroarer (*waal*). When I was first shown the *waal*, I could not comprehend the immense power it dispenses when it is animated with its sounds. A young mentor led me to it and said, 'That's it. This is the thing you have been looking for and you came in here. Now you have seen the *waal*.' I could not understand what he meant, and worse still, the humbleness of the object, made with no aesthetic elaboration on its surface, betrays nothing of its ritual significance. It was only when the ritual proceeded throughout its different phases that I discovered the power that the *waal* commands in the village, especially when it is animated.

After accepting the *bandi* into the *ngeko,* slit-gong rhythms (*tivut*) went off and the *ngeko* came alive with powerfully reverberating sounds. The rhythms indicate the clans that the *bandi* come from and they also send out a message to surrounding villages that, on that morning, new initiates have been taken into the *ngeko* to be initiated. The men of both moieties, who have been decorated, emerge from the *ngeko* and begin dancing on the ceremonial ground as secret flutes and trumpets are played inside the upper chambers of the *ngeko*. As they dance along, the dancers call out the names of all the spirit crocodiles of Iatmul (and Sawos) villages. The names of these crocodiles are as follows: Tumungumeli Mandangumeli (for Tambunum and Timbunke villages); Yaumeli Abiameli (for Mindimbit and Angriman villages); Kararau Marenyo (for Kararau and Kaminimbit villages); Suaragwi Yaviragwi (for Kewoli and Timboli villages); Suimbo Parimbe Yavarimbe (for Central Iatmul villages); Tavarambu (for Korogu and Kandingei villages); and Maviagwi Amboragwi (for Nyaurengei and Yambun villages). The names of these crocodiles relate to the primal movement of spirit crocodiles associated with each village and their stories are known in myths (*sagi*) that are owned by individual clans. In invoking the names of all the major Iatmul villages, the dance highlights the fact that beneath the cryptic cultural labyrinth of Iatmul mythology is one significant animal: the crocodile. The crocodile is the most central totemic animal of all Iatmul clans and is considered to have brought the world into existence in totemic cosmology.

After the dance finishes, a man of the leading moiety shares the betel nuts amongst all the initiated men of both ritual moieties. The leading moiety then makes its way to the *saii*. Secret musical instruments are concealed inside coconut leaves and are brought to the *saii*. The sound of the crocodile (*waal*) forces the uninitiated to keep at a distance from what is going on in the *ngeko* and they are forbidden to see it being animated. The Iatmul *waal* is for the Araphesh the voice of the *tambaran* (Tuzin 1980: 56).

> Secret sound-making devices . . . are not imitations of its voice, they are its voice . . . This is why operating these devices in a ritual setting is a supremely sacred act. It is a moment when the power of the Tambaran [crocodile] is made manifest through the agency of men, who by the same token, become godlike through the power they momentarily command. (1980: 57)

When it is animated, the *waal* is like a siren that sanctions and coordinates the movement of the uninitiated with respect to the activities of the initiation. However, the *waal* is used not only in initiation rituals but also on other secular occasions, and when its sound begins, the uninitiated are immediately made to keep away from the vicinity of where the sound emanates from.

While the men of the leading moiety make their way to the *saii*, those of the opposing moiety remain with the new initiates in the *ngeko*. For the remainder of the time spent as a *bandi*, the initiate has only the right to remain silent. The *bandi* is not allowed to laugh and joke with initiated men, let alone to enquire about anything that is going on, either within the *ngeko* or outside in village life. If the initiate reveals that he has knowledge about the different phases of the ritual, the man who has told him has breached the ethics of secrecy and would be charged accordingly. The initiates are given instructions only momentarily when they are asked to do something each day, they are not told or given the entire plan or programme of what they going to experience in the coming weeks inside the *ngeko*.

While the *bandi* (initiate) and the men of the opposing moiety wait in the *ngeko*, a man from the leading moiety makes three appearances, pretending to call them into the ritual enclosure (*bandi*).[6] The men of the leading moiety will have been making some minor preparations inside the enclosure before the initiates are brought in. While the men of the opposing moiety remain in the *ngeko*, a knowledge man from their moiety will perform a particular magic to 'cool the stomach' (temper) of the men in the leading moiety. Men of the leading moiety whip their counterparts in the opposing moiety when initiates are brought into the enclosure. Hence magic is made to make their men move faster in order to avoid being beaten severely. This magic involves use of personal names owned by the clan from which the magician originates. On this particular occasion, I saw Alois Kanuat, the eldest man and leader of the *nyamun arambandi* approaching a ceremonial post in the Wolimbi *ngeko*. Alois invoked its name and petitioned the spirit known by that name and made known his particular request. Alois then blew over some ginger leaves and betel nut, and gave them to the initiates and all the men of his moiety to chew. A short dance was then performed to quicken their bodies and make the men 'hot and active' before they took the initiates into the *bandi*.

Counter-magic was made by a man of the leading moiety in order to ensure that men of the opposing moiety are appropriately beaten. After the third false call has been made, the initiate is taken to the enclosure in the

[6] *Bandi* is the word for the ritual enclosure and is applied to the initiate who goes into the enclosure: for the period of seclusion, the initiate is also called *bandi*.

company of men from the opposing moiety. As this entourage makes its way into the enclosure (*bandi*), the area around the path leading into the enclosure comes alive with women, children, and uninitiated men who gather there to say farewell to the initiates. The mother or a classificatory sister of the initiate's father's sister (*iau*) can put on a dance as her nephew walks along to enter the *bandi* in order to become a 'man'. On this particular occasion, I saw one of Harry's *iau* dancing with the joy of seeing her nephew going into the enclosure to be initiated. Some girls or even older women related to the initiate may be heard crying softly, and others, I am told, will have tears in their eyes as they watch with fear and anxiety; uncertainty looms over the initiation of the *bandi*.

Men of the opposing moiety then enter the ritual enclosure. A man of each moiety carries one of the initiates on their back as they go into the enclosure. When the initiate and the men of the opposing moiety enter the enclosure, they must quickly identify and stop the man who is 'animating' the crocodile, otherwise the leading moiety continue to whip their counterparts in the opposing moiety.[7] A leading man of the opposing moiety will also have to put out two fires that have been set alight at the top of the entrance to the ritual enclosure. After these ritualized attacks are stopped, complaints will be heard about the pain that has been inflicted on members of the opposing moiety. The men of the leading moiety joke and laugh about what they have done, but their counterparts warn them about their revenge when they get to lead the initiation the next time. After all this noise quietens, the *bandi* upon whose request the enclosure was erected is carried out on the shoulders of one of the initiators in the leading moiety. The *bandi* is shown to the uninitiated for the last time. In this case, it was Harry who was carried out and showed before the 'crocodiles get to devour the initiates'. Upon re-entering the enclosure, 'metaphorical birds' (literally flutes) begin to sing and the process of scarification begins. In the intervening periods, when the flute music subsides, men inside the enclosure will laugh, joke, and tease the initiates. The *bandi* sits and lies down on an upturned canoe and is supported by his mother's brother. Specific 'crocodiles' are engaged to execute the lacerations on the body of the initiate. Scarification is a bloody and painful experience and the *bandi* who yells in pain receives insults, jokes, and ridicule from the initiators. The sound of the music, joking, and laughter is increased to drown out the responses to pain from the initiate. In Bateson's model of schismogenesis, a relationship of

[7] See Tuzin (1980: 62) for a comparable description of the entrance into the ritual enclosure, the ritual attack and the voice of the *tambaran*.

complementary schismogenesis comes into play in the relations between the initiators and the initiate. Initiates submit themselves to the swaggering and bullying tactics of the initiators (Bateson 1958: 130). This relationship of schismogenesis persists throughout the period of the initiation ritual until the initiates are let out of the *bandi*. It takes about an hour for a 'crocodile' to finish the work of devouring an initiate. When the incisions on the body of an initiate are completed, the initiate sits up and the name of the initiate, from his father's side, is shouted loudly by the initiators in a chorus of voices to announce that the scarification is completed. His mother's blood has been shed and he is now set to become a 'man' of his father's clan. The lacerations are cleaned and treated with particular kinds of 'medicine'. Throughout this ritualized ordeal, the metaphoric birds continue to sing in the company of other secret musical instruments, while uninitiated people gather outside near the ritual enclosure.

The initiates are then brought from the *saii* to the *ngeko*. At the sound of the 'crocodile', the uninitiated who are outside the ritual enclosure are forced to retreat into their houses. Men from both moieties then remove the sticks and palm leaves that frame and cover the ritual enclosure, and use them to hide the initiates as they take them back to the *ngeko*. This procession to the *ngeko* is accompanied by music from secret instruments. As the procession nears the house of a particular man, the names of his uninitiated sons are called out as a threat to take them into the *bandi* to be initiated as well. As they are walking, the initiates are required to walk slowly with their backs bent forward at a slightly acute angle. The initiates observe a posture of bending forward for some weeks and it is considered that such a posture helps to bring out the scars on their bodies once the scars are healed.

Inside the *ngeko,* the initiates are given specific instructions about how they should conduct themselves in the weeks to come. Particular emphasis is placed on the need for the initiates to look after the wounds on their bodies. Despite the fact that the wounds are on the initiate's body, he does not own them as yet. The incisions on his body are owned by his initiators and if the initiate is careless enough to make blood drip from his wounds, the initiate and his own moiety will be charged and penalized by the leading moiety. The initiators control the movement of the initiate in and out of the *ngeko*. Whenever he goes out of the *ngeko*, he must be properly covered with a cloth to avoid being seen by uninitiated people, because the wounds on his body are fresh and require some time yet before they are healed. The initiate must never be seen by the uninitiated until the liminal period of seclusion expires. Any deliberate attempt made by the *bandi* to be seen or to talk with uninitiated people is a very serious offence (*kuchal*) that is punishable with a penalty. The *bandi* is not supposed to talk with the uninitiated people because he is inside his male 'mother's womb' located inside the 'crocodile's nest' and 'it is not yet the time for a baby inside a mother's womb to be talking'.

After a leading man of the initiating moiety issues such instructions, the *bandi* is then shown his fireplace in the *ngeko* and is also given instructions as to how he should take care of the wounds on his body. The next phases in the ritual continue with more bullying and trickery. Details of such trickery are deliberately withheld here but generally 'the novices are subjected to a great variety of cruel and harsh tricks . . . and for every trick there is a ritual pretext' (Bateson 1958: 131). In all these instances of intimidation and playfulness, the *bandi* is expected to submit himself to the authority and command of his initiators. The initiators provide firewood and water to each *bandi*. Men from each moiety take care of the *bandi* that belongs to their opposing moiety. The *bandi* eat two meals a day. The main meal is taken between 12.30 p.m. and 2 p.m. each day and the other meal is in the evening. The main meal is taken in the *ngeko* while the evening meal is taken in the *bandi*'s residential home (*ngeio*). When going for the evening meal, the *bandi* is accompanied by initiated men and there is a small partition erected in the residential house, somewhere for the *bandi* to sleep in the night or to take his meal. The food of each *bandi* is provided by the *bandi*'s own mother or other female relatives such as a father's sister (*iau*), mother's brother's wife (*mbora*), mother's sister (*nyamei*), and in some instances a classificatory brother's wife (*tagwa*). The mother is obliged by her own intention to see her son initiated and become a 'man', and failure to provide the food to her *bandi* will result in her being prosecuted with a penalty. Whatever the weather, she has to make daily trips to the fishing lagoon to bring home fresh fish for her *bandi*. She gives money to her other female relatives in the village to buy sago at the market while she attends to fishing. She leaves her house very early in the morning and by noon she cooks a particularly delicious meal of fish steamed with coconut milk, green leaves, and baked sago pancakes. This particular kind of sago pancake is made only during initiation rituals. Her procurement of food for the *bandi* continues throughout the period of the ritual. The mother hopes that her *bandi* will be able to finish all that she has cooked for him. During initiation rituals there is nothing that pleases a mother more than for her to be told that her *bandi* is doing well in the *ngeko* and is growing from strength to strength from the food that she cooks. When my adopted mother was told that I was expanding in body size while I was in the *ngeko*, the news made her cheeks swell in pleasure and she was pleased with her efforts because the *bandi*'s body becomes the register of his mother's agency. It is a requirement that all the food that a mother supplies must be finished by her *bandi*. Of course, what is normally provided is often plentiful, and the 'crocodile mothers' who look after the *bandi* in the nest know best how to dispose of the surplus with the appropriate etiquette.

The *bandi* can sleep in the *ngeio* or in the *ngeko* during the night, but they are required to be inside the *ngeko* throughout the day. If the *bandi* sleeps in his own residential house, he must return to the *ngeko* early in the morning with his 'ritual mothers', making sure that he is not seen by uninitiated people. If the *bandi* sleeps at his house, a special partition is erected as a barrier that separates him from the uninitiated family members inside the house. Only initiated men in the house can converse with him, but they do so silently in whispers. If a *bandi* is discovered to have slept on his wounds, he will be cited for an offence and the *bandi*'s moiety will be responsible to settle the penalty imposed on them. To avoid the risk of compromising the secrecy surrounding this ritual, I will provide only a vague outline here.

There are three significant phases of the initiation ritual and each of these phases is associated with three different kinds of 'crocodiles' that perform different kinds of things on the initiates. The first two happen in the first two weeks, and the third phase is at the conclusion of the ritual, when initiates are being prepared to leave the *ngeko*. The first two phases effect a change in the posture that initiates adopt and in their body decoration. With body decoration I refer to two kinds of 'clothes' that the initiates wear while they are inside the *ngeko*. In the first week, the initiates are covered in a 'white cloth' and this is replaced with a 'red cloth' a week later. The white cloth is symbolically associated with death and mourning whereas the red cloth is associated with life and fecundity so that the change in the colour of clothes marks a progressive shift from death into life. The red cloth is also used on spears made for the *bandi* and on some ceremonial posts in the *ngeko*. The initiate, the spear, and the ceremonial post are considered analogous, so that each of them is referred to as *bandi*. Thus, when a ceremonial post is carved, it is prohibited from being seen by the uninitiated, and after the carving is completed, a process similar to scarification, the post is painted with the same coloured cloth as when a *bandi* comes back from the river after the 'third crocodile' has worked on him. On the night before a *bandi* passes out of the enclosure, the spears used by the *bandi* are brought to his residential house as a substitute for the *bandi* himself. When the spears are brought into the residential house, they provoke excitement and happiness in the *bandi*'s mother, sisters, and mother's brother's wife, and other such female relatives who may be gathering to celebrate the emergence of the *bandi* from the *ngeko* the following day.

While being secluded in the *ngeko*, there are only two occasions when the *bandi* comes into close contact with the uninitiated public. One of these occasions is popularly known as the time when the *bandi* goes on a 'picnic' in the forest. After the 'picnic' is over, the *bandi* returns to the village in the company of all the initiators, who sound musical instruments, including a 'crocodile'. The entourage arrives at the *saii* and the *bandi* is covered with banana leaves. After being adequately covered, the *bandi* is led into the village in the company of initiators who protect him from the women of both moieties in the village who seek to penetrate the procession of men to get to see and even touch the scars on the body of their moiety's *bandi*. This is a playful part of the ritual involving both men and women, and it shows one way in which all the people in the village are members of these moieties. Often the *bandi* is well protected from being touched by the women, but sometimes, to avoid being touched, the *bandi* must run at great speed to the *ngeko* where women cannot enter at this time of the initiation. After gathering in the *ngeko*, the *bandi* and all the initiated men go out to the river for a ritual bathe, which involves swimming out on the Sepik River for about 100 metres and returning ashore again. The river current is fast but the *bandi* and all the initiated men brave the waters to swim across and return. On returning ashore the *bandi* is dressed again with 'red cloth' and is then led back to the *ngeko* with the usual accompaniment of music. After this, the time when the *bandi* is to be released from the enclosure into the village as a 'man' remains very much at the discretion of the leading moiety. Most of the wounds will have healed. The *bandi* continues to observe all the regulations, and people like his mother's brothers will begin to tell him secret stories from his mother's side. It is also during the time of seclusion that initiates are thought to play secret musical instruments. Other older men from both moieties give general moral instructions and protocols relating to the conduct of relationships inside the *ngeko* and life in general. Instructions and totemic mythology are told furtively to initiates when they are alone in the *ngeko*.

The second time that a *bandi* is exposed to uninitiated people is when the *bandi* is invited to a residential house for an evening meal. If a meal is eaten at a mother's brother's (*wau*) house, then the *bandi* will be required to reward his *wau* later on. Another relative in the village may also host the meal. During such times, small children, boys, and girls, and even grown-up women, take the chance to feel the scars (*waalumi*) on the *bandi*'s back.

In the evening, when the *bandi* has taken his meal, he will sit in a dimly lit part of the house while the women and children are in another part, separated by a temporary partition. The *bandi* sits on a stool facing his 'ritual mothers' (who accompany the *bandi* on such occasions) and his initiated male host, while the women, children, and other teenagers who have gathered in the house will take turns to come up and feel the scars on the *bandi*'s back. When the wounds are healing, they are often irritating, and the caressing gives a pleasant sensation to the *bandi*. If those who are feeling the scars are joking and laughing, the *bandi* must restrain himself from yielding to the jokes and teases. He must keep still and quiet as his scars are being felt. After this is done, the *bandi* is taken back to the *ngeko* or to the house where he sleeps for the night.

When moving in the night, a *bandi* is escorted by one or two of his 'ritual mothers' and they use a torch (or fire) and the *bandi*'s spear. If they come across any uninitiated person on the way, the uninitiated person must turn his or her back to the *bandi* and avoid looking at the *bandi* till he passes them. The *bandi* is given the right of way and often treated as a 'prince', as it was explained to me jokingly. If the uninitiated people greet the *bandi* in the night, the *bandi* responds by tapping his spear. The *bandi* does not talk to the uninitiated. After a minimum of six weeks have elapsed, the leading moiety will appoint a day for the *bandi* to be released from the *ngeko*. The *bandi*, however, is not informed about when it will be. On the day prior to the appointed day, the leading moiety will summon the opposing moiety to gather as much garden food as possible. This food will be cooked and eaten by the men of the leading moiety as they stay up for an all-night vigil. During that night, the 'birds sing throughout the night' and the men dance in the upper chambers of the *ngeko*. Men of the opposing moiety take part in the dance but they do not take any leading roles. To keep awake a lot of coffee and tea are consumed, and nowadays it is common to find alcohol as well. In the morning the men dance on the ceremonial ground, while the metaphoric birds continue to sing from inside the *ngeko*. A particularly playful dance is enacted when women and girls join the men in singing. During this time, other men are preparing the *bandi* to leave the enclosure. The flute music continues to be played and comes to an end only when the first *bandi* steps out of the enclosure, dressed in short trousers, for the first time after six weeks. In my own experience as a *bandi*, I found that as I was leaving the *ngeko*, my mind raced back to all the experiences of the previous weeks and I was overwhelmed with an ambiguous combination of feelings, including joy and sadness, nostalgia and a profound sense of achievement that comes through endurance.

Before leaving the *ngeko*, the initiates are given small baskets which they keep by their sides. The baskets contain a supply of betel nuts, mustard, and lime for chewing, again for the first time since the seclusion period begins. The initiates are led from the *ngeko* into the bush and arrive back at the *saii*. At the *saii*, the *bandi* is given ginger that has had magic words spoken over it to chew and is warned not to look at anyone as he marches back to the *ngeko* in the company of everyone in the village. The *bandi* who requested the initiation goes out of the ritual enclosure and then the other *bandi* follow after. The ritual enclosure is now decorated with new and brightly coloured sago palm leaves, some flowers being attached to the palm leaves. The bright colour of the ritual enclosure symbolizes life and regeneration, in contrast to the initial enclosure, which was covered with old and dark palm leaves associated with the emotions of anger, separation, death, and mourning. When the *bandi* goes out of the enclosure, a strong feeling of achievement and excitement from heightened expectation impregnates the atmosphere outside. Shouts of acclamation and tears of joy greet the *bandi* as he walks along the footpath back to the *ngeko*. With his basket of betel nut by his side, the *bandi* keeps his head down and walks back. On the way, several female relatives, particularly the father's sister (*iau*) and the mother's brother's wife (*mbora*), may put on a dance to welcome the *bandi*. The *iau* sings her totemic songs while the *mbora* chants some of her husband's clan names and stories, and totemic plants associated with the *bandi*'s or the mother's brother's clan will be displayed.

Upon arriving in the *ngeko*, all the people gather to inspect and comment on the scars that have been incised on the *bandi*'s back. The *bandi* sits on a stool and becomes the subject of admiration and the envy of onlookers. Slit-gong rhythms now go off and the *ngeko* comes alive again with the sound of these reverberating rhythms. After a while, a *bandi*'s mother's brothers will lead their nephew to a spot out on the ceremonial ground and sing him their clan's totemic songs. As a gesture of proud attainment, one of the mother's brothers will pour and rub lime on the *bandi*'s chest and shoulders. Totemic plants of the mother's clan are planted in the ground around the area where the recently initiated *bandi* is sitting. While totemic songs are sung, other female relatives join to dance in celebration. Then a mother's brother will be seen approaching his nephew and whispers into his ear a secret name which he must not tell anyone.

After this, the *bandi* is taken back into the *ngeko* where he is instructed to not talk with any uninitiated person (except his mother) for the next five days. After the five days have elapsed, all the initiated men gather again in the *ngeko* and a bunch of betel nuts provided by the men of the leading moiety is shared amongst all of them. As the betel nut is exchanged between the men of both moieties, they also shake hands to leave behind all the tensions that have transpired between the two moieties in the course of the initiation ritual. The ritual moieties then dissolve and people revert back to their affiliation with totemic clans. The *bandi*, who has 'become a man', can now talk with anyone in the village, but he is asked to abstain from having any sexual intercourse for the next six months in order to preserve the scars on his body. He is also expected to not discuss any aspects of the initiation ritual with uninitiated people in the village in order to preserve the secrecy surrounding the ritual.

Concealment and revelation in the *bandi* ritual

To avoid compromising the secrecy surrounding the *bandi* ritual, the description here has been controlled so that a lot of explicit details have been omitted. The manner in which the initiation protocols in general are executed in Kanganamun village differs slightly from those carried out in other Central or Western Iatmul villages. This involves the manner in which initiates are cared for, including feeding and treatment of wounds, the rules governing the uninitiated seeing the initiates during the seclusion period and the general physical appearance after the ritual is completed. Internal comparisons with other Iatmul villages have not been spelt out here. The ritual age grades do not exist today in the form that Bateson (1932: 432–4, 1958: 245) described when he was there in the 1930s. Instead, what is preserved are the two generations in the ritual moieties, composed of a 'father's generation' and a 'son's generation'. Those of the 'father's generation' in the *nyamun arambandi* (the elder-brother group) are seniors to their counterparts in the *shambu arambandi* (the younger-brother group). Those of the 'father's generation' in the *shambu arambandi* are seniors to those of the 'son's generation' in the *nyamun arambandi*. In turn those who are of the 'son's generation' in the *nyamun arambandi* are seniors to their counterparts in the *shambu arambandi*. This sense of generational seniority specifies, for instance, who can give instructions to whom and other aspects of the ritual behaviour not specified here.

The ritual is generally described and talked about with much pride and a high degree of respect is accorded to men who have been initiated. Indeed, one might say that talk about the ritual in everyday discourse takes on an aesthetic form that conceals the horrifying reality of what a *bandi* is subjected to during the ritual. The ritual is a public event in the sense that everyone in the village is subjected to the stringent rules and protocols enforced by the leading moiety at the time. However, what actually happens to the initiates inside the enclosure is private—a secret matter known only by the initiator and their novices. The ritual sequence unfolds as a gradual series of revelatory moments for the initiate that culminates in his release from the 'crocodile's nest' some six or more weeks after the initial phase of detachment and scarification. Once the initiate is released back into the village—like a crocodile hatched and released into its life-world—one can only see the evidence of things done in secret on the bodies of initiated men. The time when the work of the ritual is revealed to the wider public is also the time when it is simultaneously concealed (Herle and Moutu 2004). What is shown on the bodies of recently initiated men is aesthetically compelling in that it provokes admiration and commentary from the onlookers who gaze upon the scars. This aesthetic, however, conceals the physical and psychological reality of a *bandi*'s experience. It is the secrecy surrounding this ritual, coupled with its aesthetic and masculine appeal, that carries the seductive power which persuades generations and generations of novices to be initiated into the cult.

Iatmul (and Sawos) mythology has it that, once upon a time, a spirit crocodile-man (*waal wanjimaut*) who had scars on his back visited the village. The scars on his body were so beautiful and captivating that they attracted the interest of the village people and they asked about the scarification and how they could get it on their bodies as well. The spirit man then told each father to bring a live crocodile for himself, and if he had several sons he wanted to be initiated, he must also bring a crocodile for each of them as well. Thus each man went about catching crocodiles, tied them up by their limbs and mouths and brought them into an enclosure. On the appointed day, all the men gathered in the enclosure and the spirit man unfastened and set loose all the crocodiles. When released, the crocodiles took revenge on all the men who were gathered in the enclosure. Only one man managed to escape from the enclosure, but the crocodile also bit him and his body was imprinted with marks of the crocodile's teeth. This man then inaugurated the idea of the initiation ritual, by showing the men how to make patterned incisions on a *bandi*. The scars are called *waalumi*, which literally means the 'crocodile's teeth', and they are not representations of the female genitalia as Silverman (2001: 38) interprets them.

I was not told any mythical explanation about the connection between the initiation and the mother's blood that is shed from a *bandi*. However, it is generally held that if the mother's blood is not shed, then it will have a contaminating influence on a man's physical strength and fitness. Thus, in order to 'become a man', one has to undergo the initiation. In the historical past, the initiation had a strong connection with the military strength of the village. It is during the ritual that men are trained and instilled with the discipline that prepares them for warfare against their enemies. Since pacification, the military aspect of the ritual has faded away; the physical drills that the initiates undertake during the ritual are now reduced and only some of them continue to be observed. Furthermore, there are no ecological consequences of the ritual, for example influencing fertility as one finds in other Sepik societies such as the Manambu (Harrison 1990a) and the Ilahita Araphesh (Tuzin 1980, 2001). In Iatmul, ecological fertility is bound up with the ownership of personal names, which is the preserve of totemic moieties.

The progressive sequence of the ritual is characterized chiefly by elements of surprise and uncertainty, revelation and concealment, submission and aggressiveness, mockery and ridicule. All of these are intended to instil and cultivate an enduring stamina in the character of an initiated man. The endurance is at once emotional (in terms of physical pain) and mental (with respect to a person's character and personality). It is often said that a man has to endure pain in order to endure life, in much the same way as a woman must endure pain in order to give birth to life. When discussing the photographs of the ritual in Bateson's ethnography (Bateson 1958), I was told that the photographs are only like the cover of a book. The different phases of the ritual are a gradual process of revelation, much like a narrative with a plot that is unveiled through several chapters in the book. To be initiated is to be given the privilege of reading that book, and what is described here is only a vague outline of such a book. The men's initiation ritual has its pride of place in Iatmul culture and, in everyday discourse, it is always discussed with an aesthetic that conceals its brutality so it remains as a unique experience that is known and preserved within the sanctity of ritual secrecy.

The symbolic dimension of the ritual is one that involves notions of gender transformation, death, and mourning as well as of life and generation. Men of each moiety are considered to be 'mothers' to the initiates from their opposing moiety. One moiety gives their son to be initiated by the opposing moiety and in doing so they temporarily lose a sense of ownership over their son during the seclusion period. The *ngeko* is also transformed into a 'womb' or a 'nest' in which 'crocodiles are hatched'. The womb or the nest is protected by male 'mothers', who lead the initiation and, at the same time, the other part of the *ngeko* retains a male gender and is associated with the opposing ritual moiety. Appurtenances such as ceremonial posts (both male and female) and flutes (mostly female) surround the initiate in the enclosure. During the initiation ritual, the *ngeko* takes on an androgynous form of gender, as a precondition of the fact that when one gender is activated the other is eclipsed (Strathern 1988). Finally, in the first two phases of the ritual, the colour symbolism of the 'clothes' that initiates wear are on the one hand associated with loss, sorrow, and ultimately death, and, on the other hand, life and regeneration. In death, the *bandi* sheds his bad mother's blood, gains his mother's brother's name, and ultimately he becomes a 'man' of his own paternal clan (see also Wassmann 1991: 33–5). We shall see how notions of life and death appear in the Iatmul conception in the following chapter; for now, let us return to the concerns about the ownership of ritual action.

Ownership rights in ritual action

Against the background what has been discussed so far about the initiation ritual, let us see how Harrison's notion of 'ritual as intellectual property' (Harrison 1992) can be applied to the Iatmul context. Harrison presents a comparison of material from a range of societies and observes that 'ritual is to action, as rhetoric is to discourse, as luxuries are to goods' (1992: 238). Harrison assembles a variety of examples from a range of historical disputes over ritual symbolism, and argues that an underlying concern of such disputes involves issues of property claims of an intellectual kind. He sees intellectual property as the ownership of a class of things, of their images and typifications (1992: 235). Harrison sets up an analogy between prestige goods and ritual symbolism in order to argue that ritual action is experienced in a manner reminiscent of objects which are transacted in a prestige economy such as the *kula* trade network in the Massim area. That is, the symbolic dimension of exchange relationships such as those found in the *kula* is similar to those of ritual actions. Therefore, such objects are to be understood not as what people 'own' but as what they 'are' (1992: 240). A particular theoretical concern that motivates Harrison's analysis is the contrast between economic and ritual behaviour, or between economic action and ritual action. He therefore focuses on the rivalries in economic practices such as the potlatch system and rivalries over ritual prerogatives such as the dispute over the ordination of female priests in the Anglican Church. Harrison shows that a basic feature of disputes such as that over the ordination of women moved from the 'economic, legal, familial or political status of men and women to their ritual status' and therefore it is the 'ritual roles that have been and are being contested' (1992: 228).

If we apply Harrison's analysis to the performance for tourists in Kanganamun, we find that it is not ritual prerogatives as such that are the basis of claims the men are making with respect to the performance and ownership of ritual action. All of the men concerned are initiated and are therefore entitled to the money because of their identity as initiated men. The prerogative that was exercised in that case relates to those who have rights to share and distribute that particular money. However, that prerogative was not itself under dispute but rather it was invoked to rectify what was perceived to be anomalous in the conduct of proper relations within the *ngeko*. What provided the convincing argument that money should be fairly redistributed to all the initiated men in the village was the fact that such men share a relationship of identity through their initiation. All the initiated men in the village are like members (parts) of a crocodile's body and it is during the initiation ritual that the action of moieties make visible the body of such a crocodile in their ritual action. The Kanganamun men's claim about the ownership of ritual action derives its legitimacy from an identity that they all share through their initiation. What was enacted as a spectacle for the tourists was already owned and, despite being an improvised pantomime, it was a performance that was already owned by all the initiated men and therefore it follows that whatever benefits that arise as a result of it being performed must be distributed in a manner that recognizes all the owners concerned.[8]

Revelation and concealment: *naven* and *bandi* rituals

Since the discussion above stems from ritual action, I shall now digress in order to comment upon the relationalist theory of ritual action propounded by Houseman and Severi (1998) concerning the famous *naven* ritual initially described by Bateson (1958), as well as other anthropologists who worked in Iatmul (e.g. Silverman 2001). I was not fortunate enough to witness a *naven* ceremonial during the course of my fieldwork. I was told several accounts of *naven* ceremonials, of which two were performed in 1997 and 1999. In 1997, a teenager from Kanganamun village living in Wewak town was selected to represent Wewak in the regional soccer

[8] A full exploration of this issue *vis-à-vis* issues of intellectual property rights in PNG is part of a separate project.

tournament held in Port Moresby. Although the Wewak team did not win, the Kanganamun teenager was congratulated with a spectacular *naven* performance upon his return to Wewak. That *naven* was performed by the lad's mother's brother on account of his entry into and participation in the Wewak soccer team that played in Port Moresby. The *naven* of 1999 took place in Kanganamun village. This *naven* was enacted by mothers of several Kanganamun boys who won a soccer tournament in the Eastern Iatmul village of Kararau. There the tournament was hosted to celebrate Papua New Guinea's independence anniversary. The Kanganamun team ended up as the champions of this soccer tournament. Before the Kanganamun boys returned, news of their win had already reached home. Hence upon their return home, some of their mothers went out on the Sepik River and performed a small *naven* for them to congratulate their sons for the victory.

Naven literally means 'going on view' (see Houseman 1998: 40), while *bandi* refers to the ritual enclosure from which the word for an initiate is derived. In analytical parlance, one might say that *naven* is a ritual of revelation whereas the *bandi* is a ritual of concealment. What is often revealed and concealed in these two rituals are the relationships that underlie the sexual reproduction of persons in Iatmul. There are interesting analytical themes associated with these two rituals. With respect to the duration of the rituals, the *naven* lasts only for a few hours whereas the *bandi* lasts for several weeks and involves an organizational structure and energy that outweighs the *naven* ritual. Both the *naven* and *bandi* rituals are premised on a sense of 'productive absence', which is itself an outcome of a spatial and temporal contrast between departure and return. By productive absence I refer to the fact that, in his or her absence from the village, the person honoured in the *naven* ritual would have left the village for a while and is engaged in some productive activity, such as going to the market for the first time or working in a job somewhere in town, involvement in warfare (as in the past), or getting initiated in the case of a *bandi* (see Bateson 1958: 1–10; Silverman 2001: 143; Weiss 1987: 164, 267, cited in Houseman and Severi 1998: 124). In kinship terms, *naven* brings into view relationships of filiation and affinity, whereas the *bandi* conceals the conjugal union of spouses and relationships of filiation.

In the *naven*, the celebrity would leave and go to a place outside the village such as a market, fishing lagoon, or town and, on returning to the village, the celebrity was congratulated. This then led to a financial reward being paid by the celebrity's father or patriline to the main protagonist of the ritual such as the mother's brother. In *bandi*, however, the initiate stays within the vicinity of the village but is kept confined in the *ngeko.* In being kept secluded during the initiation period, he is withdrawn from participating in the normal flow of village life and nurtured into becoming a man. On his return, the *bandi* becomes an initiated male member of his patrilineal clan. If the *bandi* loses his mother's blood through initiation, he gains a secret name from his mother's brothers which remains with him throughout his life till he dies.

With respect to the gender of these two rituals, those honoured and the protagonists of *naven* are both men and women (cross-sex) whereas the initiates and protagonists of the *bandi* ritual are principally men (single-sex). Citing ethnographic accounts of the Iatmul, Houseman and Severi argued that Bateson (1958) 'did not see that naven is *first and foremost* a ritual reserved for women and normally celebrated by women' (Houseman and Severi 1998: 121, original emphasis). Hence if *naven* is primarily a female ritual then *bandi* is effectively a male ritual. Both of these rituals bring into view the network of kin relationships and gender understandings of the Iatmul. The *naven* and *bandi* rituals play on the contrast between ritual and totemic moieties and the contrast between the *ngeko* and *ngeio* as we have seen in the previous chapter. Since *naven* is primarily a female ritual, what it reveals is that a father's sister (*iau*) has departed from her totemic clan and is married into another clan. In Iatmul understandings of analogic kinship (Wagner 1977) and analogic gender (Strathern 1988), cross-sex siblings are regarded within a lineage and clan as 'brothers'. Thus in celebrating the achievements of her brother's child in the *naven*, she is returning to her clan as a cross-sex sibling in a 'male' form. She moves in between residential houses. *Bandi* ritual, on the other hand, is a male ritual and it reveals that, from the perspective of ritual moieties, an uninitiated man is 'female' and so 'she', as it were, has to leave her residential house and be initiated in order to move in between the *ngeko* and the *ngeio* as a 'man'. This explains Bateson's confusing remark that 'novices are wives of the initiators' (1958: 131). Whereas the ritual moiety enacts a contrast between female and male, the totemic moiety sees same-sex and cross-sex siblings within a clan as unisex 'brothers'.

The *naven* ritual is a ceremonial of gender transvestism which celebrates culturally significant acts among the Iatmul and is enacted when the person honoured performs that particular cultural act for the first time or achieves a significant feat. 'The naven rite celebrates first-time cultural achievements such as spearing fish, wearing spirit masks, trapping prawns, and formerly bloodshed. Today, naven also honours the feats of modernity, including airplane travel and the purchase of a 25–40 outboard motor for a dug out canoe' (Silverman 2001: 3). *Naven* was originally described by Bateson

(1958), and his description and analysis was motivated by particular epistemological concerns. There were several philosophical intentions that underlie his analysis.[9] As he recounted in his second epilogue, *Naven* was offered as an epistemological premium to purchase explanation (1958: 280–1) for behaviour which is conceptualized as a form of communication such that interactive processes are seen as communicating particular messages. Although his concept of schismogenesis was developed prior to his fieldwork (see Bateson 1935), his experience with the Iatmul provided a definite ethnographic niche for Bateson to elaborate his theory of schismogenesis by embedding it in the nature of Iatmul ethological behaviour and eidological predilection.[10]

Schismogenesis refers to the process by which the cumulative interaction between individuals leads to a process of progressive differentiation observed in the behaviour of individuals. Bateson describes two kinds of schismogenesis: complementary and symmetrical. Complementary schismogenesis is observed for instance in the behaviour of a woman with her husband. When a husband is assertive, the wife becomes submissive and her submissiveness leads to further assertiveness and submissiveness on the part of the husband and wife respectively. An example of symmetrical schismogenesis is when a mother's brother's son (*laua*) boasts in front of his mother's brother (*wau*), prompting the latter to resort to a sexual salute called *ngarik*, which involves the *wau* sliding his buttocks down his nephew's shin (Bateson 1958: 13; Silverman 2001). Bateson's model posits that causal relations of interaction act as a feedback system where, for example, marital partners have a reciprocal effect on each other and in so doing they sustain a degree of equilibrium without which their marriage will collapse. Because a *laua*'s boasting threatens the complementary relationship he has with his *wau*, the performance of the *naven* in the burlesque form of a *ngarik* is seen as a corrective measure against this anomaly. In cybernetic terms, the *ngarik* is a 'degenerative causal loop', which directs the avuncular relationship towards a condition of complementary schismogenesis (Handelman 1978: 183). Arguing against the notion of a 'group mind', Bateson's model of schismogenesis asserts that it is the network of relationships between people, such as between affinal relatives, that facilitates integration and

[9] See Lipset (1982 [1980]) for a biographical account of Bateson's intellectual legacy.

[10] Whereas traditional Western metaphysics associate emotion with the body and intellection with the mind, Bateson (1958) attempts to forge a necessary unity by his notions of ethos and eidos and the logic of schismogenesis unveils this unity, which is facilitated through a causally interactive network of relationships.

social equilibrium. By focusing on the *naven* ceremonial as performed by the *wau* for his *laua*, Bateson intended to 'bring into view' a composite picture of the structural (kinship) configurations and the emotional and cognitive life of the Iatmul.

In an appreciative commentary, Handelman (1978) follows Bateson's observation that the *wau–laua* relationship is the pivotal relationship on which the *naven* ritual is enacted, and that this relationship cuts across two patriclans. Handelman raises the question of whether *naven* is better analysed as a ritual or as a play. 'Play', according to Handelman, 'accentuates the plasticity of ideation, while ritual emphasizes the integrity of the moral community.' Therefore Handelman goes on to suggest that the *naven* is ideally seen as ludic because it serves as 'an effective channel of metacommunication' (1978: 188).

Houseman and Severi (1998: 121) argue that by focusing only on the relationship between *wau* and *laua*, the analyses of Bateson (1958) and Handelman (1978) neglect other kinds of *naven*, such as those performed by women only or those enacted between *iai–ianan* (father's father's mother [FFM]–Ego) as described by Silverman (2001: 141–51). Through a critical rehabilitation of Bateson's model of schismogenesis, Houseman and Severi (1998) pose the daunting question of how and why action becomes ritualized. In seeking to address this question, they propound a new theory of ritual action based on the notion of 'ritual condensation'. This notion of 'ritual condensation' is 'defined as the simultaneous existence, within a single sequence of actions, of opposing modes of relationship' (1998: xii). Relationships in a ritual 'bring together in a single sequence of actions a plurality of pre-existing ties, generally drawn from a variety of domains: subsistence, the life-cycle, kinship, other ceremonial events, and so forth' (Houseman 1998: 447). The enactment of these relationships 'is systematically constrained by interactive dynamics entailing the condensation of nominally incompatible modes of relationship. Thus in the *naven* ceremony, parent–child ties and those between sexual partners, normally antithetical, are dramatically fused, as are cross-sex and same-sex relations and, more generally, the process of symmetrical and complementary differentiation' (1998: 447–8). In the *naven* pantomime, female protagonists (such as mother's brother's wife) appear in the caricatured form of vain and arrogant warriors, while male protagonists (especially a mother's brother) mock and parody pitiful widows. In their transvestism, female and male protagonists comically exaggerate the ethos (see Bateson 1958: 123–59) of the opposite sexes respectively. A mother's brother puts himself in the place of his sister, while a father's sister puts herself in the place of her brother. By following through Bateson's depiction of Iatmul ethos, Houseman and Severi (1998) raise the question of why is it necessary to become the 'other'.

They suggest that 'what . . . gives this theatre of passions its recurrent character is social necessity' (1998: 23) based on a relational form that hinges on two particular characters, the *wau* (mother's brother) and the *iau* (father's sister) who represent marriage alliances of the Iatmul. This is because 'the interaction between wau and laua involves a confrontation between the sexes and a conflict between matrilateral kin (including men) and patrilineal kin (including women)' (1998: 60). Accordingly 'the relationship between the characters of wau and laua turns out to be necessarily implied by the relationship between the *wau* and *iau*' (1998: 61, original emphasis). Unlike Bateson and Handelman, who focus on the avuncular relationship and how *naven* rebalances the ambivalences of this relationship, Houseman and Severi argued that the *wau* and *laua* relationship is an effect of the ritual and does not constitute a pre-existing sociological context for the ritual (1998: 116). In short, Houseman and Severi adopt a structuralist-inspired interpretation of the ritual based on the primary atom of kinship. They argued that if *naven* ritual is a symbolic behaviour, then 'symbolism comes into being through the condensation of two contradictory relations in accordance with a complex of schismogenetic process . . . If the word symbol signifies anything which takes the place of something else, then naven is a context which produces symbolism for the very reason that each protagonist literally takes the place of another' (1998: 250). In imitating the opposite sex, the social aim of *naven* 'is not so much to reproduce the image of men and women, and vice versa, as to combine contradictory images of the opposite sex in order to receive in return an analogous elaboration of one's own image' (1998: 250). In *naven*, therefore, one sees the dissolution of the singular self through an orientation towards becoming the 'other'.

Anticipating ontology

In my view, Houseman and Severi indeed managed to arrive at what is at the heart of Iatmul existential ontology, except that they have fallen short of specifying who is that 'other' self and in so doing they sustain the epistemology of symbolic representations. To specify who is that 'other' requires a view of the gendering of kinship among the Iatmul, an issue that will be raised in the following chapter. As is evident in Strathern's account of gender relations (Strathern 1988), Melanesians like the Iatmul present their gender through an analogy based on same-sex and cross-sex relations. The Iatmul term *nyamun shambu* applies to both same-sex and cross-sex siblings and it does not differentiate between the sexes, and so I have been using these terms to mean 'elder brother younger brother'.[11] Thus when a father's sister (*iau*) imitates her brother, or when a mother's brother (*wau*) imitates his sister in the *naven*, he or she is simply becoming 'the other brother' and s/he is her/himself that 'other brother'. What the *naven* ritual reveals through the contingency of symbolic representation is *an ontological disposition towards becoming the other brother.* In contrast to Houseman and Severi, I argue that, ontologically speaking, there is no representation involved here. Since the father's sister is a cross-sex brother to her brother, in comically assuming the character of her brother, she is not representing her brother but rather she is herself that other brother appearing in a different relational form. The self-same internal relation is instantiated in another form (see Strathern 2001b, 2005). With this in mind let us consider how the theory of ritual condensation applies to the *bandi* ritual.

There is a ritual kinship established in the *bandi* ritual in which men of the leading moiety become the 'mothers' of the initiates while men from the *bandi*'s own moiety are the 'fathers' of the initiate. Within each of the moieties are two generations, one being the father's generation and the other a son's generation, and a relationship of complementary schismogenesis is observed amongst these moieties. The two generations in the ritual moieties mirror the two generations found in the kinship system based on intergenerational siblingship. During the initiation ritual we encounter a situation in which aggressive initiators intimidate the initiates, who are passive and submissive to the authority of their initiators. The kin relationships involved in the *bandi* ritual are those between the *wau* and *laua* as well as the *iau* (father's sister) and *kangit* (nephew). Contrary to Houseman and Severi, who hold that the avuncular relation is an outcome of the atom of kinship, I argue that it is a relationship based on analogic kinship whereby the mother's brother and his sister are identified, and therefore the mother's brother takes care of his sister's children (see Bateson 1958). The mother therefore appears in the form of her brother in the initiation ritual, comforting her child who is being initiated.

[11] In some contexts the term *nyangai* is used when someone is addressing a sister or a classificatory sister, but it is also a generic term that could mean females outside of a kin relationship. I am conscious of the analytical problems that the term 'brother' might bring. This translation runs the risk of invoking an unintended masculinized image of fraternity that is absent in the Iatmul relational matrix.

The ethological differences between sexes that are evident in secular life take on an exaggerated form and are enacted particularly by men of opposing moieties with respect to their initiates. Whereas the leading moiety is active and assertive, the opposing moiety is passive and solicitous, and the same behaviour is evident in the relationship between initiates and their initiators. In being initiated, the *bandi* ritual inducts men to become parts of the body of the 'crocodile' (*waal*), which is the community of initiated men in the village. Just like the primal crocodile which opened up its mouth to birth the world, the *bandi* ritual is based on an oral and not a genital mode of birth, such that in devouring the initiates (*bandi*) the initiated (*waal*) give birth to new crocodiles. 'This twofold identification of the initiators *and* the novices with the totemic crocodile is constructed on the basis of a condensation of opposites in which the act of devouring and that of birth are simultaneous' (Houseman and Severi 1998: 159, original emphasis). In order for an action to have its effect, relations have to be separated (Strathern 1988: 191–224), i.e. initiates are separated from the rest of the village and brought into the enclosure and female kin are separated from their male kin in order to be married. Thus what we see in this ritual is that the initiated is separated from the uninitiated and is submitted 'to an operation in which the act of being born and that of being devoured become one' (Houseman and Severi 1998: 161). At the beginning of the *bandi* ritual, the old dark green palm leaves that adorn the enclosure have a dull outlook, which conveys a sense of loss, mourning, and bereavement because of symbolic death. However, when the initiates eventually come out of the *ngeko*, the ritual enclosure is decorated with brightly coloured palm leaves conveying a sense of triumph over death. The two major phases of the *bandi* ritual commence with symbolic death and culminate in life and regeneration when the *bandi* emerges from the enclosure. Death and life are simultaneously present as a necessary unity of opposition embodied by a *bandi*. With this in mind, the following chapter will consider Iatmul understandings of the human 'person'.

4

Nyamun Shambu: An Ontology of Brotherhood

. . . these patterns[of thought] are expressed in contexts of the relationship between brothers.

(Bateson 1958: 248)

In the last two chapters we have seen how ritual and totemic moieties appear and function in Iatmul social and cultural life. The contrast between the men's house (*ngeko*) and residential house (*ngeio*) provided an image by which one could visualize the flow of social relationships in an Iatmul village. In terms of Bateson's model, we might say that the totemic moieties are a function of opposition and that this opposition is sustained in a relationship of symmetrical schismogenesis, whereas ritual moieties are a function of unity and are premised on a relationship of complementary schismogenesis. However, as we have also seen, there is as much conceptual opposition and unity within totemic moieties as within ritual moieties. In Chapter 3, reference was made to how the colour symbolism in two phases of the *bandi* ritual is conceptualized in terms of life and death. This chapter returns to that thematic concern and utilizes two particular vignettes based on conversations that emerged during two different occasions of death in the village. These two dialogical encounters unveiled what might be described as the Iatmul version of the 'fractal person' (Wagner 1991), based on the Iatmul notions of *nyamun shambu* or the elder/younger brother. Situating this idea of personhood in an Iatmul context provides an analytical perspective to compare the nature of the naming system in Iatmul with that of its immediate neighbours, the Manambu (Harrison 1990a).

Nyamun shambu and the concept of person

One day in May 2001, a woman named Pamari came back from the fishing lagoon and, as she was approaching her house, she heard the agonizing sounds of wailing and sobbing by women who were mourning the death of an elderly woman, Maria. After leaving her things in the house, Pamari came out and, meeting me on the pathway outside her house, she asked who had died. When I said it was Maria, Pamari told me that she had encountered Maria's ghost (*kayik*) at her garden, which was next to Maria's near the fishing lagoon. Pamari said that when she was checking the melons in her garden, she saw the shadowy figure of someone who was sitting on Maria's part of the garden with her back towards Pamari, and therefore she could not see her face. Thinking it was Maria, Pamari attempted to talk with her but was suddenly overwhelmed by a paralysing numbness that made her mouth and her entire body become heavy and too weak to manage a word or even to do anything physical. In the twinkling moment when she closed and opened her eyes, the numinous and shadowy image of that person had vanished and Pamari was left with chilling goose bumps that made the hair on her skin stand up in fright. Immediately after that, Pamari left the garden and returned to the hut beside the lagoon where other women from the village had gathered. Because of beliefs associated with encounters of another person's *kayik*, she kept to herself what she had just seen. It was only when she returned home that she confirmed her suspicions that Maria had died and that was why she (Pamari) saw Maria's image at the garden near the fishing lagoon. Since they were good friends, Maria's spirit had gone to the garden to inform Pamari of her death. Pamari had checked on her (Maria) in the morning when she laid sick in bed. The garden they worked together, the food they shared, and the abiding friendship that they had made her spirit appear in that disembodied form in order to inform and alert her friend of her imminent death and separation. As Pamari reported this to me, her breath shortened and the well of emotions within her precipitated in clouds of tears that rolled from her eyes and she made her way to her friend's house for mourning. Later on one of Maria's sons, Luke Kamangari, told me that his mother must have died from retributive vengeance executed by clan spirits from other clans.

I then relayed this account from Pamari to one of my mentors, who explained that all grown up people have a *kayik* and this *kayik* can sometimes leave the body (*mbange*) in dreams or it can be extracted from the body through sorcery. He explained: 'that is why when a person is asleep, he or she must be woken up carefully, slowly, because if his or her *kayik* has gone out of the body during sleep, a sudden disturbance to the one who is sleeping might result in the death of that person'. My interlocutor also told me the story involving Maria's own husband, Yimbun, during a time when an initiation ritual was held in the village. When he was still alive, Yimbun took pleasure in imposing an arduous penalty against the 'elder-brother group' in the ritual moiety because of an offence committed during the ritual. The penalty required the men of the 'elder-brother group' to bring a fresh coconut with the taste that Yimbun particularly preferred. Yimbun also demanded that when the coconut is harvested, it must be carried from the crown of the palm to the ground. Now this is the typical idiosyncrasy of a ritual elder who demanded that the coconut has to satisfy his personal taste in order for the penalty to be settled. Not knowing which coconut would yield the specific taste that Yimbun preferred, several coconuts were climbed and nuts were taken to Yimbun, and finally one of them was accepted. Angered over what they consider a ridiculous penalty, a man of the 'elder-brother group', who was knowledgeable in magic and sorcery, extracted Yimbun's *kayik* and put it into a basket of fish, which was then taken by a woman to a market in the Sawos village of Marap. During that time the woman was away for the market, Yimbun was sick for a week and it was only after she returned from the market and gave him sago to eat that he was well again. Yimbun revealed this after he saw a dream regarding his illness. Another story involves the spirit of a man who had emigrated and settled in Bumbu, a squatter settlement at the fringe of Lae city in Morobe Province. Stories emerged that soon after that man died, his *kayik* was sighted in various places in the settlement, and it also frightened and chased away some Kanganamun people who went to have their bath by the Bumbu River in Lae. In the village I am told that the *kayik* of a dead person sometimes chases away people in their gardens or capsizes their canoes on the river or lagoons.

It was in this context that my interlocutor told me that life and death are a pair of brothers. Life (*yuphut*) is the 'elder brother' and death (*undumbu*) is the 'younger brother'. This conceptual understanding is concretized in the image of sleeping and swimming. If a person sleeps and passes away in death, then it is the younger brother (death) who has assumed precedence over the elder brother (life). Similarly, death is analogous to someone who swims out on the Sepik River and never returns, whereas life is when the person who swims out returns ashore again. As the 'elder brother', life is slow, restrained, and prolongs itself, while death, the 'younger brother', on the other hand, is swift and quick to assert its dominance in taking over and terminating life, the 'elder brother'. This conception of life and death makes the Iatmul 'person' appear as an embodiment of 'paired brothers' who are ontologically looped in a perpetual and alternating process of return and becoming the other brother. In other words, whether you are asleep or awake, dead or alive, whether one is the elder brother or the younger, one is always in a perpetual state of returning to become the other brother. If one takes this notion of an alternating pair of brothers to its ultimate logical conclusion, we might see that each of the brothers in the pair contains another pair, and this sense of a paired metaphysical necessity continues on recursively in a process of infinite regress and returns momentarily in the form of becoming the other brother. We shall see how this conceptual understanding of paired brothers appears in the naming as well as the marriage system in Chapter 5. But in the interim, if we recall the discussion in the previous chapters, we will have seen how this notion of paired brothers appears in a variety of forms and is retained across domains of different scale and complexity befitting the image of a 'fractal person' in a holographic worldview (Wagner 1991, 2001).

With this particular ethnographic vignette and analysis in mind, I would like to look at a similar concept of 'person' provided by Harrison (1990b), which appears amongst the Manambu, in order to make a comparison. The concepts of *kaiyik* (image; soul; spirit) and *mawul* (heart; emotions) that the Manambu use in articulating their idea of a 'person', are exactly the same as those often used by the Iatmul, but there are some minor variations that need to be highlighted. The important point is the manner in which the concepts of *kaiyik* and *mawul* appear to behave with the characteristic dispositions of the Iatmul notions of *nyamun* and *shambu*, the elder brother and younger brother. Harrison describes the Manambu person as an embodiment of 'Spirit' and 'Understanding'. These concepts parallel the manner in which Bateson (1958) described the ethological contrasts between the sexes and the contrasting personality types discussed in Chapter 2. The comparison below synthesizes the accounts of Bateson (1958: 123–59) and Harrison (1990b) together with what my Iatmul interlocutor told me, in order to relate it to the wider sociological and existential ontology of the Iatmul.

It was in anticipation of a sociological account of men's initiation rituals amongst the Manambu (Harrison 1993) that Harrison provided an exegesis of the Manambu concept of 'person' (1990b: 351–63). A theoretical motivation underlying his exegesis was to offer an approach in which men's initiation rituals in Melanesia could be explained in sociological terms. Harrison proposes that such an approach should encompass the symbolic and political significance of rituals, as well as issues of gender relations, hierarchy, and equality, and identify the constructs that people themselves use to articulate their understandings of rituals. His exegesis shows in a very illuminating way how the Manambu 'person' appears as a microcosm of the social relations which compose him or her. Expanding on the Manambu notions of *kaiyik* and *mawul*—which refer to one's spirit and affective dimensions—Harrison shows how these notions are continuous with the wider dialectical relationships between masculinity and femininity, amorality and morality, politico-ritual hierarchy and domestic-secular equality. The analytical categories of Spirit and Understanding are used to describe *kayik* and *mawul* respectively. Associated with these categories are opposing tendencies or characteristics that define a 'person', such as passive and active, autonomous and dependent, assertive and solicitous, etc.

'Understanding', Harrison explains, 'is the faculty by means of which the individual is aware of social obligations and connections and apprehends them as having a moral force' (1990b: 352). 'Spirit, on the other hand, is the individual's life force, a kind of élan conceived as the source of physical growth and well being, of self-assertion and self-will, and of certain mystical thoughts' (1990b: 352). Understanding has a moral quality and is oriented towards the conduct of proper relations with others, whereas the spirit is self-introjected and is therefore amoral. The Manambu 'person' appears as an embodiment of an internal dialectic oriented towards projects of individual pride and self-gain as well as having an inclination towards compassion and respect for others. Furthermore: 'The Understanding hears in the sense of being passive in its orientation towards others . . . The Spirit, on the other hand, speaks, it is active, autonomous and assertive' (1990b: 355).

The Manambu notions of *kaiyik* and *mawul* have similar connotations for the Iatmul. In both the Manambu and the Iatmul context, the term *mawul* has several meanings but in general it refers to the soft or inner core of a plant or an animal. With respect to humans and animals, it refers to the liver and, in the sense in which it is being described here, 'mawul is the seat of an individual's affective response, thought and knowledge'. It is one's sentimental capacity and the quintessential hallmark of an individual's moral and social person and, in its association with 'hearing', it covers a wide 'range of ideas—comprehension, obedience, pity, desire—all of which ... [imply] the capacity to identify with others' (1990b: 354). *Kaiyik*, on the other hand refers to one's soul or spirit, shadow, and in other contexts it also refers to carvings, painting or photographs.

> The Kaiyik is the source of the individual's capacity for motility and spontaneous action and of physical and mental energy. It can wax and wane in

> strength, and it can be removed by sorcery or spirit attack causing lassitude, illness and eventually death . . . A kaiyik on the loose is a public nuisance, as it plays irresponsible and sometimes frightening pranks: scaring travelers in the bush . . . capsizing canoes. (1990b: 354)

The *mawul* is not detachable from an individual's body whereas *kaiyik* is. When it is not detached, 'kaiyik is the source of one of the most admired qualities an individual ... can possess ["sharpness"]' (1990b: 354).

Both men and women are composed of *kayik* and *mawul*. A *kayik* grows in proportion to the age of an individual and babies do not have a *kayik* comparable to those of the adults. The affective quality of the *mawul* is often associated with women, for instance mothers in Iatmul are generally entreated with a sentimental and affectionate phrase such as '*nyamei una mawul a*' which means 'mother you are my liver'. The association of *mawul* and women is also revealed when death is experienced in the village. Women mourn and sing lamentations based on totemic chants that recall the life and character of a person who is lost in death. Men do not mourn in the way women do and indeed only a few of them mourn during funerals. Bateson (1958: 156–9) relates these contrasting attitudes towards death with the contrasting ethos of Iatmul men and women. The sociological parallel of Manambu's Spirit and Understanding would be the contrasting ethos that Bateson (1958: 123–52) described for Iatmul men and women, as well as the personality types and behavioural dispositions associated with each of the two types of men's houses discussed in Chapter 2. Bateson observed that generally speaking Iatmul 'men are occupied with the spectacular, dramatic, and violent activities which have their centre in the ceremonial house, while women are occupied with food-getting, cooking and rearing children—activities which centre around the dwelling house and gardens' (1958: 123). It was in this light that I used the contrast between *ngeio* and *ngeko* to describe the flow of sociality in Kanganamun village in Chapter 2. In Manambu, Harrison noted that the 'kaiyik' is associated with spirit, amorality, masculinity, autonomy, assertiveness, and the politico-ritual domain while *mawul* is connected to understanding, morality, femininity, domesticity, dependence, and solicitude, etc. The same is true of the Iatmul. However, women in both Manambu and Iatmul societies do assert themselves where they see it fit and proper. Among Iatmul, for instance, women are renowned for initiating sexual encounters with men (see for instance Bateson 1958: 144)[1] and, in some historical accounts,

[1] During my fieldwork, I also heard numerous stories about women who take initiative in organizing sexual encounters with men.

women also play an active role in warfare assignments (1958: 145–7). The ceremonial antics enacted in the *naven* ritual invert the conventional ethos associated with women, and so we find women appearing to be boastful and arrogant while men become like pitiful widows provoking laughter and compassion. In the *bandi* ritual, it is the mother's brother (*wau*) who acts as a mother by showing compassion through caring and comforting his nephew during scarification. With respect to the personality types and behavioural dispositions, we have seen that, by virtue of their totemic affiliation, there is a relationship of symmetrical schismogenesis that prevails between the pair of brothers called Kimbianmeli and Kisameli. In addition, issues of ownership claims often provide an elicitory trigger for schismogenic differences to burst into episodes of conflict and violence that perpetuate the progressive differentiation amongst the totemic moieties in Kanganamun village.

As we have also seen, Kimbianmeli and Kisameli are not just types of men's houses, they are also a pair of brothers. In Iatmul totemic mythology, dark coloured things such as plants and birds are generally associated with the 'mother/earth' totemic moiety, which is connected to Kimbianmeli *ngeko*. On the other hand, bright coloured things are associated with the 'father/sky' moiety, which is connected to the Kisameli *ngeko*. The *bandi* ritual plays on this contrast between the two colours to depict death and life as a pair of brothers that converge upon and are embodied by an initiate. It is apt to see that the colour symbolism of the *bandi* ritual assumes a form of figure–ground reversal (Wagner 1986). That is, in totemic understandings, a dark colour is associated with the 'mother/earth' moiety (*nyamei nimba*) whereas the bright colour is associated with the 'father/sun' moiety (*nyowi nimba*). The 'mother/earth' moiety is the younger-brother and the 'father/sun' is the elder-brother moiety. The colour of the ritual enclosure at the beginning of the ritual is dark, and dark colours are generally associated with the younger-brother totemic moiety. But when the ritual concludes, the colour of the palm leaves that adorn the ritual enclosure are bright, the colour that is generally associated with the elder-brother totemic moiety. However, in the two significant phases of the ritual, the cultural connotation of these two colours is reversed. In the first phase of the ritual after the initiates are lacerated, they are given white 'clothes to wear'. Notice that white is a bright colour that is conventionally associated with the elder-brother totemic moiety, but in this ritual context it becomes associated with symbolic death, which the Iatmul consider as the younger brother. In the second phase of the ritual, the initiates are 'adorned with a reddish-coloured 'cloth'. Red is a dark colour that is normally associated with the 'mother/earth', the younger-brother totemic moiety. But in putting on this 'red-coloured cloth', the initiate undergoes a symbolic transformation from death into life. The initiate is now considered alive after being devoured and birthed by the crocodiles. In sum, then, the ritual sequence is modelled on the same logic of being oriented towards becoming the other brother.

Harrison notes two particular kinds of string bags used by initiated men of Manambu, which are bound up with their social identity. One of them, called *kwasembi*, is made by the initiates' female kin and presented to men after their initiation, while the other is an ordinary looped bag. The *kwasembi* is associated with a man's *kaiyik* whereas the ordinary one is for social purposes and is associated with his *mawul*. Initiated Iatmul men are also given string bags after their initiation and such bags are provided by the initiate's 'ritual mother' (*nyamengu*) who looks after the novice during the initiation. This bag does not carry the same significance it does among the Manambu. As we have seen in the previous chapter, the object that has a close analogical relation with an initiate amongst the Iatmul is a spear. This spear is also called *bandi* and its movement between the *ngeko* and the *ngeio* portends the imminent appearance of the *bandi* from the ritual enclosure. When this spear is brought into its residential house (*ngeio*) on the eve when initiates are to be released from the enclosure, female relatives of the initiate celebrate the forthcoming emergence of their *bandi*, who has been initiated into becoming a 'man'. The spear and the man share the same meaning through their participation in the word *bandi* and so the appearance of the spear, which is an analogue of its human counterpart, motivates a private celebration inside a *ngeio*, and this moment of initial jubilation precedes the public celebration that takes place around the precincts of the *ngeko* the following day.

The significant difference between the Manambu and Iatmul is that while the *kaiyik* is the source of the focus of men's initiation rituals among the Manambu, it is the body which is at the core of Iatmul *bandi* ritual. The initiation rituals augment immanent capacities and shut off the 'hearing' senses of a Manambu man so that he becomes aggressively violent and forceful in the pursuit of his self-seeking aggrandizement. The same augmentation happens to an initiated Iatmul man but, through the process of initiation, the body becomes something like a 'receptor' that is able to sense and receive particular messages from different clan spirits, particularly the ones that are called *wagan*. However, an initiated Iatmul man cannot be in dialogue with the clan spirits without the appropriate use of totemic names (*wansikundi*) from his or his mother's clan. He uses such names to invoke and call forth particular spirits whose powers he will utilize to pursue particular objectives, such as sorcery, fighting, or love magic, etc. While it refers to the system of totemic names, the etymology of the term *wansikundi* makes reference to hearing. *Wan* is the ear, *si* refers to names and *kundi* refers to talking or the mouth, the organ by which clan spirits are invoked. The initiation ritual allows a man's body to become receptive to information coming from clan spirits and this information is not 'heard' but 'felt' through the body. In contrast to Manambu, it is not the ritual as such that augments the fecundity of a man, because the Iatmul would locate the mystical powers of an initiated man as coming from clan spirits. Whereas the initiated Manambu man asserts himself through 'talking', his Iatmul counterpart would combine both 'hearing' and 'talking' and receives information from the spirits by 'feeling' his body.

In Harrison's analysis, the Manambu keep ritual and morality separate, whereas the Iatmul unite ritual and morality. It is said that the 'eyes' of one's clan's tutelary spirits (*wagan*) are upon the initiated men and their manner of conduct matters significantly. That is, if an initiated man chooses to learn and make sorcery and magic, the *wagan* will easily respond to his invocations and subsequent manipulations. On the other hand, an initiated man is also expected to show appropriate moral conduct. 'He should always walk on the *wombuno*', the ceremonial ground. In this context, the ceremonial ground is a metaphor of moral conduct and it extends beyond the confines of a village to anywhere that an initiated man may go. These subtle differences between Manambu and Iatmul are probably connected to the fact that, in organizational terms, the Manambu conflate ritual and totemic moieties while these are kept distinct amongst the Iatmul.

If Harrison connects the Manambu notion of *kaiyik* with ritual and *mawul* with mundane social life, I suggest that *kaiyik* and *mawul* take a sociological and ontological form amongst the Iatmul with respect to their notion of 'paired brothers', the *nyamun* and *shambu*. In sociological terms, this pair of brothers appears most concretely in the two distinct forms of men's houses and in the way in which *ngeko* and *ngeio* structure and organize the flow of social relationships. In Bateson's model of schismogenesis, one might think of this notion of paired brothers in terms of symmetrical schismogenesis, for example in the relationship between two opposing totemic moieties exemplified in the personalities of Kimbianmeli and Kisameli, or in the pairing of ritual moieties. Finally, if life and death are considered as a pair of brothers embodied in all humans, then it follows that the Iatmul 'person' is ontologically oriented towards becoming the other brother with the conceptual potential of infinite pairing. Because of the fact that this notion of paired brothers replicates itself as a pattern that appears in a variety of contexts, such as ritual and totemic moieties, kinship and gender, naming and marriage systems, and music, this Iatmul notion of the embodiment of paired brothers is best seen as a 'fractal person'.

Nyamun shambu and the fractal person

This kinship between life (*yuphut*—elder brother) and death (*undumbu*—younger brother) is strikingly different from the way in which the German philosopher, Martin Heidegger (1962), conceives of the metaphysical project of Being. Heidegger (1962: 279–311) assigns death with the sovereign and gravitational force of individuation and complete totalization. As he explains it, human beings nurse and possess within themselves the potential for their own individual deaths. Death is a metaphysical necessity that imposes an arbitrary yet irrevocable demand against any possibility of representation or substitution. That is to say that no one else can represent any of us in our own individual deaths. When death intervenes, death itself is never terminated but it is rather realized as that ultimate possibility of our being which has been outstanding so far in our lives (cf. Dreyfus 1997: 209–12). As I understand it, Heidegger's conception of death is also employed to illustrate a Hegelian proposition that Being and Nothingness are one and the same. So long as a person is still alive, his or her identity is open to a constant process of revision and redefinition. Employing a language of transaction, Heidegger describes death as that which liquidates the balance that has always been outstanding and reconciles the question of Being in the abyss of Nothingness. The biographical career of someone's life achieves its completion in death. What someone's life has been about becomes completed as a settled matter because, upon death, the transaction is completed and all the outstanding balance left so far in the sum of one's life is liquidated (see Hoffman 1993: 195–215). Hence what Heidegger calls *Dasein* is but a Being-towards-death.

Such a conception of Being has been a subject of a critically illuminating exchange between two Melanesianists who differ in their theorization of Melanesian ontology through a contention over the processual notions of 'being-towards-death' and the 'being-towards-beginning' (see Mimica 1993: 79–95; Weiner 1991, 2001: 55–8). The description of the Iatmul person described here is committed to the ontological view that a 'person' is always oriented towards becoming the 'other' and that this 'other' is not an external other but rather an internal relation. In Wagnerian terms, the Iatmul notion of paired brothers composes the 'fractal person', the being which is 'never a unit standing in relation to an aggregate, or an aggregate standing in relation to a unit, but always an entity with relationship integrally implied' (Wagner 1991: 163).

The idea of a 'fractal person' was offered as a critical alternative to the manner in which the Western metaphysical opposition between society and individual was unwittingly allowed to install itself as the hegemonic voice of reason in the anthropological imaginations of Melanesian societies. The context in which Wagner writes is situated in a critical attempt to rethink the typological contrast between 'big man' and 'great men', characters that are at the centre of political and ceremonial life in many Melanesian societies. The original impetus to the characterization of the fractal person came from the fictitious image of a cyborg—an entity which is part-man and part-machine—that M. Strathern (1991) appropriates from Haraway (1985) to conceptualize the Hagen big man as neither singular nor plural. Since the notions of big men and great men incorporate a problem of scale, Wagner extends this argument with mathematical imagery in order to conceptualize the contrast between singularity and plurality exemplified by the manner in which big men appear to be simultaneously individuals and corporate entities such as a clan or lineage. Wagner transforms this apparent analytical problem of an entity occupying two positions at once (singular/plural; individual/corporate) into a solution.

As a recursive motif, the idea of fractal personhood is discernible in several contexts, such as in notions of geneaological enchainment (so that person as human and person as lineage are identifications of this process of enchainment); through the commonality of shared language (and talk, in particular, is the primary medium in which fractality is expressed); and in naming practices. One of the examples that concerns us here in this book is the manner in which Wagner describes Daribi naming practices (see Chapter 6) in order to exemplify how Melanesians conceptualize existence as identity through analogical reasoning. It is in naming that the identities of people are known and circulate like *kula* and *moka* valuables, since names are at once individual and collective. Underlying Daribi naming practice is a notion of congruence based on a relationship of resemblance that betrays a sense of equivalence or a notion of identity that is based on contingency. Wagner extends this notion of congruence to conceptualize economic exchanges and the political activities of big men (1991: 166).

To concretize his argument that the fractal person is neither singular nor plural, nor sum nor part, Wagner cites instances from several societies in PNG, but specifically assembles ethnographic examples from three different geographical areas. The three ethnographic examples include holographic ideas about reproduction evident in ritual and myth amongst the Gimi; the system of enumeration and intimations of infinity among the Iqwaye; and notions of elicitation and containment among the Barok. The Gimi example shows a holographic model based on a metonymic conflation of the contained foetus with the penis contained in copulation. A man is a penis with a penis but a woman has a penis within her body. 'The set of substitutions constituting a woman's internal penis, from the holographic foetus within a foetus to menarche to that of impregnation and pregnancy, is also the coming into being of legitimate procreation and kin relationship out of its incestuous opposite' (Wagner 1991: 168). Amongst the Barok, the holographic model appears in the ideas of elicitation and containment practised between exogamous matrimoieties, particularly through replicating in various ways the image of *kolume* (containment) and *gala* (elicitation). Accordingly one could see the Manambu (Harrison 1990a) concept of *ndja'am*, the reciprocal exchange of feeding and nurturance involving the exchange of women, names, magical and ritual services amongst particular sub-clans in the same light. Wagner's third example concerns the counting system of the Iqwaye, which will be a subject of comparison with the Iatmul in Chapter 5. The Iqwaye example demonstrates a congruence between the body of a Iqwaye person and the cosmos at large. In Wagner's terms, an Iqwaye person is a totality in the same vein as the entire cosmos and the act of counting or reproduction is a replication of this image of totality through the device of scale retention.

In sum, through offering a particular conception of inherent totality—that is based upon 'analogic cross-sections through which the whole grows itself'—Wagner's notion of the fractal person is offered as an alternative approach to two theoretical issues: one concerns the metaphysical assumption about the relation between the individual and society, and the other concerns the issue of representational metaphysics. In terms of the latter, Wagner notes that if the notion of fractal person summons the image of a holographic worldview (see Wagner 2001), then holography itself is not an ethnographic phenomenon but rather a mode of understanding. 'In no case is the holography a matter of direct presentation; it is not perceived in the material so much as it is re-perceived as the sense of indigenous intention to show phenomena in their self-constitution' (Wagner 1991: 170). This has implications for the former, which Wagner explains as follows:

> Reperception implies that the holography will not be apparent in the kind of organic thought that distinguishes kin terminology as 'social' (or 'cognitive'), factionalism as 'political', horticulture as 'technological', or that postulates an integration of groups, functions or categories into a larger social fabric. The crucial element is the fractality that prevents the differentiation of part from whole, that keeps the imageries of understanding from collapsing into the individuals, groups and categories that constructionism bundles into wholes greater than the sums of their parts. (1991: 171)

Reperception is not an interpretative stance, nor a mode of social constructionism based upon an epistemological plane of explanation, but an immanent social form. Thus, when I was told that Iatmul conceptualize life and death as a pair of brothers, my informant could be seen as describing such a mode of immanent humanity. His explanation involves reducing the scale in which the Iatmul conceptualize the world notionally in terms of the paired brothers: *nyamun shambu*. In its diminished version, a human person is an embodiment of paired brothers endowed with the conceptual potential of infinite pairing. But when magnified, the paired brothers appear in the form of totemic and ritual moieties, and, at the cosmic level, the heavens and the earth are mythologically imagined as the jaws of the primal crocodile that brought everything into existence through the separation of its body.

Indeed, as Harrison observes for the Manambu, it is conceptually and practically impossible for the sky to exist without the earth. 'The social world of Avatip', as it is in Kanganamun or other Iatmul villages, 'is divided in such a way that the idea that groups require each other comes close to being a kind of *necessary* truth, not only a *contingent* one' (1990a: 65, my emphasis). We shall deal with one such concern about *necessity* and *contingency* in Chapter 6, when we consider the naming system of the Iatmul and the Daribi. The question that emerges from the discussion is that if a fractal person 'is an entity with relationship integrally implied', what is the ontological status of such a relation if life cannot exist without death, sago without fish, and the sky without the earth? For Wagner, the integral relation implied in the concept of a fractal person is actually a foil of reperception, 'the certainty of a subjectivity witnessing its own perception' (2001: 38), much like Pamari who witnessed the apparent form of Maria's *kayik*, with its back towards her at the garden by the lagoon.

With all this in mind, and recalling the proposition that names play a crucial role in understanding the concept of a fractal person, let us now turn to a comparison of the nature of personal names as it is found amongst the Manambu and the Iatmul. We begin with Iatmul names and how they are connected not only to the question of life and death but also to the practical concerns which reign over the ownership of resources.

Names are thicker than blood: existence, identity, and the ownership of resources

Iatmul names are located within the province of totemic moieties. Recalling the reproductive relations that compose a person, all Iatmul individuals are given a minimum of two names, from both sides of their parents. They are also given several other names but only one of those names is used throughout most of his or her lifetime. The mother's name, called the *apan si*, returns to the mother's clan once the bearer of that name dies. This is because an *apan si* cannot be inherited as are the names from one's father's side, which are called *nyait si*. A patriname or a *nyait si* is reincorporated into the stock of names that are owned by a clan and used again when a new child is born into the clan in question. *Apan si* or the matriname, on the other hand, returns to its owners, the mother's clan. Concomitant with this notion of the returning of names to their respective clans is the belief that when a person dies, he or she goes and live in the world of the dead (*undumbu ngei*) under the name that comes from the mother's side, whereas the patriname is reincorporated into a person's own clan. Thus the returning of names to respective clans is both an issue of ownership and a question of the ontological identity that one assumes through the name that one has to live, either in this human world (*yuphut ngei*) or in the world of the dead (*undumbu ngei*) (see also Bateson 1958: 233; Wassmann 1990: 32). The names are already there prior to one's birth, and after being born, one is given particular names to be used throughout one's biographical career. When the bearer of that name eventually dies, the name continues to live on after death. Since the names exist prior to, and are constitutive of one's existential identity as an individual person or clan member, and since the names survive posthumously, I have therefore described this quality using the phrase *names are thicker than blood* (cf. Sahlins 1976: 10).

To add more complexity to this scheme of ontological onomastics, Iatmul also believe that life and death are totemic realities owned by the two totemic moieties. The following ethnographic vignette elucidates this clearly. In 2001, Makwat was a vibrant young woman of 24 years old, married to Francis Wariangijang of the Samiangwat clan which is part of the *nyowi nimba*—the elder-brother totemic moiety. Makwat fell ill all of a sudden and within a matter of days she was gone. The sudden and abrupt end to her life left the villagers in shock, disbelief, fear, and bereavement. Francis and Makwat had four young sons at the time of her death. The villagers were consumed with fear and grief at the loss of Makwat. In those freighted moments of emotional density, villagers described their experience of this loss and the ensuing fear (about death-inflicting spirits in general and Makwat's ghost in particular) as if they were naked and tactile sensations that could be experienced in a physical sense much like a weight on one's body.

In the days that followed, many men commented that her death was probably the result of retributive vengeance, or that her father was deliberately using her death for instrumental purposes, to 'stand on her grave' in order to be able to make magic and kill people through summoning and invoking her spirit using her name after her death. Makwat's father, Tobias Wali, flatly and categorically denied this allegation, and sought various traditional means to vindicate himself. When the events of her life and biographical career were recited during the mourning, Makwat's husband, Francis, reported that a few hours prior to her death, he bumped into a 'dark blackish shadowish man' (spirit figure) on the pathway leading into their house when he was returning from his classificatory mother's house, where their children were being cared for on account of his wife's illness. Given that his wife was lying ill in the house, the encounter with such a spirit figure was a bad omen. Thus Francis rebuked and shouted curses to that spirit before he entered the house to attend to his wife, but it was already too late. A few hours elapsed and Makwat left him and the children. Francis believed that the 'spirit' (*undumbu*) he encountered on the path was the one that came and took away the soul (*kayik*) of his wife. When Francis produced this account, James Noru, who is a classificatory mother's brother of Makwat, told me that it is highly likely that the spirit Francis encountered was indeed the 'undertaker', a totemic spirit of his moiety known by the name Kambaimbange, who had come to receive the spirit of Makwat as she entered into the world of the dead. But Kambaimbange is not only an undertaker, he is also credited with bringing the world into existence. Bateson (1958: 233) was shown a carved representation of this mythological character in the Eastern Iatmul village of Mindimbit, and reported this as follows:

> Kava-mbuangga, the wagan who set his foot upon the mud and created dry land, is a representative of both the living and of the dead; and there are myths of his visit to the land of the dead. A figure of him . . . in Mindimbit was painted in two colours, the right hand side of the figure in ochre to

> represent living flesh, and the left-hand side in black to represent stone, kava (paralysis, or 'pins-and-needles') which creeps over the body in death. Thus in the figure the two sides of the Kava-mbuangga's personality are diagrammatically shown.

The two colours which represent life and death are embodied in the figure of Kava-mbuangga, known in Kanganamun as Kambaimbange. The two colours, ochre and black are dark colours which are both connected to the younger-brother totemic moiety, *nyowi nimba*. The paralysis that Bateson describes is similar to the paralysing numbness that ran through Pamari's body when she encountered the ghost (*kayik*) of Maria at the garden near the lagoon. This sort of paralysis that Pamari encountered is a near-death experience and is the closest approximation of what a human body becomes under the condition of death. It was when we were discussing this mythological character, Kambaimbange, that James Noru told me that life and death are also held as totems of the two totemic moieties we have seen already. Life is generally considered as a totem of the elder-brother totemic moiety (*nyowi nimba*) while death is owned by the younger-brother moiety (*nyamei nimba*). James is not only a classificatory mother's brother (*wau*) of Makwat, but also a man of growing erudition in Iatmul totemic philosophy. James agreed with the connection drawn between names that people use and identities they assume within this ontological framework of dual 'planes of existence' (see also Bateson 1958: 237), since the names are at once the identities of mortal and immortal beings.

It was Bateson who first observed for the Iatmul that their 'naming system is indeed a theoretical image of the whole culture and in it every formulated aspect of the culture is reflected' (1958: 228). Indeed the holographic pattern of paired brothers that we have seen thus far is also replicated in Iatmul names. Bateson glossed this pattern in terms of siblingship. 'Everything and every person has a sibling and the polysyllabic names are so arranged in pairs that in each pair one name is the elder sibling of the other' (1958: 243). The names are composed of polysyllables and are arranged in pairs in the lists of names that individual clans own. Each list of names has a series of names which are organized as paired brothers: *nyamun shambu*. Each list consists of several pairs of names with an average range of 10–12 pairs. The names could be of either two same-sex or two cross-sex siblings, but in each pair, the first name is the elder and the second in the pair is the younger-brother name. Wassmann reports the same situation in Western Iatmul when he observes that 'the names are arranged in pairs. The first name of the pair "is" the "elder brother" (*nyamun si*) . . . the second "is" "younger brother" (*suambu si*)' (1991: 225). Each name in a pair bears some resemblance to the other name. Such a point of congruence is based either on gender, or on a genealogical or analogical relationship designated by the name of any elder and younger sibling. Such names may also refer to the shadowy aspect of the same name. These names are not created anew: the names were given when the totemic cosmology was established, and each clan has its own list of names which refers to their cosmological heroes, totemic appurtenances and particular kinds of activities in cosmological creativity. The precise details of what their cosmological heroes did are held as part of body of esoteric knowledge that is owned by each clan and such knowledge is jealously guarded. Each name has a gendered dimension and the suffix of each name determines the gender of that name. However, since the Iatmul present their gender understandings through an analogy between cross-sex and same-sex siblings (see Strathern 1988), Iatmul names also replicate this pattern of gender through the fractal notion of paired brothers. In Chapter 5 we will see how this naming system is tied up with Iatmul marriage practices and ideas about reincarnation.

Iatmul names are bound up with their mythological understandings of the world and they do not invent names anew, as we find amongst the Daribi (as we shall see in Chapter 6). Consequently the names and the literal meanings of these names remain constant and endure as they have been known originally. Although the names and their meanings remain the same, most names betray the impression of perpetual movement or activity. Bateson observed that the etymologies of most names are based on a kinaesthetic imagery that betrays a sense of processual motion. These personal names are also place-names (toponyms). All aspects of their cosmology are endowed with personal names including celestial and terrestrial configurations such as flora and fauna. When a particular name is bestowed on a person, that act of bestowing is simultaneously an act of ownership, particularly if such a name is also the name of a piece of land, waterway, lagoon, or of particular clan spirits connected to particular bodies of knowledge. Thus a name of a lagoon, waterway, or a mountain could also be the name of a person and the clan that owns the name also owns the lagoon, waterway, or mountain, etc. The meanings of these names are not derived from arbitrary geographical features but they narrate a history of cosmological creativity and endow the places with a particular kind of specificity and identity. In light of this, one could say that Iatmul place-names are what some theorists have described as *incident names* and *possessive names*. They are incident names in so far as they recall a specific event associated with particular locations or a set of activities. They are possessive names because they recall the involvement of individual cosmological heroes with the particular location in question, so that the names indicate ownership and control (Barber and Berdan 1998: 117). To assert its claim to a particular lagoon or waterway, a clan may bestow the name of that lagoon or waterway on one of its children, especially a newborn child. In so doing the clan is laying a claim of ownership both to the name and to the particular resource that has the same name as the person who bears that name.

For instance, at the time of my fieldwork, there were competing claims over the ownership of a small stream that runs through a part of Kanganamun village, effectively inserting a generally accepted physical boundary between the two totemic moieties. The two clans which have an interest in the land area and the stream are Yabu and Lenga. Yabu belongs to the elder-brother moiety, while Lenga is a clan of the younger-brother moiety. Their competing claims have existed for some time and there are no efforts to fully resolve the question of who actually owns the stream and the tracts of land along the stream. However, in the meantime, Job Bangranduapan, who belongs to the Yabu clan has given the name of the stream, Agurogu, to one of his dogs and this shows that Job is making an explicit claim of ownership over the stream. But there is also another reason why the Iatmul bestow names on dogs, pigs, and cats. This is because sometimes such names are names of very powerful clan spirits, and when the names of the spirits are used without careful propitiation, this may provoke the wrath of such spirits, which can cause infirmities, illnesses, and even death. As a precautionary measure, or a risk aversion strategy, people bestow names of clan spirits on their domestic animals, and if such animals do well in surviving, then these names are later taken and given to their clan children.

Another example of how names are connected with the ownership of particular lagoons may be illuminating. In 1997 a serious allegation of theft arose as a result of conflicting claims of ownership over the fishing lagoon called Takaripi. This lagoon is located some kilometres away on the southern bank of the Sepik River, near Maringe, a Central Iatmul village. As we saw in Chapter 2, the system of ritual and totemic moieties transcends individual villages, with occasional variations in certain practices but, with respect to the theme of *nyamun shambu*, it must be noted that Iatmul villages are also paired as brothers. Thus Kanganamun is the elder brother of Maringe, which is considered the younger-brother village of Kanganamun. Their spirit crocodiles are famously known in Central Iatmul as Wani and Kabak. Wanikanawimeli is the elder brother of Kabakmeli the younger-brother crocodile. It is these two brother villages that are now disputing each other's claim of ownership over Takaripi lagoon.

According to people in Kanganamun, the lagoon is owned by clans of the Wolimbi *ngeko*, but due to its proximity to Maringe the people of Maringe have been using the lagoon. Allegations emerged that some men from Maringe village destroyed fishing nets and stole fish caught in nets owned and deposited in the lagoon by Kanganamun women. A meeting was held between the men of the two villages at the local government station in Pagwi, located further upstream in the Western Iatmul area. When several Kanganamun men stood up, during that meeting, to explain and assert their claim to the lagoon, they were shouted down by men of Maringe village, primarily because they claimed that those particular Kanganamun men did not know and own the names that are connected with this lagoon. However, according to my adopted brother Vincent Yarme, of the Samiangwat clan in Kanganamun, when he stood up to talk, his clansmen (*yaranga ndu*) in Maringe village recognized that Vincent had a genuine claim and agreed with the general view he proffered that people of both villages should use the lagoon together.

The Samiangwat clan both in Kanganamun and Maringe villages claim that they are the owners of Takaripi lagoon. By this they mean that the have the list of names that are connected with the ownership of this lagoon. Generally, however, it is believed that the names belong to 'spirit crocodiles' that guard the lagoon. Anyone who has the right to invoke the names may summon the 'spirit crocodiles' to wage an attack or cause havoc on people who are not supposed to be fishing in the lagoon. These names are derived from totemic myths (*sagi*) held by the Samiangwat clan (although other Iatmul clans are likely to have their own versions of the stories and names). Although I have seen the full list of names connected with this lagoon, I hesitate to reproduce all of them here due to ongoing disputes over it. Instead I shall mention only two pairs of names in order to illustrate how names appear in lists and how they are connected to the ownership of resources.

. . .

Ngundawa	Luheingundawa
Karingundawa	Ndambiangundawa

. . .

Ngundawa refers to the water woman while *Luheingundawa* is the whirlpool water woman. These two women stir the waters and cause a whirlpool in the lagoon. It is believed that in order for the lake to maintain its viability, the waters in it must always be kept in motion. *Karingundawa* is the woman who is responsible for the swift tide and the strong current of the water on the river. *Ndambiangundawa* is the woman who deepens the lagoon. These two women cause the water to go around and around swiftly in a whirlpool. Below is a photograph of Cathy Karingundawa of the Samiangwat clan in Kanganamun village (Figure 4.1). Although Cathy is now married into the Uriap clan and has several children with her husband, the name she has as Karingundawa has not moved with her in marriage but is retained and owned by her clan. In the event that her Samiangwat clan goes into a dispute with another clan in the village or elsewhere, Cathy's own biography and her clan's totemic claim to the name Karingundawa will be used as the basis of their claim. So, in a typical debate, a Samiangwat man would point either to Cathy or her children and probingly ask: 'Tell me who is this? Is this not Karingundawa? Is this not the child of Karingundawa? For all this time, people in this village have known her with this name. Karingundawa. She is a mother now and has children.' The children bear evidence to the fertility of their mother and her clan and the rightful use of the name. No great harm or misfortune has visited her or her family. The bestowal of the name Karingundawa has not angered spirits who are known by that name. By giving the name Karingundawa, Cathy's father, Akanawi, has deliberately made an explicit claim of ownership over Takaripi lagoon. The bestowal of that name is an act of ownership.

Because humans and spirits are known by the same names, they belong to the same clan. Hence Karingundawa is both a spirit and a human incarnated in a particular clan person. Cosmological activities are said to be executed by clan spirits. It is the particular kinds of actions performed by these women that become the image that names both the spirit women and their human counterparts. The actions the spirit women perform are extremely vital and necessary to keep the lagoon from drying up through a process of sedimentation—lagoons which are stagnant and immobile will dry up easily. I have also provided the meanings of these names in order to illustrate what Bateson means by a visual imagery of kinaesthetic, which forms the descriptive content of many Iatmul names. While the names refer to a processual motion engendered by the activities of the spirits, the meanings of these names are held constant throughout time. Against this background, let us consider the system of personal names amongst the Manambu (see Harrison 1990a) and the Iatmul.

Figure 4.1 Cathy Karingundawa of the Samiangwat clan in Kanganamun village

The Iatmul and Manambu system of personal names

The Manambu are close neighbours to the Iatmul in both geographical and cultural terms, and they share a similar preoccupation with the ownership of personal names which are tied to the ownership of resources. While much of what Harrison discusses regarding the Manambu has close parallels with the Iatmul, subtle nuances differentiate the two societies and these differences might be analytical as well as ethnographic. In both societies, totems are referred to as ancestors. In Iatmul, totems are called *nyait ngwal*, a kinship term which literally means 'father grandfather' and makes reference particularly to two generational lines (*mbapma*) within a clan. *Nyait ngwal* and *mbapma* are also bound up with two kinds of bones (*ava*) which carry the human skeletal structure. These two bones are the spine (referred to as *ngwal ava* or *nyamun ava*) and the pelvis (which is called *nyait ava* or *shambu ava*). The two *mbapma* or generational lines are distinguished by their connection to the two kinds of bones, of which one is the elder-brother bone (*ngwal ava*) and the other the younger-brother bone (*shambu ava*). A man and his grandson belong to the same *mbapma* and therefore are of the same elder-brother bone (*ngwal ava*), while the man's son belongs to the other *mbapma* and is aligned with the younger-brother bone (*shambu ava*). Contrary to Bateson (1932: 26), who thought that the *mbapma* system does not relate to marriage, in my view it is intrinsically connected to the *iai* marriage system. Because of the fact that male members of a clan belong to two different generations (*mbapma*), women go in between these generations of men during marriage. *Mbapma* is connected to *nyait ngwal* in the sense that, within every clan, fathers (*nyait*) belong to one generation and their children belong to another who are of the same generation as their FF (*ngwal*, i.e. father's father). Thus Ego and his FF are brothers while Ego's son and father are also brothers. A man would normally take his father's names and bestow them on his own son, while his father's sister's names are applied to his daughter. 'Theoretically, a man is re-incarnated in his son's son; and a woman in her brother's son's daughter' (Bateson 1958: 18). We shall see how this happens when we consider Iatmul understandings of intergenerational siblings in Chapter 5.

Lévi-Strauss (1973; cited in Harrison 1990a: 52) sees totemism as a human tendency to impose categorical order upon experience, totemism being connected to systems of classification as an epistemological practice. The Iatmul notion of totemism is not based on classification but on the juxtaposition of a pair of kin relatives who are internally related to each other as brothers.[2] Thus the notion of *nyait ngwal* juxtaposes *nyait* (F) who is a brother to his FF and *ngwal* who is brother to his SS. Furthermore, Lévi-Strauss (1966; cited in Harrison 1990a: 73–6) sees totemic cultures as being inherently static and resistant to change. In the preceding section I have shown how totemic names of the Iatmul thrive on an imagery of processual motion, and, as I will come to argue in the following chapter, it is the institution of 'ownership' that sustains the dynamism of Iatmul totemic cosmology.

Harrison refers to a pan-Manambu totemic clan system which transcends all the Manambu villages and observes that: 'Clanship provides the basis for trading and visiting throughout the Manambu territory as well as

[2] The Iatmul notion of juxtaposition is drawn from the metaphor of sago shoots which emerge from the same stock but grow and spread side by side with each other. The Iatmul totemic system is conceptualized in this vein. See for instance Bateson (1958: 266) and Leenhardt (1979) for juxtaposition as an epistemological practice in Melanesia.

for the transmission of totemic and ritual lore' (1990a: 18). A comparable totemic clan system pervades the entire Iatmul (and Sawos) region of the middle-Sepik area. Every Iatmul village has a Sawos partner with which they would exchange their respective fish and sago. Since sago and fish go together as pairs so do their villages. The Iatmul share the same totemic cosmology with the Sawos through their common myth of origin and so the same mythological lore and series of names exist in both societies. Thus if one were to approach the Iatmul and Sawos region from the perspective of their naming system, then it would appear that the entire region is an ensemble of names, and what lies beneath this interlacing system of names is a constellation of a network of relationships.

Whereas the Sawos are a land dwelling people, the Iatmul and the Manambu are riverine societies and derive their economic livelihood largely from a domestic fishing economy. This local fishing industry feeds into a regional trading network of barter and market exchange (see Gewertz 1983). Iatmul and Manambu villages continue to have trade relationships with their neighbours. While money is becoming the dominant form of currency in these economic exchanges, the exchange of goods for other goods goes on concurrently with monetary transactions. In religious terms, Christianity has become well entrenched in both societies and has supplied an additional stock of names which has lessened the conflict over the theft of names in both societies. As I have noted in Chapter 2, Christianity has fed into the local political situation that exists amongst the totemic moieties in Kanganamun. Many of the Iatmul and Manambu now live outside their villages, either as employees of some sort or as settlers squatting at the fringe of urban areas. Repatriation of income into the villages from educated and wealthy members of these societies is more evident amongst the Manambu than the Iatmul. For instance, in the main Manambu village of Avatip, one can see a number of high-rise and permanent buildings and satellite dishes which have been built and installed there. In terms of modern economic wealth, the affluence of Avatip has no parallel in any of the Iatmul villages. In terms of education, both societies have many educated people and currently the villages of Avatip (Manambu) and Kanganamun (Iatmul) boast of two doctorates between them. However, illiteracy is threatening to increase in Central Iatmul villages. Administratively, the Manambu belong to a different constituency and electorate from the Iatmul.

On the environmental front, both societies experience seasonal inundation which lasts for about 4–6 months annually. However, while the Manambu give themselves to gardening and sago production—their gardening is often connected with complex ritual processes—the Iatmul do very little gardening and depend heavily on trading with their Sawos neighbours for their supply of sago. The Iatmul do not have access to land such as is available to the Manambu, where the cultivation of yams is integrated into a male initiatory cult (Harrison 1990a: 14–16). There are variations in the ritual practices which focus on birth, marriage and death, and male initiation between the two societies. The yam harvest ritual of the Manambu is not found amongst the Iatmul. The Iatmul continue to practise their famous *naven* ceremonial (see Bateson 1958; Houseman and Severi 1998; Silverman 2001). Male initiation which involves the scarification of the bodies of initiates continues to be practised in Western and Central Iatmul villages, whereas such a practice (see Harrison 1990a: 78–9, 100) is no longer undertaken by the Manambu and in Eastern Iatmul. The senior ritual grades of the Manambu male cult, associated with yam cultivation and the beating of novices, has no parallel amongst the Iatmul. In Manambu, members of specific ritual grades initiate novices into the men's cult, whereas in Iatmul it is the ritual moieties that take turns to initiate novices.

The analytical categories that are used in the ethnographies to describe the social organization of the two societies also differ. With the Iatmul, we find totemic and ritual moieties and clans, whereas amongst the Manambu one is dealing mainly with sub-clans. The naming system of Iatmul is located within the province of totemic moieties, with clans from these two opposing moieties owning some thousands of personal names. Such names are owned by sub-clans that have a moiety-like form amongst the Manambu. There is also a major difference between the societies in terms of male initiation practices and totemism. With the Iatmul, the ritual and totemic moieties are independent of each other and there is no congruence between them (see also Bateson 1958: 4). Totemism and the ritual practices of male initiation are brought together amongst the Manambu, and so a ceremonial debate over the theft of a name culminates in an initiation ritual. The debate over the stealing of names culminates in a men's initiation amongst the Manambu, but any parallel to this is absent in Iatmul. These litigious debates over the theft of names by which sub-clans seek to assume control are implicitly disputes over the ownership of ritual prerogatives, which therefore casts 'ritual as an intellectual property' (Harrison 1992).[3] Since the ritual and totemic moieties of the Iatmul are separate

[3] After reading the Manambu ethnography by Harrison (1990a), it will be evident that Harrison's influential essay on 'ritual as intellectual property' derives its inspiration from his Manambu material.

universes of interaction, the claims of ownership within Iatmul moieties would be routed through separate ways and outcomes.

Both societies are patrilineal in cast with strong ties of matrifiliation, and residence after marriage is patri-virilocal. In procreative idioms, bones are derived paternally while flesh and blood are derived maternally. Ties with one's mother's clan are very strong and formalized through matrinames. The bestowal of names by one's mother's brother (*wau*) recognizes and establishes a constant series of exchanges between an uncle and his nephews and nieces. All names are patrilineally inherited and, as I understand it for the Iatmul, the names are the 'inalienable possessions' (Weiner 1992) of each clan, and every clan (or sub-clan in the context of the Manambu) has several thousands of personal names. The Iatmul matrinames, or those which are derived from one's mother's side, are distinguished from those of one's father's side (or patrinames) by their suffixes. A male matriname ends with the suffix '*apan*' (which Bateson had taken to be *awan* as it used by the Eastern Iatmul), while a female matriname ends with the suffix *iesi*. For instance, Ganjayimbunapan and Ganjayimbuniese are names that belong to a pair of cross-sex siblings, and their mother belongs to the Suaru clan which owns the aquatic bird *ganja* (tern) as a totem, while the term *yimbun* refers to the upper course of the Sepik River beyond the Manambu territory.

In his comparative essay on the system of personal names between the Iatmul and Manambu, Harrison (1985) noted that, in both societies, the names from one's mother's side are connected with death. Apart from matrinames, the Manambu have a practice of bestowing bereavement names called 'dirt-taking names', which are given by one's mother's kin when they bring food to the house of their mourning relative. These names are described as 'dirt-taking names' because they refer to the funerary custom in which a bereaved is smeared with dirt as a sign of mourning. The bereaved is called by that name during the period of mourning and bereavement. A Manambu person would have several bereavement names throughout the course of his or her lifetime and the name returns to its clan after the mourning period is over. The Iatmul matriname is susceptible to threats from sorcery because it is this name that is used by sorcerers to practise sorcery on its bearer. Often the secret name from one's mother's side that is given particularly to men after their initiation is used in sorcery to kill the bearer of that name. The Manambu matrinames are bestowed as protective capsules over the bearer of that name, offering safety from any malicious harm that might come from the bearer's clan folks who have died recently. Iatmul matrinames render the bearer of such names susceptible to sorcery and are associated intimately with death, while Manambu names dissociate the bearer of such matrinames from ghosts and obviate the possibility of death (1985: 141).

In both societies it is the names which grant rights of ownership to particular clans or sub-clans (in the case of Manambu), and those who own the magical powers associated with such names can impose ecological restrictions against the exploitation of resources. Harrison (1990a) provides a rich ethnographic account of the manner in which the Manambu people use, control and argue over the ownership of personal names. Harrison was fortunate to witness several cases of conflict and the debate in which such conflicts were resolved, therefore his ethnography is saturated with a historical depth lacking in the present study, mainly because I did not witness any such ceremonial debates over names, except for one single dispute, which emerged about the time I was about to leave the field. Harrison's ethnographic account explains how the ownership and use of personal names provides a strategic resource for political actors to assert influence over other clan groups, shows how the conflict over names is executed and resolved, and traces how the ownership and perennial theft of names have implications for the political evolution of society.

The concept of 'society' as a transcendental totality imposes itself as an analytical constraint within which Harrison's analysis is organized. He describes 'society' as 'a transcendental, relational totality with sub-clans and their funds of ritual power having a timeless reality independent of its members' (1990a: 4), and the political process which underlies the history and cosmology revolves around such a metaphysical conception of 'society'. Because each patrilineal group in Manambu has specialized hereditary functions in magic and in ritual, such groups have to collaborate through exchange of women, names, and specialized types of knowledge(s) in order to maintain what Harrison describes as a 'total world order'. The hereditary powers are derived from names which are a set of totems. The personal names individuate both the group and the person, reminiscent of the character of the fractal person we have seen already. The exchange of women between different sub-clans is continuous with an exchange of names—an 'onomastic exchange' based upon an idiom of uterine kinship in which groups feed and nurture one another. Marriages are often strategically organized not only to ensure the demographic viability of individual groups but also to get names. Unlike Iatmul, Manambu agnates within a sub-clan compete with each other and so each sub-clan has a relationship of mutual interdependence with groups with which they intermarry. The internal relation amongst agnates is fraught with rivalry and competition.

This is not the same with Iatmul clans and sub-clans. In light of Iatmul dualist thought, Bateson made the following observations:

> While the clans are nominally grouped together in pairs as 'elder' and 'younger', the members of the clans also devote a great deal of energy to symmetrical competition in pride of ancestry and, as a result, the types of dualism are tangled together. We may suggest, very tentatively, that the statement of elder and younger brotherhood between related clans perhaps mitigates the symmetrical competition between them. (1958: 271–2)

Because of the internal rivalry within Manambu sub-clans, their individual leaders therefore appear as calculating strategists who relentlessly seek the control of names to enlarge their renown and that of their group. Through the idiom of uterine kinship and reciprocal exchange between groups, kinship, marriage, and ritual are projected onto the plane of cosmology, so that the transactions of individuals and groups has the appearance of a 'visible form of a vast, invisible connubium that forms the timeless pattern after which living people must marry' (Harrison 1990a: 58). Although Manambu marriages appear to resemble a cosmological pattern, the manner in which Harrison depicts its internal workings is, however, too calculative to resemble anything like the Iatmul form of prescriptive marriage called the *iai-ianan*. As we shall see in the following chapter, the Iatmul *iai–ianan* is based upon the transmission of names and marriageable spouses whose identities are, in turn, based upon the image of the paired brothers, *nyamun shambu*. The Iatmul marriage and naming systems are patterned upon the recurring image of the fractal person and not on an economically expedient scheme of marital and political strategizing as one encounters among Manambu.

The other ethnographic difference between these two societies with regard to their naming system is that the Manambu appear to have a finite or limited stock of names, while the Iatmul have an abundance of comparable names (see also Wassmann 1991: 63). Implicit in the ethnography that Harrison (1990a) provides of the Manambu naming system is a sense of continuity between a limited number of names and a limited number of reproductive resources, such as land and fishing lagoons. In this vein, Harrison notes that the Manambu people:

> . . . think there is fixed, finite number of personal names in the world, which have existed since the world's creation. The names were neither created by human beings nor can they be changed or added to. Together with natural species, the landscape, the ritual system, and the social groups whose immemorial property the names are, they were brought into existence by the

> totemic ancestors and are simply the objective properties of the total world order . . . The 'message' of Avatip totemism is that the world of everyday life exists in counterpart to another, the world of the totemic ancestors described in myth, and that these are the basic parallel categories of the world order. (1990a: 55)

Hence we find a situation in which sub-clans compete against one another, not only to control the ownership of ritual prerogatives and the subsequent manipulation of cosmological ideas, but also with a concern to ensure the demographic viability of their particular sub-clans. In addition to this, Harrison observes that since ritual prerogatives and cosmological claims are vouched for in terms of personal names, 'cosmology and ritual are conceived to form a closed, finite universe of personal names, ritual powers and other forms of immaterial property that men treat as having a reality transcending themselves; and second, that men compete politically on the basic assumption that those resources, and the status they confer, are limited and of scarce value' (1990a: 4). There are two analytical differences here. The first is that the Iatmul do not have a sense of 'closure' which appears to be the case with the Manambu. As noted in Chapter 1, Iatmul villages continue to grow and sub-divide, creating colonies in different places throughout the region, and nowadays settling in squatter settlements in urban areas might also be seen in this sense of an endless ramifying stock of clan groups. This image of an 'open' system (cf. Tresch 1998) with a tendency towards constant proliferation of clan groups is aptly captured in Bateson's botanical metaphor of the rhizome.

> The natives see their community, not as a closed system, but as an infinitely proliferating and ramifying stock. A clan will grow big and it will subdivide; a village will grow big and it will send out colonies. The idea that the community is closed is probably incompatible with the idea of it as something which continually divides and sends out offspring 'like the rhizome of the lotus'. (1958: 249)

Because villages and clan groups are always paired as brothers, their constant proliferation into new colonies always retain the same pattern of 'paired brothers', so that the proliferation of groups at the macro-sociological level of groups such as clans and villages is identical with the infinite pairing that is instantiated in Iatmul names and conception of personhood in ontological terms. Second, in describing names as a 'strategic resource' for political action, Harrison renders the Manambu names as an instrumental currency whose value is coined in the economic factory that supplies means and end (1990a: 3) relations, and makes value a function of scarcity. This analytical view inserts a conceptual disparity between 'source' and 'resource', and I suspect that this disparity might be one rationale behind the economics of scarcity. If names are people and if names are also mountains and waterways, thinking of names as resources is merely an instrumental approach to the conceptual dilemma posed by limited means and unlimited wants.

When a Manambu magician (*simbuk*) or his Iatmul counterpart (*sipundu*) calls forth the abundance of fish and mayflies on the Sepik River, he does so through the magical power of names (1990a: 47). For instance, during a visit to the Yenjan village, few kilometres upstream from Kanganamun, I met with Keman Kaman, an old man of erudition and oratory. He told me that if I visited him on Sunday, he would prepare a meal of mayflies and baked sago for me. Whether their appearance was predictable according to local ecological knowledge is another question but Keman spoke with utter certainty that there would be mayflies on Sunday. Sure enough, the following Sunday there was an abundance of mayflies that congregated on the river and his wife had gathered the insects and roasted them in leaves over the fire as a special delicacy. He told me that the 'mayflies came to dance on the *wombuno*', the ceremonial ground around the men's house. He explained that there is an invisible *ngeko* under the Sepik River and the invocation of the names associated with the mayflies is comparable to the 'rhythms that are beaten from slit-gongs in the *ngeko*' that summon people for a ceremonial gathering. In invoking the totemic names, he aligned the mayflies with the slit-gong rhythms, causing the mayflies to assemble on the part of the river just below the village. The point here is that the names are not only the means to have access to 'resources', they are also the source of such resources, and the task of a knowledgeable man is to establish the alignment that releases abundance.

As I understand it, the abundance of names amongst the Iatmul is not continuous with the limited number of resources available to them. That is, while resources such as lagoons, tracts of land, and forested areas and waterways are limited in number, names outnumber such resources. The Iatmul have no concern about how many names they have but with what names they own. When I probed several men over the possibility of enumerating the names which are owned by individual clans, my probing was made irrelevant by the simple response that 'there are too many names and how can we count them'. My adopted father recited over 500 names (some of which I have written down) of his clan, and his classificatory brother, who lives and works in Wewak town, had with him four note books which are populated with lists of names that are owned by their clan. My crude estimate is that the two men hold about 2,000 names between them. Bateson

(1958: 222) noted that a learned Iatmul men of erudition may keep somewhere between 10,000 and 20,000 polysyllabic names in his head, and may be able to recite them at any one time, but some of such names also belong to other clans through the interconnection between names and stories. It is not clear from Bateson whether the figure he provides is for the number of names within an Iatmul village, or whether the figure was for a moiety or clan. Harrison (1990a: 59), however, mentions that the Manambu village of Avatip mobilizes about 32,000 such names. In both societies, clans and sub-clans do not have enough members to bear all the names that they have. Finally, with respect to the continued life and use of names, what Harrison observes for the Manambu is also true for the Iatmul: 'names represent, implicitly, the idea of all its past, present, and future members. The members change as generations go by. But the names they "occupy" ... are, supposedly, fixed names of the sub-clans' members forever. As personal names for human beings, ... the names are classes, each in principle is occupied by an infinite series of individuals in succession' (1990a: 59).

From relationship to infinity

I have described the Iatmul (and Sawos) region as an ensemble of names, and beneath these names is a network of relationships. By this 'network' I refer to the fact that, distributed throughout this region, are namesakes—*wasari* (see also Bateson 1958: 244). I shall call these *wasari* same-names instead of namesakes because Iatmul *wasari* are relatives who share a common totemic denominator. Same-names come from either side of one's parents. Such living men and women are also the *wasari* of totemic ancestral spirits (see also Harrison 1990a: 56) and, amongst the Iatmul, it is always important that each name must 'match' the person who is given it.

Explained to me in *Tok Pisin*, the notion of 'matching' in Iatmul naming practices is critically important as it betrays a law-like rule or relationship of necessity. One night, while explaining the connection between a name and a name bearer, a mentor explained this notion by pointing to a pair of boots. He said that the pair of boots I wore must match my feet, not in terms of size but that the right one must be worn on the right foot and the left on the left foot. Otherwise, he explains, this will cause a friction which might give me a painful blister on my feet. The interlocutor employed an analogy from the shoes and feet—which are based on a relationship of paired necessities—to explain how a name should match the person who is given that name. By this he means that the name and named *must* belong to the same clan. People who use names which belong to other clans might have problems such as illnesses or infirmities within their clan or family, since the name they use is not identified with them totemically.

Accordingly, one could only find one specific name in a village and the minute one finds people from the same village of different clans who have the same name, it means that one of the clans has stolen the name from the other. People with the same names (*wasari*) are properly found in different villages. And, as I have stated above, these *wasari* are kinsfolk who are related by totemic descent. Kinsfolk, identified through their shared totemic co-substantiality, are obliged to look after one another, for example, by way of providing food and accommodation when such relatives undertake visits to the village of host relatives, and the help is reciprocated later in return visits. When a man of erudite knowledge in one village dies, the clansmen in that village consult knowledgeable men of their clan in other villages to replenish their knowledge of names and stories of their own clan. The sharing of knowledge amongst clan members of different villages facilitates reciprocal exchanges between such relatives. I have seen exchanges of food and other comestibles going on between three men who are *wasari*: Luke Kamangari of Kanganamun; Peter Kamangari of Parimbe, and Peter Kamangari of the Sawos village of Nangusap. Luke Kamangari tells me that often his Sawos *wasari* would supply him with sago even if he didn't bring him any fish, and when his Sawos *wasari* visits Kanganamun, he will stay with Luke until he returns to his village with some fish provided by Luke's wife. Luke's wife has also been selling, in Kanganamun, sago that belongs to her husband's Sawos *wasari*, and the money that is earned is then sent to their Sawos relative after all the sales are completed.

In the context of name disputes, knowledgeable debaters may be sourced from other villages to help in the attempt by a clan to assert its claim of ownership over a specific name that is under dispute. The existence of same-names in other villages is amongst the best evidence a clan may use to justify its claim to the disputed name. Knowledgeable *wasari* from other villages may themselves be part of the team of debaters who will speak on behalf of their clan in the village in which the ownership of a particular name is being contested. For instance, there is now a name, Tanginwuli, which is under dispute by two clans in Kanganamun village. Jack Kapi, who is the father of one of those small boys who has been named Tanginwuli, told me that he has sent word and invited two namesakes of his son to come to his aid in debating the ownership of the name Tanginwuli. Both of these men are of the same clan as Jack, but one of them belongs to the Sawos village of Marap and the other to the Central Iatmul village of

Sotmeri. Both men have accepted the invitation and are looking forward to the debate. At the time I left the field, a date was not yet set for such a debate.

Against the background of what has been discussed so far, I would like to pose some general theoretical observations regarding the ownership of names amongst the Iatmul in anticipation of the discussion in the two following chapters. Initially we have seen that the Iatmul version of the 'fractal person' is a pairing of brothers who are notionally looped in an ontological process such that each is always becoming the other and that this pairing is endowed with the conceptual possibility of infinite pairing. The theoretical issue that emerges is that if '*relationship*' is integrally implied in the constitution of a fractal person, and if pairing can continue *ad infinitum*, what then is the *connection between relationship and infinity*? In comparing the Iatmul with the Manambu I have made two pertinent observations. One is that the Iatmul (and the Sawos) region is a constellation of relationships and this observation lends an ethnographic basis to the view that Iatmul names contain relationships. The other observation stems from the fact that while the names are valuable to both the Iatmul and the Manambu, the Manambu appear to imagine a limited or finite supply of names whereas the Iatmul imagine they have an abundance of such names. This leads again to the general theoretical question about the connection between *relationships* and *infinity*. It is because of such a theoretical realization that I am calling for an ontological theorization of ownership and relationships. The two following chapters aim to embed such a theorization in ethnographic material.

5

Names and the Temporal Life of Ownership

In every village you will find the living embodiments of the ancient mythology—the man who bears the name of the founder of the village. He will straighten his shoulders as he tells you, 'I steered the canoe which brought my clan to this place.' And another man will stamp on the ground as he says, 'I am Kevembuangga. I put my foot on the mud and made it so hard that people could live. But for me there would be no people.'

(Bateson 1946: 121)

'I am Tanginwuli. My name is Tanginwuli. I have always been known by this name in this village. Why then have you taken my name? It is my name and you have stolen it.' These were the words of Joseph Saungombi, an elderly man in Kanganamun village. Saungombi had become furious when it was brought to his attention that the name Tanginwuli had been given to a male child who was born to Jack Kapi and his wife Sarah. The two men belong to opposing totemic moieties in the village. Jack belongs to a clan called Uriap, which is a part of the younger-brother moiety called *nyamei nimba* or the 'mother/earth people'. Saungombi, on the other hand, belongs to a clan called Wanigo which belongs to the elder-brother moiety called *nyowi nimba* or the 'father/sun people'. Previously in the history of the village, as Saungombi would argue, the name Tanginwuli was used by a man of the Wanigo clan who had since died. Although that particular Tanginwuli died without leaving any descendants behind, the coconut trees that he planted on the mounds along the sides of his residential house and two posts, which are remnants of his house, remain standing on the site where it was built. The remnants of the house together with the plants are located in the residential area of the Wanigo clan. The coconut trees and the remaining posts are visible and tangible reminders that recall the life and person of Tanginwuli as a man who belongs to the Wanigo clan in the village. Therefore, as far as Saungombi and his Wanigo clan are concerned, the name Tanginwuli is theirs.

After he had learnt that the name Tanginwuli had been given to Jack's child, Saungombi confronted Jack at the residential compound of his clan, Uriap. Saungombi aired his claim in a fiery complaint and accused Jack and his clan of stealing the name Tanginwuli. For their part, Jack and his clan took the accusation of theft in silence and with equanimity in order to prevent a polarization around the conflicting claims and to avoid revealing the basis of their claim too prematurely before a ceremonial debate over the name was called for. Jack however replied with the assertion that the name Tanginwuli is also his clan's and issued the challenge that, if Saungombi cared about it, he should show cause as to why he claims otherwise. Some time after Saungombi had made known his complaint against Jack and his Uriap clan, a young man of the Wanigo clan, Tippon Gawi, had a male child born to him and his wife Miriam. Tippon and Saungombi are clansmen (*yarangundu*) and are related to each as classificatory brothers. Saungombi is the oldest and the most knowledgeable of the men in his clan. Thus when Miriam—Tippon's wife—gave birth to a male child, Saungombi saw the occasion as an opportune moment for them to assert their claim of ownership over the name Tanginwuli by bestowing that name on a son of their clan Wanigo. This is similar to what Harrison (1990a: 127) reports of the neighbouring Manambu. That is, a claim to the ownership of a name is not made in some abstract manner but in the most concrete way of actually naming a child. However, in order to do so, the clan must have a child of its own. Although Saungombi had proclaimed that he himself is Tanginwuli, the birth of the male child to their clan provided the opportune moment for his clan to assert their claim in direct opposition to Jack and his Uriap clan.

Consequently there were now two young boys, each of them in 2001 about 5 years of age, who shared the same name. These boys belonged to different clans of opposing totemic moieties. A situation like this is far from being normal in any Iatmul village. Two people of the same village should not share a name.[1] In the event that a situation like this arises, it means that one of the clans in question has stolen the name from the other. At the time this book was written, the conflicting claim of ownership over this particular name was not yet resolved. Apart from Saungombi's initial outburst, there has been no formal attempt organized by either of the two clans to

[1] For similar concerns with same-names in different Sepik River villages, see for instance Harrison (1990a: 56) and Telban (1998: 127).

resolve this tussle of ownership. Since this conflicting claim has remained unresolved for the last seven years, it could continue for some time as yet. A formal attempt would involve staging a ceremonial debate with the litigious intention of getting one of the claimants to relinquish their claim of ownership. In the intervening period, both of the clans have been keeping a close watch over each other regarding the possible physical consequences of naming their two sons with the same name. First, this is because Iatmul believe that there is a mystical connection between a name and its bearer, which makes it inadvisable to remove a name from a person unless it is sanctioned by the outcome of a ceremonial debate. Second, it is believed that if one of the clans has wrongly appropriated the name from another clan, there would be physical manifestations of the friction between mystical agencies associated with that name and the bearer of that name. A person and the name he or she is given must match each other, much as a pair of boots for a person's feet. If the matching pair does not work out, 'frictions' will result in the form of illnesses or defects that will be experienced either by the name-bearer or by other members of that particular clan or lineage.

I want to take a momentary anchorage in the account to enter into a description which I hope will clarify further some of the aspects of totemic names and the connection to kinship and marriage practices. I have hinted at the possibility of conceptualizing relationships in ontological terms. To this I end, I identify and employ four Western philosophical concepts—immanence and transcendence, necessity and contingency—and hope to concretize the nature of this conceptual approach through introducing further ethnographic material from neighbouring societies. Opening with a discussion of Iqwaye (Mimica 1988) and Iatmul, I hope to show how the ontological issues of immanence and transcendence are located in social relations. After this, the discussion moves to a consideration of the issues of necessity and contingency as they appear in the context of kinship and clan organization amongst the Iatmul (Silverman 1996) and the Manambu (Harrison 1989). A theoretical dimension of this discussion concerns the manner in which time and relationships function in affecting and coordinating the behaviour of ownership. Since Iatmul names are generally considered as abundant in stock, and since they serve as vectors of integral relationships, another theoretical interest of this chapter relates to the question of the connection between relationships and infinity that emerged in the last chapter. Our discussion therefore begins with an analytical concern with infinity among the Iqwaye; the overall discussion proceeds from a concern with numbers to names.

Intimating the relation as an infinite being

'For every Iqwaye really numbers are human beings.' This evocative and powerful observation is excerpted from Mimica's fascinating ethnographic account of the counting system and the cultural meanings of the category of number as it is lived and articulated by the Iqwaye (Mimica 1988: 73). Mimica describes a symbolic homology between numbers and human beings whereby the manner in which things are enumerated is analogous to the way in which human beings reproduce themselves sexually (1988: 92, 104). The central aspect of the Iqwaye's counting system is predicated on the irreducibility of the human body, which serves as the seat of proper numbers. This is because, among the Iqwaye, counting—much like the sexual reproduction of persons—has cosmological foundations, and the category of number is therefore bound up with the cosmic realm such that the essence of number is the corporeal man (1988: 104).

Mimica describes enumeration as a cognitive process predicated upon the human body so that:

> . . . the body, as well as the relationships between the bodies that counting presupposes, are of a conceptual order which any actual corporeal person or persons may come to represent concretely. By assuming the deictic function in the acting of counting, the speaker ... incarnates and fully accomplishes the meaning of the concept. (1988: 26)

The human body or the concrete human person therefore becomes the microcosmic locus of the universe as whole. 'The corporeality of man is also the physical realm of cosmos. They are bound up in their complete unity because Omalyce is simultaneously himself and the cosmos' (1988: 77).

Since human beings are co-extensive with the cosmos in their primal origin, 'the *immanent* human is also the *transcendent* world' (1988: 100, my emphasis). The body assumes an ontological function (Merleau-Ponty 1962) of synthesizing the immanent world of sociality with a transcendent world of cosmic reality. Given that the counting system of the Iqwaye is objectified in the corporeal form of human bodies, and since the Iqwaye style of enumeration always closes in on 'one', each Iqwaye person—like their cosmogonic ancestor Omalyce—embodies 'oneness' (Mimica 1988: 104, 123). In their cosmogonic myth, the body of the primal man, Omalyce, ruptured and formed the earth and the heavens and the humans within it. Omalyce emerged to embody simultaneously man and the cosmos. He then took mud and created the first men and gave them personal names after the manner of fingers on his hand. These men are individually different but are like clones who share an identity of being 'one' with each other as with Omalyce himself. By the names they had, each of the five men instantiates the splendour of Omalyce's creativity, since they were in metaphorical terms the fingers of the 'one' man Omalyce.

Fingers appear prominently as metaphoric referents for human beings. If an adult Iqwaye person is asked about many children he or she has, that person would answer by referring to the number of fingers on his or her hand (1988: 61). Personal names of the Iqwaye are sourced from individual patrilineal descent groups (PDGs). Iqwaye men are bestowed with both patrinames and matrinames, while women are given only matrinames. Furthermore there are two birth-order series amongst the Iqwaye which are sex-specific. A male Iqwaye person will have two names which end with birth-order suffixes while a female will have a patriname with a birth-order suffix. The birth-order suffixes of the Iqwaye names are actually finger names.

Like their counting system which always returns to 'one' so too does their birth-order series, which is 'modeled on the anatomical unity of the human hand'. Furthermore, since the birth-order implies consanguinal relatedness, children emerging from a maternal womb imply that the 'metaphorical significance of the birth-order suffixes is not simply—humans as fingers—but *brothers and sisters* as fingers which, as such, represent the hand(s) of a higher whole, their male genitor, father' (1988: 61). The birth-order refers to the emergence of children from the genetrix and the finger-names refer to the genitor. Birth-order and finger-names operate by a sexual and procreative idiom (1988: 59).

The Iqwaye system of birth-order is closely bound up with their style of enumeration. In association with birth-order suffixes, finger-names bring into play the seriation of fingers as numerical units. In the same way that siblings are different from and unique in relation to each other, so are fingers on a person's hand, yet these siblings are of an identical and substantial kind. 'Fingers and siblings', therefore, 'constitute a thoroughly systematized configuration in Iqwaye culture. Their seriation through naming as distinct segments of the hand complements that of the expressly numerical binary seriation . . . The finger-names as birth-order suffixes, symbolize the fingers of the male genitor who, in the Iqwaye culture, is posited as the bisexual and the self-created being' (1988: 64, 69). Since hands carry a gendered inflection and have sexual meanings, Mimica suggests that 'each hand is a sexual male procreative whole, in relation to which fingers are its male and female children' (1988: 69). Thus the Iqwaye system of enumeration is bound up with a dense substratum of cosmological and sexual meanings.

Therefore in metaphorical terms, 'numbers are human beings and they are appropriately generated like them' (1988: 92).

Inspired by a Husserlian species of phenomenological ontology, Mimica's interpretation is based on the metaphysical dialectic of part–whole relationships and his descriptions show how a part is equivalent to the whole, in other words a part is as whole as the whole. Mimica uses the term 'partialised whole' to describe this. As a mode of non-quantifying enumeration, a salient epistemological feature of this counting system lies in its intellectual tendency to employ analogical relationships in order to arrive at an equation of totality. For instance, one rope of shells is equivalent to a line of warriors. 'The warriors are counted and determined as a whole (rope) in terms of its constitutive parts (shells), yet they are determined in terms of the unity of that concrete whole—one rope of shells' (1988: 17). The system of enumeration is described as a process of totalization in which 'each completed cycle of enumeration is a totalisation of the multiplicity of units into the single whole' (1988: 94). Such a process of totalization transforms plurality into singularity or many into oneness (1988: 56; see also Wagner 1991: 166–7).

For instance, a finger is part of a hand as a hand is to a man. The fingers on a hand become 'one' hand, so do two hands become the hands of 'one' whole man. The basic numerals of the counting system are 1 and 2, which are fused together into a dyadic seriation which forms a binary logic. Hence the numbers on a finger follow 1–2–1–2–1 and when it comes to the fifth finger, the numerical term for 5 is also the term for 'one' hand. 'One single finger like one body are already symbolic equivalents of the entire cosmos. Thus one by itself is already the intimation of infinity' (1988: 95). The highest possible number in Iqwaye, therefore, is a function 'of the relation between the humans and the cosmos. And their relation is that of unity and oneness' (Mimica 1988: 93).

Given the fact that the Iqwaye counting system subsists on two basic numerals, 1 and 2, which are fused or synthesized into the creation of another 'one', Mimica compares this sense of one-twoness with Brouwer's notion of 'twoity' to highlight what he describes as the temporal life of numbers (1988: 125–38), akin to the temporal life of human beings. Criticizing the way much of Western mathematics makes enumeration too abstract and devoid of a historical character, Mimica argues that, due to its cosmological foundations, the totalizing mode of Iqwaye enumeration presupposes an intrinsic relation between number and temporality. A logic of binary fission, similar to its kinship manifestation, provides a rhythm that temporalizes Iqwaye enumeration. 'The binary rhythm of succession reproduces the primordial rhythm (temporality) of the cosmic process of self-generation. Out of the one emerges two, from which emerges one, and so on. This self-propagation . . . is the pluralisation of . . . its composite parts (the digits). The totalised parts in turn fuse back into the original unity of the one' (1988: 136–7). Since numbers are reproduced in a way that is analogous to human beings, let us now take a view from the perspective of kinship.

The ontology of brotherhood and fatherhood: names, kinship, and marriage in Iqwaye and Iatmul societies

Since Iqwaye enumeration involves the interdigitation of hands and toes, and since hands are inflected by gender and carry sexual connotations, I have rehearsed the description here in anticipation of the comparison below with Iatmul names. A common model of prescriptive marriage prevails amongst the Iqwaye and Iatmul societies. This involves the marriage of a male Ego with any of his classificatory father's mothers (FM). In Iqwaye, such a woman is called '*ate*' while the same is called '*iai*' among the Iatmul. The women in these marriages originate in the clan from which a male Ego's FM was taken. A principle of alternating generation regulates this model of marriage. It therefore appears that, in every lived generation, there is only one generational gap between generations.[2] In both societies, one generation belongs to a group of parents (genitor/genetrix) and the other belongs to children (progeny/consanguines). One generation belongs to Ego, his father's father (FF) and his son's sons (SS) whereas the other generation belongs to Ego's son (S), father (F) and father's father's father (FFF).

The main difference between the two societies relates to the ontological emphasis that is placed on 'fatherhood' and 'brotherhood'. The names and marriage practices which follow the pattern of each alternating generation arise in Iqwaye because emphasis is placed on the identical relationship between genitor and progeny, such that when a genitor begets his son, he begets his own self in the social sense that his son is also his classificatory father. In the Iatmul situation, the emphasis is placed on a sense of 'brotherhood'. Amongst the Iatmul particularly, a male Ego and his paternal grandfather or father's father (FF) are related to each other as classificatory brothers, and Ego will address his FF by the kin term '*nyamun*', which

[2] For a comparative ethnography that deals with this one-generational gap between generations, see Hugh-Jones (1979).

means elder brother, while his FF will address Ego as '*shambu*', which means younger brother. Since Ego's S and F are classificatory brothers, Ego's son marries one of Ego's classificatory mothers and Ego's son becomes a social father to Ego. All of Ego's classificatory mothers are potential wives to Ego's son and this is the basis of the Iatmul prescriptive form of *iai* marriage (cf. Bateson 1932; Houseman and Severi 1998; Korn 1971; Rubel and Rosman 1978; Silverman 1996, 2001).

There have been several critical and insightful ethnographic interpretations of the Iatmul kinship and marriage situation. However, I argue that the notion of 'brotherhood' might help to resolve some of those ethnographic puzzles. As will be explained below, the Iatmul *iai–ianan* marriage involving the marriage of a male Ego and his father's mother's brother's son's daughter (FMBSD) and father's mother's brother's daughter (FMBD) (see Bateson 1958: 88–92; Harrison 1985: 142–3; Korn 1971: 86–9; Rubel and Rosman 1978: 34–8) involves a pair of women who are classificatory sisters. That is, a father's mother (FM) and her brother's daughter (BD) who address each other as *iau* and *kangit* are marriageable to their *ianan*. In their own clan, these two women would be considered as *nyamun* and *shambu*. Since there is a growing body of literature on Iatmul marriage practices, I offer a general commentary.

Houseman and Severi (1998) and Silverman (2001) provide the most recent interpretations of the kinship and marriage system of the Iatmul, in order to establish their interpretations of the *naven* ritual. Houseman and Severi (1998) revisited what Forge (1971), Korn (1971), Rubel and Rosman (1978), and Stanek (1990) said of the symmetrical and asymmetrical forms of Iatmul marriages. Symmetrical marriages refer to sister exchange, while asymmetrical marriages refer to the prescribed *iai–ianan* marriage. Through this Korn (1971) and Rubel and Rosman (1978) analysed Bateson's data to illuminate Lévi-Strauss's notion of elementary structures and reciprocal exchange relationships between affines (cf. Strathern 1984b). Houseman and Severi (1998) extended an observation by Forge (1971) that the symmetric and asymmetric systems of marriage correspond respectively to asymmetrical and complementary schismogenesis as described by Bateson (1958), showing how these contrary orientations relate to the relational contradictions evident in the *naven* ritual. In revamping Forge's observation, they argue against Bateson's insistence on centring his interpretation on the avuncular relationship between *wau* and *laua*. They state that the *wau–laua* relationship is an outcome of the relationship between wife-givers and wife-takers, and do so by focusing their interpretation of the *naven* ritual on the characters of the *wau* (mother's brother) and *iau* (father's sister). It is from the simultaneity of the opposing relationships between *wau* and *iau*, associated with their transversal antics in the *naven*, that they propound their theory of ritual action based on the notion of ritual condensation.

Silverman (2001) discusses a class of *naven* rituals performed by a set of affinal relatives called *iai–ianan* in which the ritual culminates in a repetition of the marriage of affinal relatives of the previous generation. Swayed by Freudian psychoanalysis, Silverman interprets the *iai–ianan* marriage which follows the *naven* ritual in the language of oedipality. That is, when Ego (*ianan*) marries one of his FM (*iai*), Silverman sees that such a marriage acts as a facility for Ego's father to take back his mother. He focuses on the metaphoric voices of masculinity and motherhood to present what he calls the 'meanings and misfortunes of masculinity' (2001: 176–7; see also Mimica 2003). This class of relatives called *iai–ianan* are actually looped into a prescriptive form of marriage. Silverman argues that when an Ego marries one of his classificatory FM, Ego's father returns to his mother with an oedipal yearning. Silverman declares this as an existential tragedy for the Iatmul. However, if we bear in mind the connection between the ontology of brotherhood and the *iai–ianan* marriage as explained above, the *iai–ianan* marriage can best be seen as an ontological relation that is concretized in marital arrangements and therefore there is no tragedy for the Iatmul.

Recognizing a similar scheme of preferential marriage in both Iqwaye and Iatmul societies, Mimica (2003: 37) asserts that: 'the truths of the father and son are their own respective mothers. Qua *iai*, "a woman who walks the same house path" as her paternal grandmother [. . .] this form of matrimony replicates itself indefinitely, both in structure and in [personal] names'. In personalized terms, Mimica explains: 'my father married his own *iai* (FMBSD) who give birth to me, i.e., his own father: I can marry my own *iai* (FMBSD) and give birth to him, my son who is my father. The circle is closed' (2003: 37). A man who marries his *iai* becomes a (social) father to his own father. The Iatmul *iai–ianan* marriage involving the male Ego and his FMBSD and FMBD is thus based on a pair of clansmen who are classificatory brothers through the logic of alternating generations, and a pair of women who are classificatory sisters based on the logic that collapses preceding generations. This logic of the collapse of generations and the marriage system is also connected to ideas about reincarnation and the transmission of names. This explains Bateson's general observation that a man takes his father's names and applies them to his son and his sister's names are bestowed on his daughter (Bateson 1958: 18). This is based upon of the collapsing and merging of generations into the two generational sets mentioned above. When a man begets a son, his son becomes his social father through the logic of the *iai–ianan* marriage. That is, the man's son's son can marry the man's mother's classificatory sisters, who are classificatory mothers to the man. Because the son's son's wife is classificatory mother to the man, the man's son becomes a father to his own father from the perspective of the son's son. When a man begets a daughter, the daughter becomes a sister to the man from the perspective of the man's sister and by giving his sister's name to his daughter, the sister becomes reincarnated in the form of her brother's daughter. The premise upon which this is based is the paired brothers notion of *nyamun shambu*: elder brother and younger brother.

According to this ontological premise, female members of the same clan are sisters while the male members of the same clan belong to a generation of fathers and sons. 'A sister, regardless of age, always addresses her brother as *nyamun*, the term used by a man for his elder brother only. But between siblings of the same sex, the terms *nyamun* (elder sibling of the same sex) and *shambu* (younger sibling of the same sex) are always employed' (Bateson 1958: 243). Both same-sex siblings and cross-sex siblings address each other as brothers. The terms *nyamun shambu* are used by same-sex siblings depending on their genealogical seniority, but with cross-sex siblings, a female member, irrespective of her age, addresses the male relatives of her clan as *nyamun* (elder brother), who in turn address their female members as *shambu* (younger brother). These particular kin terms illuminate Iatmul *iai–ianan* marriage. Internally within a clan, all females are brothers and all males are fathers and sons. There is no generational gap amongst women of the same clan because they always 'go in between clans' by marrying into clans outside of their own. As far as the *iai* marriage goes, it is with respect to their potential spouses that women within a clan are defined as sisters. Internally women are considered 'brothers' within their clan while externally they are sisters who could be married into other clans. And that is precisely why Ego's son can marry anyone of Ego's FM's classificatory sisters who are of the same clan. Ego's son and F are brothers while Ego's mother and the women of her clan are sisters who are therefore marriageable by a set of classificatory brothers in the alternating generation. The following cases illustrate my arguments.

During the ritual in which I was initiated, my adopted mother, Marimbunjin, provided me food while I was inside the ritual enclosure. She was helped by the wife of one of her classificatory brothers. My mother's brother's daughter, who was about 4 years of age, always accompanied

Marimbunjin when they brought me food. The little girl would tell her father, James Lanjin, that she was helping her elder brother (my mother) to feed their *bandi* who was inside the enclosure within the *ngeko*. After I was released from the enclosure, I had to provide a small recompense in appreciation of my mother's brother and his wife for their help in looking after me. On that occasion, I heard James Lanjin tell his daughter to follow her 'elder brother' (my mother) to our house to help wash dishes.

On an earlier occasion, I was surprised one day to hear my adopted mother, Marimbunjin, referring me to her brother's daughter as one of my mothers. Normally this relationship between father's sister (*iau*) and her brother's children (*kangit*) is called *iau–kangit*. But on this particular occasion, Marimbunjin was sick and could not make her daily trip to the fishing lagoon. She thought of me and was worried that we might not have any fresh fish for the meal that evening so she went to Betty, her brother's daughter who was married into the Wanigo clan and residing nearby. Marimbunjin spoke to her niece thus, saying: 'You know we have someone staying with us and it is not good that we do not have any food this evening. I am sick and will not go the river. But when you go and get some fish today, please do think of us and bring us some.'

After returning from the lagoon that day, Betty came to Marimbunjin's house with some fish. As she entered the residential area, she called out saying: '*nyamun, nyamun*'. However, my adopted father, Yarme, recognized Betty's voice and replied saying: 'Why *nyamun, nyamun*? I am here, why not come to me?' But Betty replied saying: 'Look at yourself first. You are too old and slack and there is no man in you.' Meanwhile my adopted mother, who was still sick and lying in bed, overheard the sexual jokes between Yarme and Betty and instructed me, saying: 'Go and see your mother Betty and take the fish from her.' After Betty departed, I asked why Betty, who was Marimbunjin's brother's daughter, was addressing her father's sister as her 'elder brother'. Through a shorthand explanation Marimbunjin offered that Betty was her 'brother' and therefore she (Betty) was also my mother. Marimbunjin was paraphrasing what Bateson had previously described through the notion of 'identification' based on a system of analogic kinship (1958: 39; Wagner 1977). This process of kin identification operates on a basic syllogism expressed in propositions such as: 'A mother gives food to her children. A mother's brother is identified with his sister. Therefore a mother's brother gives food to her children' (Bateson 1958: 25). The deduction of such a syllogism enabled Bateson to provide his initial interpretation of the *naven* ritual, where the identities in question involve the ceremonial role of the mother's brother (*wau*) and the father's sister (*iau*).

The Iatmul emphasis on 'brotherhood' also has mythological underpinnings. Its corpus of myth is replete with narratives about the elder brother and younger brother (see Bateson 1958: 242–3, 248; Wassmann 1991). We have seen how this pattern replicates itself across different domains in Iatmul thought and culture. Bateson describes this pattern in terms of direct and diagonal dualism, in line with his model of complementary and symmetrical schismogenesis (1958: 271). In direct dualism, for instance: 'everything in the world can be grouped in pairs, such that in each pair one component is an elder sibling, while the other is a younger sibling of the same sex' (1958: 239). Diagonal dualism, on the other hand, appears in the manner in which ritual moieties are organized in initiating novices, or in terms of the pair of men who marry each other's sisters (1958: 238). In terms of direct dualism, marriage therefore appears like a technology that separates internally related siblings in order to generate life through the sexual reproduction of clans. And when life (elder brother) is brought forth, it also summons its opposite, death, the younger brother. When accomplished, death allows the Iatmul person to simultaneously inhabit two separate worlds by virtue of the pair of names people have. Among the Iqwaye, death dissolves the corporeal person and reabsorbs him or her into earth (cosmic body), which is the primal ground of being.

> Through the operation of kinship marriage, and sociocentric classification, only the *transcendent* sociocentric identity of every human being can be and is perpetuated. In short, through the corporeal dissolution the person is reabsorbed into the earth, that is the metaphysical substantiality of the cosmic being ... and as such the concrete human being is consumed by its metaphysical *transcendent* (Mimica 1988: 99, my emphasis).

This sense of metaphysical transcendence, perpetuation, or reincarnation which Mimica articulates works out well in the context of the *ate* marriage of the Iqwaye, which parallels the Iatmul *iai–ianan* marriage. Mimica notes that an outcome of this model of marriage in Iqwaye is that the kin term for 'father'—*miqwa*—becomes self-reciprocal. Since Ego marries his classificatory FM, his genitor father will call Ego a social father. Mimica explains that the three men—Ego, F, FFF—are 'related patrifilially as the genitor and progeny are fathers to each other. What oneself is to another, that other is so to the oneself' (1988: 88). The same may apply to the Iatmul situation too, given the fact that in Iatmul Ego's son and father are related to each other as classificatory brothers, and if Ego is the eldest son in his family, his son is given the name of his FF; and these two men are not only identified as classificatory brothers but Ego's son is also considered as a reincarnation of his FF.

Mimica explains that the *ate* marriage is a culmination of the kin and sociocentric classification among the Iqwaye, as well as having the ontological significance of intimating the cosmological basis of procreation as described in the myth of Omalyce. Mimica explains the birth of progeny to the genitor in a sociocentric sense, especially when the progeny marries a genitor's classificatory mother. The Ego, F and FFF are united in their consubstantiality and are also connected through the relationship of progeny and genitor. The emphasis on 'fatherhood' among the Iqwaye, as Mimica explains, is grounded in cosmological understandings since 'fatherhood is the expression of the ontological desire ... for self-completion; a desire to render the man in relation to woman the original oneness, a unity unto and in itself' (Mimica 1988: 89).

In sum, while the Iqwaye and Iatmul share a similar model of prescriptive marriage, the ontological emphasis in Iqwaye is placed on a notion of 'fatherhood', whereas the Iatmul conceive it in terms of 'brotherhood'. What death does in both societies is to intimate that primal unity in which metaphysical transcendence and immanence are simultaneously articulated as 'one' (see also Bateson 1958: 236). In Iqwaye this becomes concretized when a corporeal person is reabsorbed into the earth, while in Iatmul death is paired in a kinship with life such that the question of transcendental cosmos is also found in an immanent world of social relations, and the person inhabits both worlds simultaneously through the names.

As I understand it, personal names among the Central Iatmul are not transacted along with the women who move between clans in marriage (cf. Bateson 1958: 228), as is the case among the Manambu (Harrison 1990a). Generally names remain as possessions of individual clans and only women move between clans through marriage. However, there are some names that may be given away to be used by a person from another clan within the same totemic moiety. This happens mainly for a person holding a mortuary feast for a dead person, who can then assume the right to use the names associated with the deceased. Such names are those which are of the 'same rope' as owned by deceased. That is, such names belong to the same list of paired names used by the deceased. Often a decision is taken between the men of a deceased's clan and the person who sponsors the mortuary feast, so that the parties concerned are clear about what names are given away to the other clan. In most instances, if the deceased is a woman, then it is only the feminine names that are given away while the masculine names remain, or vice versa.

Silverman (1996: 43) describes a major difference between the Eastern Iatmul, Central Iatmul and Western Iatmul naming practices. He noted that when the last surviving member of a clan dies, the names of the deceased's clan are redistributed throughout the village. Such a practice does not prevail in Central and Western Iatmul. In general, when the last surviving member of a clan dies, the names of that particular clan continue to survive as a token reminder of that clan. However, it would be a clan belonging to the same totemic moiety and clan association that would assume the right to use the names of the clan which is now extinct. In Kanganamun village, while the clan Mbei does not have any more surviving clan members, its stock of names is being used by the Yabu and Kembiam clans, who belong to the same clan association (Walgem) as Mbei. The reason for this is given below. The difference between Eastern and Central (and Western) Iatmul has been part of an interesting development in the ethnographic theorization of the formation and dissolution of clan groups among the Iatmul and Manambu societies, to which I now turn. I hope that the discussion will anticipate the issues of necessity and contingency that will be raised in the following chapter.

Names are thicker than blood

Writing from the context of his understanding of Manambu, Harrison (1989: 5) observes that: 'When an Avatip clan dies, it only goes out of action, not out of existence.' Harrison is describing how the totemic cosmology of the Manambu is able to transcend time and the limitations of human finitude, and the vicissitudes of demography. With his customary style of comparative anthropology (see for instance Harrison 1985, 1992, 1995), Harrison makes an interesting contrast between what he calls Highland and Lowland political systems of Papua New Guinea. Seeking to contextualize Lindstrom's distinction between 'wealth-based' and 'knowledge-based' politics, Harrison suggests that, while they share a similar function as symbolic economies of prestige, the Highland political systems are based on wealth whereas Lowland systems are based on knowledge. Harrison describes the ceremonial debate over the theft of names among the Manambu as comparable to exchange systems of the Highlands societies. While material wealth is mobilized and exchanged in the Highlands, it is words that are the medium of exchange in Lowland political systems.

Concomitant with this contrast between wealth-based and knowledge-based political economies is an ontological assumption that underlies the formation and dissolution of social groups in the Highland and Lowland societies. The basic ontological feature of these two kinds of political systems is that Highland social groups emerge and dissolve themselves through a myriad of contingent situations whereas in Lowland societies, such as Manambu, social groups exist as an a priori necessity. Harrison observes that Highland societies do not have elaborate totemic cosmologies, and their clans are independent political and territorial units which carry out war, marriage, and exchange relationships with other such groups. Furthermore, they have a flexible agnatic charter that allows them to easily incorporate outsiders. And when such groups live together, it is their co-residence and locality that is very much at the heart of their creativity and self-definition. Land is a major source of economic and political strength and identity. To live off a group's land is like being fed by substances of the group and persons are incorporated into other groups through a form of non-agnatic recruitment (Harrison 1989: 4).

Lowland societies such as the Manambu (and Iatmul) have totemic systems characterized chiefly by the ownership of a series of personal names. Clan groups are divided over the sorts of names (and stories) which they own with regard to their totemic cosmologies. A clan owns several thousand names and these names are a central part of a clan's patrimony. The sharing of agnatically inherited names is at the heart of self-definition and group identity. It is not land as such that provides them with the greatest economic resources but rights in trading relationships (see Gewertz 1983). Every Manambu village (Harrison 1990a: 19), like Iatmul villages, has traditional trading relationships with their particular surrounding neighbours from whom they acquire food and other items as well as ritual or totemic knowledge. Regular markets are held every week where people engage in trade and exchange, and there is a 'pan totemic' relationship between villages which have such trading relationships (1990a: 18).

Using an analogy, Harrison describes the Highland clans as a physical substance and their members as the pieces of this particular substance. 'It is a syntagmatic, bodily, physiological symbolism, that represents co-membership as a fleshy contiguity created from shared food and gaining of livelihood from shared land' (1989: 4). A Highland clan involves the sum total of its members acting together in concerted socio-political and economic activity. The contiguity of its members living and working and coordinating their efforts together provides the context for both group and individual self-definition. In the absence of actual numbers of people making up such groups, the groups simply do not exist as a category. It was in this light that Harrison employs the notion of contingency with regard to the social process of group formation in Highland societies.

With Lowland societies (such as Manambu and Iatmul), membership is given primarily through the naming system, and these names are 'given' to an infinite range of individuals who are known by such names throughout their successive careers in life. The names survive the death of each individual bearer and live on because they are 'thicker than blood' (cf. Sahlins 1976: 10; Schneider 1984).[3] Owing to the totemic cosmology instantiated in the naming system, Harrison observes that the social group in Lowland societies exists as an ever-present, static, and transcendent reality which survives through time despite its members coming and going in life and death. Harrison has therefore employed the ontological notion of necessity to describe the nature of social formation in Lowland political systems.

The comparative model proposed by Harrison (1989) concerning social formation in Highland and Lowland societies has received ethnographic criticism from Silverman (1996) who worked in the Eastern Iatmul village of Tambunum. Silverman points out that Harrison's framework cannot apply easily to a polity which is decisively magical and argues that:

> The dynamics that underlie the ontological foundations of Melanesian polities . . . are too complex to be adequately encompassed within a dichotomy . . . [S]ociety requires human agents to embody . . . mystical and cosmological categories. Persons become the totemic referents of their names and in this way (re)constitute the cosmos through human action. Yet the ideology of Eastern Iatmul tacks between realism and nominalism. In some contexts the cosmos is alleged to be fixed and separated entirely from social life. In other contexts human action is acknowledged to create totemic categories. In all cases, however, these claims, whether realist or nominalist, are ultimately political rather than ontological. That is to say, statements concerning the structure of the cosmos and the totemic system are tied to specific politico-ritual disputes and strategies. (1996: 32)

Silverman made an important call to take heed of local idioms of the body and how that relates to the way in which people construct their understandings of social reproduction. He therefore describes a symbolic homology between the human body, cosmology, and society. Much of Silverman's account of the Eastern Iatmul use of totemic names shows

[3] The phrase 'names are thicker than blood' is appropriated from a Fortesian epigram cited by Sahlins (1976: 10), who discusses a debate on kinship models that went on between Peter Worsley and Meyer Fortes in which the former argues that 'manure is thicker than blood'.

similarities to the use of these names in Central and Western Iatmul. However, I find that Silverman has mistakenly conflated the totemic and ritual moieties, and therefore the sorts of interpretations he provides of the Eastern Iatmul are open to question. Below are some of the general points that he makes which are comparable to the situation in Central Iatmul.

Silverman recites a very familiar myth of origin which tells of how the world was created by the agency of the wind blowing over and stirring the waters in a primal ocean. It was the primal activities of the wind that brought the world into being. The version I am told in Kanganamun describes the wind as a crocodile-cum-spirit-man with a personal agency. This primal man was simultaneously wind, water, and mud. As the wind, the primal man was blowing over the waters in a way reminiscent of the biblical account of the Spirit of God hovering over a primal ocean. Silverman, with his bent towards psychoanalysis, interprets the primal wind as a phallic gust, and invests the water with an aura of femininity by treating it as a chthonic womb (Silverman 1996: 36, 2001: 15–46). He described this myth of creation in an idiom of cosmic procreativity analogous to the way in which humans reproduce themselves sexually.

After the creation of the cosmos, cosmological heroes emerged from a hole in the ground in a place called Mivimbit, which is located near the present-day Sawos village of Gekorobi, north of Kanganamun. These cosmological heroes set about their (various) acts of creativity, which resulted in the establishment of various environmental features such as mountains, lakes, waterways, and bush tracts, as well as celestial configurations such as the moon, the stars, and the sun. After the heroes emerged from the ground, each made tracts and went along their individual routes in a primal migration (see Wassmann 1990, 1991), and at the places where they stopped and carried out particular activities, they bestowed personal names. The clans which now own such names also have ownership rights over such environmental features. And the lists of totemic names which individual clans now have make reference to and intimate this primal creativity, and these agents and places. Each clan has its own set of names which it inherits from preceding generations. However, the names are not entirely independent from each other because there are interconnections between clans, even between clans of opposing totemic moieties. For instance, in Kanganamun village, I am told that there are some names which are held in common between the Lenga and Samiangwat clans, despite the fact that the clans are from opposing totemic moieties. Lenga and Samiangwat clans cannot dispute with each other over the ownership of particular names. There is a basic agreement between these two clans that the Lenga clan can use names which they share with the Samiangwat clan only in villages where there is no Samiangwat clan and the same rule, but vice versa, is observed by Samiangwat clan. But when these two clans are found in the same village, such as in Kanganamun, the names they use follow the dictates of precedent so that the names which are of the same 'rope' (lists) and have been already used by one of these two clans cannot be used by the other.

Although there is no correlation between economic inequality and the ownership of names in Eastern Iatmul, the names provide clans with use-rights to land, waterways, and fishing lagoons. Furthermore, 'men in Tambunum do not attempt to manipulate the totemic system in order to increase their access or deny access to social rivals' (Silverman 1996: 34–5), except that the manipulation becomes concretized in conflicting claims of ownership when rival groups mobilize and assert their claims to a name under dispute. If this is true for the rest of Iatmul, one can see that the totemic system allocates people into groups with particular jural responsibilities for the things they can and cannot own in terms of their names. There has been a general decline in the number of disputes over names in the Iatmul region in general, and I would attribute this to the influence of Christianity in terms of religious beliefs and the introduction of a new set of names. The last reported dispute in Kanganamun village was in 1987 and it was debated in the neighbouring Parimbe village.

Whereas success in the past history of war, magic, and sorcery is based on the use of personal names to engage the powers of clan spirits, success today in education and business is not attributed to the use of personal names. I did come across instances where men blew spells over their carvings in order to attract and induce art dealers and tourists to buy them. In two of these instances, the carvings were sold and the carver attributed his success not only to his creativity but also to the help of his clan spirits, which he had invoked through the spell.

I should now turn to the criticisms that Silverman has of Harrison's model. Silverman argues that 'personhood' in Eastern Iatmul presupposes that persons in their corporeal form act upon a social world because, without bodies, persons go out of existence and cannot act. The same applies to a clan group. Thus, if there are no living descendants of a particular clan, the names of such a clan are distributed throughout the village after the death of its last surviving member. Silverman cites Stanek's (1990) observation that such a practice is not found in Central Iatmul. Silverman reports that: 'the lineage that sponsors a funerary rite then acquires the totemic names that defined the deceased group. Typically, names remain within the same patriclan, transferring only to other lineages. But sometimes men from different clans jointly sponsor a funerary rite, dispersing the names throughout the village' (1996: 43).

Silverman therefore argues that when a clan goes out action, it also goes out of existence. The group that owns such names dissolves and its names are incorporated into other clans within the village. I cited the example of the Yabu and Kembiam clans in Kanganamun who have now taken over the use of names that were once owned by the Mbei clan, which has become extinct. Regarding the incorporation of the names of a clan which is going out of existence, it would be more apt to say that, for Central Iatmul, clans do not die but take on a different form through being reincorporated into other clans which assume the ownership of their stock of names. Throughout Iatmul,[4] villages and clans are paired as brothers, and the surviving brother clans will assume the ownership of the names, stories, and other resources that are owned by the clan which has now died. Clans therefore behave in the way that is reminiscent of the Iatmul fractal 'person' described in Chapter 4. If we recall the fact that Iatmul conceive of life and death as paired brothers, with life as the elder brother and death as the younger brother, death in Iatmul can be seen as way of becoming the other brother. Thus it follows that if a person is a clan and clan a person (in the logic of fractal personhood), we can see that clans such as Yabu and Kembiam are behaving in that way. Yabu is the elder brother and Kembiam is the younger brother clan and both are now using the names of the Mbei clan, which is their younger brother clan in their clan association. Through death, clans such as Yabu and Kembiam are taking on the names of their younger brother clan. One brother clan is becoming another brother clan. This is in the same vein as the Iatmul 'person' who is ontologically oriented towards becoming the other brother. Although Silverman aptly reminds us that personhood in Eastern Iatmul presupposes persons who act upon a social world in their bodily-being, I argue that the bodily conception of the person is too 'bounded', and therefore restricted, to encompass the complexity of ontology of brotherhood described here.

The Eastern Iatmul people do not practise initiation rituals any more. During my fieldwork, I came across one elderly man of Tambunum village who still had the 'crocodile marks' (*waalumi*) imprinted on his body, but none of the present-day Eastern Iatmul villagers practise initiation ritual. According to Métraux, who also worked in Tambunum in the early 1970s,

[4] See Métraux (1978) for Eastern Iatmul, Stanek (1990) for Central Iatmul, and Wassmann (1991) for Western Iatmul.

men's initiation rituals ceased to be practised in Tambunum even before the outbreak of the Second World War in the 1940s (see Métraux 1975: 295). In the absence of this initiation ritual in Eastern Iatmul, Silverman appears to have given his own view about the nature of ritual and totemic moieties in Iatmul. His discussion of the connection between names and bodies (2001: 52–4) is illuminating but takes for granted the critical debate over nature and culture (contra MacCormack and Strathern 1980). That is, he proceeds with the explicit view that biological reproduction is a feminine concern whereas symbolic reproduction is the preoccupation of men. This view holds the view that nature is to culture as female is to male (cf. Strathern 1988: 3). Silverman readily cites Hogbin's famous phrase that 'men play flutes and women bear infants'. I am pressing this criticism strongly because it is within the scope of such reasoning that Silverman describes the famous ritual of scarification. Silverman interprets the ethos of Iatmul masculinity (Bateson 1958: 123–41) as a mask that conceals an inner oedipal compulsion towards femininity and takes the scars incised on the bodies of initiates as representations of 'the breasts and genitals of women and female crocodile spirits'. It needs to be mentioned here that the scars are famously known throughout the Iatmul as *waalumi*, meaning the 'crocodile's teeth' and there is no place within the ritual that accommodates Silverman's observations. The incisions which eventually become scars or colloids that adorn an initiate's body actually represent several parts of the body of a spirit crocodile.

The final criticism that Silverman has of Harrison's model is with respect to time. Silverman feels that Harrison has described the Manambu totemic cosmology in a manner that has made it seem static and transcendental. As examples, Silverman cites the descriptive content of names such as the 'vines that float down the river' or the 'wood that flows down the river'. Silverman is referring to the kinaesthetic imagery of Iatmul names and argues that such idioms of perpetual motion, as expressed in names, lend themselves to a fluid ontology (see for instance Goldman and Ballard 1998) in contrast to the static Manambu cosmology. However, Silverman does not acknowledge that the meanings of such names remain the same over time and that they will always have the same totemic referent relative to a specific clan. What remains constant and static is the literal meaning of these names while their esoteric significance is open to constant manipulation (see Harrison 1990a). Much of the body of Iatmul myth is replete with images of keeping still and movement (see for instance Wassmann 1991: 115). And for that matter, the Eastern Iatmul area as a whole is known as Woliagwi, which means the floating grass island whose movement becomes halted when it is anchored. In the opening pages of this book, I made reference to the image of a canoe fastened to a pole to keep it from drifting away. In the Iatmul concept of the 'person' described in Chapter 4, life and death are also contrasted with sleeping (rest) and swimming (motion). However, as I have shown, sleeping anticipates waking up again in much the same way as rest anticipates motion (Weiner 1988). In the same vein I have also discussed how Iatmul names express the kinaesthetic imagery that Bateson mentions. While these names are involved in this immanent world of human sociality, they also have an enduring life and meaning that transcends the life of the individuals that bear these names. Let us now turn to a consideration of how time appears in the context of name ownership, in order to say something about ownership and relationships.

The temporal life of ownership

Many ethnographers of Melanesian societies have noted the use of the first-person pronoun in respect of the kinds of claims a person may be making regarding his or her group. Although this may provide interesting insights into the nature of personhood and social agency (Rumsey 2000) or understandings of temporal synchronization (Iteanu 1998), I refer to such a cultural practice with respect to how ownership is intricately rooted in time.

Ethnographers of the Sepik River area provide illuminating accounts of claimants who, in disputes over the ownership of names and other resources, assert themselves in an inclusive sense both with respect to the language couched in the present tense and in presenting themselves as the very people who embody in a physical-substantial sense the evidence of their claim. Telban (1998) wrote in this vein about the Ambonwari who live in the Karawari area. Telban's exegetical strategy expounds upon the Ambonwari notion of *kay* and how—through its manifestation in kinship, naming, marriage, and exchange practices—it embodies a temporal process that summons notions of the past and the future into the present now. Inspired by Bourdieu's notions of embodied practice and habitus, Telban describes all aspects of human bodily practices, material and technological contraptions as inseparable from *kay*. In explicating this notion of *kay*, comparable also to the familiar Melanesian notion of *kastom*, Telban shows how the embodiment of relations bears the imprint of past historical encounters which are relevant for the contingencies of the present and concerns for the future. This notion of *kay* allows Telban to articulate a vision of temporality that dances on an extensive temporal continuum. This perception of temporal continuity is linked to the identity-forming potential of *kay* and its concomitant embodiment in human bodily practice, habits, and technological accessories. Telban (1998: 139) makes the following observations in view of the kinship and marriage practices of the Ambonwari.

> In Ambonwari kin terminology, the emphasis upon 'ancestral paths', and the putatively eternal nature of 'exchange partner' and 'ritual inaugurator' links between descent groups all suggest both the anticipation of the future and conformity with a perduring past. The duality is nowhere more clear than in the perpetual reproduction of alternate generational identities, which seems both to negate time by collapsing the past and the future and yet, through the intervening, adjacent generation, to separate and guarantee both.

The temporal duality that Telban refers to is that between the present and either the past or the future. He explains that this duality exists as necessary aspects of how *kay*, as a process of embodiment, is articulated in social life and practices by 'dancing through time' for an eternity (1998: 228). Commenting on the use of the first-person pronoun he observes that, 'In disputes or during speeches, a man from the Crocodile-1 clan often says, "I, I, I, I am Kapi." . . . By saying, "I am Kapi", a man says "I am the one who came here first", "I am the one who owns this place", "I am the father of this place"' (1998: 152). The claimant appears to be simultaneously the referent in the claim and the claimant as well, and on other hand he is also an individual man as well as the clan as a whole.

In describing the ceremonial debate over names amongst the neighbouring Manambu, Harrison (1990a: 161–2), made the following observations:

> The debating-ground has a colourful, carnival-like appearance, as each side tries to present as impressive a visual spectacle as possible. Sometimes, men act out an episode from myth in order to emphasise their claims, using 'props' and a few assistants from the audience, and the debate becomes a kind of competitive theatre. Men describe the acts of their totemic ancestors always in the first person and the present tense, as though trying to re-create the mythical past on the debating-ground. . . . A speaker does not say, for instance, 'my ancestor created such-and-such a mountain' but 'I am creating that mountain', or even 'I am that mountain'.

In my view, this use of the first-person pronoun in claims of ownership exemplifies the simultaneous interplay of immanence and transcendence which are concretized in the contingencies of a present claim of ownership. This shows that ownership is always a claim made in the present. The nature of Manambu and Iatmul totemic cosmology shows that ownership acts like a gravitational pull that embeds the transcendental reality of totemic understandings within the present immanent world of human sociality.

I came across similar pronouncements during my fieldwork in Kanganamun as well. For instance, in a heated debate between Tobias Wali and Yarme Mambingawi, my adopted father, over the ownership of crocodiles in a particular fishing lagoon, I heard both men referring to themselves as the mythic and historical figures which they are referring to when they seek to demonstrate the validity of their claims. Tobias Wali argued that it was a man of his clan who was taken by a crocodile at the lagoon called Wombungusat. And so he argued that it was 'his head' that had been taken and therefore he and his Graken clan are the ultimate owners of this lagoon. He insists that any clan that takes food from the lagoon without respecting the Graken clan must be prepared to pay for 'his head' that went down in the lagoon. Yarme, on the other hand, argued that it was he, by which he meant his totemic ancestors, who created and walked about the place which is now the lagoon. Therefore he argued that he and his clan are also entitled to use the lagoon. Tobias presented himself as the person whose life was taken by a crocodile in the lagoon while Yarme asserted himself as the cosmological hero involved in the creation of Wombungusat. Although Tobias is using a historical incident and Yarme is using a cosmogonic argument, both of them employed the same idiom of the first-person pronoun.

Since we are back in Kanganamun, we might return to the story of Saungombi that was introduced in the beginning of this chapter. We find that Saungombi asserts himself as the Tanginwuli whose name is now 'allegedly stolen' by Jack and his Uriap clan. Saungombi did not say Tanginwuli was a man of his Wanigo clan who built his house and planted trees in such and such a place. Saungombi presented himself as the very referent of the name: 'I am Tanginwuli. My name is Tanginwuli.' Through the sharing of 'totemic consubstantiality' (see Harrison 1990a: 48), Iatmul clans who are identified by a particular set of totemic names see themselves as being 'one' (cf. Mimica 1988). Through asserting his claim of ownership over the name Tanginwuli, Saungombi epitomizes the 'fractal person' who is simultaneously the individual and the clan Wanigo.

When I pressed Jack Kapi and his younger brother, Cyril, over the name they had given their son, Cyril, who is a practising apprentice in totemic mythology, made the following remark:

> If you look carefully at our stories (*sagi*), you will find that we are the same line. We are one people. We were like two fish that were hanging on the same rope and then we were separated and came out here from Mivimbit. The point is to explain why we were separated and how it happens that we are here together as people of one village.

Cyril's remarks resonate closely with Bateson's observation that underlying Iatmul dualist ontology is a particular notion of monism:

> On the whole, it would seem that the belief in multiplicity is lay and exoteric, while the details of the basis of monism are an esoteric mystery for the erudite. This does not mean that the general concept of monism is a secret. When two clans are striving over the ancestral ownership of a name, a man may declaim in open debate: '*One* father, *one* mother, *one* root—that is the sort of people that we . . . are.' (1958: 236, my emphasis)

In Western Iatmul, Wassmann (1990: 32) made the following observations concerning primal migration and the emergence of totemic names which merit quoting at some length:

> At each place visited by the migration . . ., the clan group founder leaves behind a few men and women. He assigns them an animal, plant, or some other object into which they can transform themselves; thus each place has its own 'totem'. This 'totem' and all the objects of the place receive names of their own, which are arranged in pairs in long lines. The inhabitants of the village are also given names. The 'totems' assigned in this way form the basis of the present totem system. Most important of all, the names used at that time form the stock of present names. The whole stock of names from the past is used for the present; persons, men's houses, dwellings, canoes, dogs, and pigs all bear names drawn from this stock. Thus there is a close identification between all persons and things of the present with those of the past. The person of today is defined by his (ancient) name in the sense that he figures as a reincarnation—albeit a frail one—of the primal being of the same name . . . The use of the names causes the two periods to coincide and expunges the linear-genealogical succession. This is made very clear when, for example, one of the important men of Kandingei, Wolindambwi (the name is that of one of the ancient migrants), rises to his feet during a heated debate in the men's house and calls out excitedly, 'I, I, Wolindambwi, I took part in the ancient migration!' . . . Furthermore, through the use of ancient names the person of today finds himself simultaneously in both times.

This passage from Wassmann describes the association of names with primal migration and how Iatmul names in general intimate cosmological events, localities, objects, or particular implements, as well as the totemic beings associated with such names. In addition, Wassmann makes an apt observation concerning the capacity of Iatmul names to synthesize or bring together the mythical past with the contingencies of the present. Although, the temporal notion of a 'future' is not explicitly mentioned, it is left implied as a necessary component to the temporal life of ownership.

Conclusion

The discussion in the last two chapters has focused on issues of kinship and marriage amongst the Iqwaye and the Iatmul, as well as on the nature of social formation in Iatmul and the Manambu. The Iatmul do not have a counting system comparable to that of the Iqwaye, but their marriage and naming system, and the sense of being 'one' are very similar and intimate primal origins that closely resemble the Iqwaye cosmology. In using Western philosophical concepts of transcendence and immanence, I have tried draw attention to the manner in which time becomes ontologically constitutive of ownership. The ownership of personal names in Sepik River societies thrives on a rhythm of temporality which operates through recalling the past, and collapsing the past and the future into the contingencies of the present. Ownership appears as a historical and biographical phenomenon and its autobiography is one that intimates the biography of its claimant. Just like Tanginwuli who is recalled as man from of the Wanigo clan and who had a house and planted coconuts in his *yaranga*, ownership invokes and advocates the biography of its claimant as the basis of its legitimacy and moral persuasion. Second, ownership comes into being through a biographical trajectory that necessarily integrates the lives of social others because of its ability to differentiate and identify owners.

Finally, towards the end of this chapter, the notion of simultaneity exemplified in the context of a name-ownership dispute renders ownership with the cast of transience. Like the Iatmul who makes himself inhabit both times at once, cosmological and contemporary, and who defines himself simultaneously as an individual and the clan, ownership is also historical and contemporaneous as much as it can be individuating and collectivizing. Given the contingency of existential moments of the 'now' (Gell 1992: 227, 1998: 238; Mimica 1988: 133; Telban 1998: 42–3; Weiner 1999: 249–52), ownership is essentially a concern that always comes into play in the present moment, but its power lies in synchronizing prior and relevant historical circumstances and relationships to assert itself with an outcome that is generally persuasive and sometimes litigious. At an abstract level one could see that ownership behaves in a very synthetic way in terms of bringing together both historical circumstances and how claimants are related to one another. I suggest that this synthesizing behaviour of ownership is concomitant with the synthetic function of relationships which make people such as Saungombi and his clan 'one' because the 'one man is also many men' (Strathern 1991). The theoretical concern with 'one' in the case of Iqwaye and Iatmul societies also illustrates a metaphysics of 'oneness' (Strathern 1988: 274) evident in the character of a fractal person with relationships integrally implied. If such a relationship can bring many into one, as did Saungombi and his clan, what then is the status of such a concept of relationships in ontological terms? Since Saungombi is both individual and clan, both referent of and claimant to a name, name ownership appears to embed cosmological transcendence with the immanent world of human sociality simultaneously. Through focusing on the temporal life of ownership exemplified in Iatmul names, with its attendant concern with the past and the future synchronized in the now, I have tried to implicate how one might conceive of relationships as the ground of infinite being.

6

Naming and Necessity in Iatmul

To get from the name to the name of the name, we must go through the process of naming the name.

(Bateson 2002 [1979]: 174)

> It is the *ngeko* that is attracting the tourists to the village and therefore it is appropriate that the tourists visit, take pictures, and carry with them memories of our *ngeko* so that they can make and lift the name of our village to grow up big. And when our name grows big, more and more people will come here.

These are the words of Kambonamak, an elderly woman in Kanganamun village. As we saw in Chapter 3, she made these observations with respect to the visits they receive from tourists and art dealers from time to time. Her observations are not about Iatmul personal names but something more akin to fame, prominence, or reputation comparable for instance to the 'fame of Gawa' (Munn 1986). However, in the matrilineal Gawa, people are given several (a minimum of four) personal names from both their parents' sides. One of these names has to be from the mother's clan while others are idiosyncratic. Because people in Gawa (1986: 105–9) are involved in the *kula* trade (Malinowski 1922), the *kula* valuables are often given the personal names of their owners and their names travel and circulate with the valuables, spreading their fame throughout the region through the transactional process of exchange. As a name travels around, it climbs up the ladder of fame, which then causes shell valuables to return to their owners. This is the sense in which Kambonamak is talking about the need to enlarge the name of the Kanganamun men's house, so that it can travel out through the visitors, and return with more and more visitors, such as tourists who might be able to leave some money in the village through the sale of carvings and other handicraft objects that people make.

Kambonamak's observation lends a quality of elasticity to Iatmul names. Through its enlargement, the name will grow big and absorb new moments of transactions with visitors to the village. This sense of elasticity also appears in the manner in which Wagner (1991) has described the place of names in the constitution of the 'fractal person' in Melanesian societies. 'Regardless of their range of denomination, whether personal or collective, names are but names, but it is a name that is at once the individual and collective aspirations of the big men. A Daribi friend once observed, "When you see a man, he is small; when you say his name, he is big"' (Wagner 1991: 163; see also 1972: 85). In Chapters 4 and 5, we have seen how Iatmul names appear both in the sense of being simultaneously individuating and collectivizing (exemplified in the story about Saungombi and his Wanigo clan) and in their holographic permutation (given the fact that Iatmul names are also paired as brothers). The discussion that follows in this chapter takes the form of a comparative study about the process of naming amongst the Daribi, Iqwaye and Iatmul societies in PNG. In between the discussion on the Daribi and the Iqwaye is a philosophical discussion of *naming and necessity* (Kripke 1980). I have used Kambonamak's observation as a rhetorical conceit that sets the stage for a discussion of the Daribi naming system, but the theoretical intention of this chapter is to suggest how the category of relationships can be conceptualized as a metaphysical necessity in ontological terms. I will therefore attempt to concretize this in terms of naming practices. We begin with the Daribi situation.

Daribi and Iatmul systems of personal names

Wagner (1972: 85–106) details how the Daribi names are created, used, and passed on as social heirlooms. His discussion opens with an exegesis on the Daribi notion of a '*poai*', which refers to relationships of congruence and resemblance (see also Wagner 1986: 14–17, 1991: 163–4). Persons who embody such relationships are said to be *sabi* (namesakes). In comparative terms, the Iatmul *wasari* (namesakes or same-names) are not based on any such relationships of similarity or congruence, but on the fact that the *wasari* are individuals who belong to the same clan and who are residents of different Iatmul villages. There must always be one living instantiation of a personal name at any given time in an Iatmul village and, as we have seen, others who are known by the same name must belong to a different village and must belong to the same clan or clan association, and will therefore define each other as *yarangundu*, literally meaning 'clan-man' which implies that the people so named belong to the same clan. This happens because Iatmul clans are spread out throughout the region like the 'rhizome of the lotus'. Iatmul *wasari* are citizens of different villages and so it follows that the minute you find two people from different clans sharing a name, such as the name Tanginwuli that we encountered in Chapter 5, it means that one of the groups in question has stolen the name from the other. Amongst the Daribi, the nature of the *poai* relation is such that individuals and animals that share a name do so because the name is a point of congruence in which their identity is contrived. A Daribi name designates the correspondence between a name bearer and the source of that name, and often it is the point of congruence or a relationship of resemblance that serves as the source of that name. In Iatmul, however, a name is sourced from a totemic origin and the bearer of that name must already have a relationship with a putative totemic ancestor or cosmological hero.

Wagner describes several different situations that provide the kinds of contexts for the names that the Daribi create and give themselves. In general, these situations have the effect of enabling people to extend their *poai* relations to generate identity. For instance, attributes that individuate a person—such as personal attributes and skin colour—can serve as indices of the correspondence out of which a name is created and bestowed on a person. Since *poai* relations metaphorize identity, 'the naming system applies a potentially infinite range of metaphorical correspondences to social ends'. The Daribi employ a variety of techniques to generate metaphors, and the metaphoric link, which is the *poai* link, is that which represents a person's identity (Wagner 1972: 86). In general, Daribi names are created out of the contingencies of social life and experience. Iatmul names however are not created out of any kind of contingency such as one encounters in Daribi. Iatmul names are bound up with cosmological antecedents and they do not emerge from the seeming arbitrariness of historical contingency. Daribi names are either created or imposed on a person. When names are imposed, the metaphor which names a person is created through applying the name of a plant, animal, or some other cultural elements to generate a new *poai* relation. For instance, the name of a brightly coloured bird maybe used to metaphorize a certain kind of aesthetic quality, which is then bestowed on a person. Iatmul names are also names of plants and animals, terrestrial (land tracts, mountains, waterways, lagoons) and celestial configurations (sun, wind, moon, stars, etc.), domestic implements (such as knives, baskets, nets, stools, platforms). The names in Iatmul came together with the establishment of the cosmos and of man's place within it and they do not create names anew.

Another example that Wagner gives about Daribi naming comes from dreams. A father would see something in a dream, and in that sense he saw a name in that dream. When he wakes up and recalls that dream, the father then names his child after what he saw in the dream. Another example that Wagner gives is about the perceptive abilities of small children. Thus a toddler for instance may be asked by its mother to bring to her a particular implement such as a bamboo knife which is lying somewhere in the corner of their house. If the child recognizes the implement by its name and takes the implement to its mother, the name of such an object is then given to the child (Wagner 1972: 88). This second example carries epistemological implications for it raises the question of whether the child had known (innately) beforehand the name of the bamboo implement and is therefore able to bring it to its mother. For Wagner, cognition is bound up with meaning (1986: 3–4) and names of implements such as a bamboo serve as an externalized register of cognitive processes (see also Gell 1998: 221–58). The toddler and bamboo example also raises the question of whether the child was unnamed prior the event of collecting the bamboo implement that names him. For the Daribi, the named (*poai*) and the unnamed (*poziawai*) provide an infinite range of the possible names that could be bestowed on children.

In both the Daribi and the Iatmul names also have a gendered dimension. In Iatmul the gender of the name is expressed through the suffixes; both matrinames and patrinames carry their own suffixes which fix the gender of the names. However, since Iatmul names always come in pairs as siblings, both names in a pair are considered as brothers irrespective of their gender. In Daribi however, the gender of the names is based largely on what may be described as internal and external relations specific to a group of people. Women tend to be given names which are associated with personal adornment and other such paraphernalia connected to domestic activities and hairless animals, whereas males are given exotic names from foreign languages and places including those from hunting expeditions, feathered animals, and body parts.

Some Daribi names also assume a functional role in recollecting different kinds of historical events and experiences. A name taken from a particular tree, land form, etc. may be bestowed on a child to recall sentimental affections that the child's father or mother may have about his or her place of origin. A Daribi parent who once had infanticidal intentions at the time his or her child was born may give a name to recall the kinds of emotions and series of actions that were engendered at the time of the child's birth. A mother may give her child a name that recalls the fact that during the time after the child's birth, she ran short of food and she had problems with feeding herself and the child, and so, in recalling that momentary period of hunger, she may name her child after that experience. Iatmul names do assume a function of recollection but they operate under a complex regime of memory reproduction.

Because of their cosmological antecedents, Iatmul names mediate between a transcendental world of reality and the immanent world of human action and sociality as we have already seen in Chapter 5. For instance, after the death of Makwat described in Chapter 4, I witnessed and participated in the mourning. Makwat's female relatives, particularly her father's sisters (*iau*) and her mother's sisters (*nyamei*) were lamenting by chanting totemic songs. As they mourned and wept over her body, they would call out the name of the deceased and relate it to other names and stories in their respective totemic clans. Iatmul name songs (see Wassmann 1991) recall where ancestors came from and the kinds of activities they executed. When they are sung in mourning, the songs ponder the possibility of what the deceased would do with his or her totemic accoutrements (such as a canoe, a knife, a fishing net or spear), for a person's biography is imbued with such implements and places. When such songs are sung in lamentation, the singing generates a mood of contemplative silence and causes great sorrow and brings tears from the eyes of mourners. The silence is broken with intermittent sobbing, accompanied with short narratives that recall moments of interaction with the deceased when she or he was still alive. All this causes more tears to precipitate like streams of emotional rain water falling down from their totemic clouds. On this particular occasion I heard women describe their continuous accumulation and shedding of tears as tributaries that feed water into a lagoon owned by Makwat's mother's clan.

Daribi also inherit names from their deceased relatives and sometimes they bestow the names of a living person upon their children as a token of respect. Such names have the incidental effect of creating a new *poai* relation, except that the relationship between the human *sabi* (namesakes) assumes precedence over that name which is verbalized; that is, when a person is named after a *sabi*, the thing that is signified by the name is utilized to metaphorize the relationship between two people. By contrast, in so far as the Iatmul names are totemic in origin, they cannot be given to people in the same or a different clan in the same village. As it is with the Manambu (Harrison 1990a: 61), no coevals within the same clan and village can be namesakes. To bestow a name of a living person on a child who comes from the same clan and village is to deny the existence of the living relative who is already known by that name. To give a name that is currently being used by a living clan member in the village is to imply that the said person known by that name is no longer alive. It also means that the clan is trying to get rid of that living person. Names can only be reused when the bearer of that name has died. The only names that are used nowadays with an unproblematic number of same-names (*wasari*) among members of the same clan or village are foreign names, such as those introduced by Christianity. It is unproblematic to have several Christian namesakes in the same village or clan. This is because introduced names cannot affect the kinds of totemic identities that only Iatmul names carry. Introduced names are not capable of being owned as valuable possessions because they carry no cosmological significance.

Daribi names have two simultaneous properties. First, they objectively designate elements such as trees, birds, and land forms; and, second, the designations are then used as metaphoric names (Wagner 1972: 98). Because of name transmission, the names that Daribi transmit are merged with those who previously have these names, so that a particular name 'acquires a social value, and in its transmission the sorrow of death and parting is expressed through continuity, just as continuity is only achieved through death and disruption' (1972: 98). Furthermore, the Daribi names which are inherited genealogically tend to dilute the original metaphoric significance of such names and so, in the long run, they come only to express social continuity. In Wagner's notion of figure–ground reversal (Wagner 1986), when metaphoric (or figurative) names lose their significance, they become lexical (or literal) names. The metaphoric and the lexical frame each other as necessary opposites, with each of the pair in such dialectical relationships being indispensably constitutive of the other. The reverse process by which a metaphoric signification becomes a lexical signification is, according to Wagner, 'the second-order trope of perception' (1986: 127). We shall return to this presently; first we insert a comparative point from the Iatmul. Despite being inherited, Iatmul names do not lose their literal and metaphoric qualities: both the literal and figurative (esoteric) significance of Iatmul names endures, and it is the esoteric significance of these names which forms the subject of ceremonial debate, which is carried out through innuendos and metaphoric allusions known only by men (and women) of erudition. If the diluted meanings of Daribi names express social continuity, the continuity in Iatmul is cosmological. This is clearly revealed, as we saw in the previous chapter, in how claimants of ownership assert themselves as the very persons who exist in the myth.

This particular sense of temporal continuity (which Harrison [1990a] describes as atemporal and transcendental for the Manambu) is also linked to an implicit theory of reincarnation which underlies the Iatmul ontology of brotherhood. Let me reiterate this in order to bring out the argument.

First, we must recall the fact that the pattern of thought that keeps on repeating itself across domains of different scales amongst the Iatmul is the notion of *nyamun shambu*—elder brother and younger brother. This recursive pattern is also replicated in the naming system, so that Iatmul names are paired as siblings of which one is the elder brother and the other is the younger brother. Second, the notion of paired brothers is also the one that organizes the transmission of names and the Iatmul type of prescriptive marriage called *iai–ianan*. Third, we have also seen how generations are collapsed in a way similar to the manner in which temporal notions of the past, present, and future are synchronized in the language of the present tense, along with the concomitant use of the first-person pronoun. Thus we can now repeat that since a male Ego and his FF are considered brothers: 'A man takes his father's name and applies them to his daughter . . . Theoretically, a man is reincarnated in his son's son; a woman in her brother's daughter' (Bateson 1958: 18). Through the transmission of the names from the grandfather to the grandson, the grandfather (elder brother) is reincarnated in his grandson (younger brother) and the father's sister (elder brother) is reincarnated in his brother's daughter (younger brother). Although the identity each of them has is not absolute, the contingency of their identity is borne out of an internal necessity premised upon the ontology of brotherhood. Naming and necessity in Iatmul is therefore embedded within this scheme of ontological understanding. By necessity I refer to a rule-like metaphysical law that is neither natural nor cultural but relational, and the term 'relational' is used here in the specific sense of 'fractal personhood'.

This is very different from the situation among the Daribi, who allow the contingencies brought about by different events and accidents in life to create names. For instance, the name of the bird that is crying at the top of a tree under which a birth is taking place can be taken and bestowed the child after its birth. Such a name would recall the simultaneity of the two events: the birth of the child and the bird calling on the tree. Despite the fact that the name of the bird is given arbitrarily, it is the metaphorization of the simultaneity of the birth and the calling of the bird that transforms an arbitrary situation into a relationship that is non-arbitrary. It is the contingency of these events that provides the contextual background which informs Daribi names. Wagner (1972: 103) explains that:

> The names of Daribi groups, like those of individuals, are developed from incidents expressive of individual associations and proclivities, and not as extensions of pre-existent naming-series . . . The effect of Daribi name-transmission is to preserve and perpetuate identities as idiosyncrasies of the 'line' or group, just as identities themselves are generated by the metaphorizing of individual idiosyncrasies. Thus whether we consider individual or group names, and whether we are concerned with the bestowal of names and the relations that this engenders, or with name-transmission, the Daribi naming system emerges as a means through which the individual and the incidental is retained and expressed.

The Iatmul on the other hand have a pre-existent name series which they use in giving to people. Apart from the name transmission associated with the *iai–ianan* marriage described above, some situations may cause people to choose which names to bestow on people. For example, when I first arrived in Kanganamun village, my adopted father pondered thoughtfully over what name was appropriate for me. After about a week had elapsed, he bestowed on me the name Walindanmeli, who is the cosmological hero of his clan credited with the establishment of the world and man's place within it. The name literally means 'wind' or 'white man', both of which are associated with the elder-brother totemic moiety. Totemic mythology has it that, after establishing the cosmos, Walindanmeli went off to live in the place of the dead people (*undumbu ngei*) and this place is also the place of the white people (*nyowi nimba*). Since I had gone to the village as a student from England, and since my adopted father had already been a visitor in the United States of America, he thought it appropriate to give the name Walindanmeli to me because of the fact that my going there from England recalls aspects of his clan's totemic mythology. In calling me (*nywait kwia se*) the name Walindanmeli, the name assumes a function of recalling cosmological heroes and primal events. Iatmul names such as Walindanmeli are about a world of transcendental reality which is not removed from but is embodied in the immanent world of human sociality (see also Harrison 1990a).

Wagner's rendition of Daribi naming system is bound up with a concern about the innovation of meaning that is contingent upon symbolic or representational forms of signification. Wagner (1972) delves into the contrast between lexical and metaphorical signification to elucidate his theory of meaning. Lexical signification, he explains, is based on an arbitrary relationship between the signified and the signifier, whereas metaphoric signification is based on a determinate and non-arbitrary relationship (1972: 4–5; cf. Leach 1976: 9–16). Accordingly, he sees metaphorical signification as an innovation based upon lexical signifiers and explains that:

> In ordinary lexical signification the relation between the signifier and the signified is supplied by convention alone, hence it is arbitrary and cannot be said to convey meaning except in a tautologous sense. Such a signifier becomes meaningful in a nontautologous sense only when it is extended to form a metaphor, that is, when a word that already signifies some element is used to signify another, thus creating (mediating) a relation between the signified elements. Thus a lexical signifier refers to a specific element, but a metaphor signifies a relation. (Wagner 1972: 169)

The difference between these two forms of signification is that the lexical encodes and classifies things such as dogs, trees, etc., whereas metaphorical signification institutes a non-arbitrary relationship between the signified and signifier through the creation of analogies and contrasts. Nonetheless, lexical signifiers function as the ground upon which metaphorical signification is figured, and the alternation between these two forms of signification constitute the figure-ground reversal.[1] Thus, for instance, take one of the famous ethnographic expressions of the Bororo man who says that 'I am a parakeet' (Wagner 1972: 7). 'The metaphor *extends* the notions of "man" and "parakeet" by drawing them into a new relation and a new meaning' (1972: 6, original emphasis). In so doing, the metaphor suspends the conventional understandings of 'man' and 'parakeet', and, through setting up a contrast and analogy between such lexical terms, it creates a new relationship of meaning which is based on the non-arbitrary relationship between such symbolic referents. It is also in this sense that Daribi names seem to have an elastic capacity to expand and contract through the transmission and flow of analogies and contrasts to generate meaning and identity.

Wagner's theory of meaning is based largely on metaphorical signification, although he notes that metaphors may lose their metaphoric properties and precipitate into lexical ones.[2] While metaphors are generated out

[1] Figure-ground reversal is, for Wagner (1986), the trope of perception based on the analogical argument that meaning is akin to perception. Wagner has since moved on to institute a dialectical shift from conceptualizing meaning as perception (2001) to perception as technology (2006).

[2] On this note, Wagner (1986: 12) sets up a captivating metaphoric analogy between money and symbols. Whereas money is the currency and medium of commodity exchange, symbols are the academic currency of anthropological theorization. Just as money loses its value, so do symbols lose their meaning. Meaning appears in the form of value, just as money appears in relation to commodities. Epistemology becomes a matter of explaining how this value

of suspending conventional symbols, both lexical and metaphorical signification are involved simultaneously in the construction of meaning. Emulating how meaning is invented through the dialectical interplay of invention and convention (see Wagner 1975), Wagner's rendition of Daribi practices of signification is a critical innovation upon the structuralist vogue that inspired a good part of earlier anthropological understandings of cultures such as those of Melanesia (see Weiner 1988). His insistence on the dialectic of the literal and figurative, or the lexical and metaphoric, gives meaning and identity a function of change and innovation. The metaphoric innovation that Wagner describes for the Daribi, however, is precipitated by a contingency of one sort or another. This is also a crucial difference that distinguishes Daribi from Iatmul naming practices. A concomitant outcome of the sense of contingency that informs Daribi naming practices is an impulse to innovate upon the conventional schemes of signification. Because it exists as a kind of metaphysical necessity, Iatmul totemic cosmology does not allow for metaphoric innovation in names, save that in specific circumstances clan members may select from a pre-existing series of names to name someone. I have also observed that the nature of name transmission amongst the Iatmul is connected to an implicit theory of reincarnation, as well as to the prescriptive system of marriage called the *iai–ianan*. Because the *iai–ianan* marriage is the conjugal instantiation of the ontology of brotherhood, the names that are transmitted through this marriage are informed by this same rule of metaphysical necessity.

Now, speaking of metaphysical necessity, Wagner (1986: 15) has a footnote in his book on self-referential symbols in which he notes that the notion of 'assumptional relationships' evident in Daribi names recalls the views expounded by the philosopher, Saul Kripke (1980) on the question of 'naming and necessity'. A brief discussion of Kripke's theory will follow shortly, but first let me recap on the manner in which names appear in Wagner's theory of self-referential symbols. Wagner (1986: 16) treats names as symbols and symbols—such as words and other gestural or visual forms—as names, and then he recapitulates on the manner in which literal and figurative significations work. At one level, names are points of reference for the thing named and, at another, a name contains the relation

---

operates. However apt this may seem, the analogy between money and symbol as the respective icons of meaning and value is prone to run into a problem of epistemological incommensurability. The locus of this incommensurability lies in a disjunction between perception and calculation and one way to phrase this clearly is to ask about how one could measure meaning in the same way as we calculate value.

between the symbol and the symbolized. The former involves classification of names into groups, whereas the latter involves names which are juxtaposed and expanded analogically (1986: 14). Daribi names take the form of analogical metaphors. The metaphors function as vehicles of meaning and they expand analogically to become like perception (1986: 10, 18–19).

The notion that meaning is akin to perception is developed as a critique of the Saussurian notion of the 'sign' as a sensual mediator between concept and percept which underlies abstraction as a constitutive process of semiotic innovation. By focusing on metaphors, Wagner discards the Saussurian notions of signified and signifier and this is executed through the dialectical alternation between invention and convention, microcosm and macrocosm (1986: 14, 18–19, 30). Wagner uses the example of a name by which a man is known as 'sulphur-crested cockatoo'. Since such a name is that of a bird which bears some resemblance to the man, the name serves as an index of a 'socially recognised "as if" relationship' between the man and the cockatoo. The name therefore becomes a function of this assumed or 'as if' relationship. Wagner (1986: 15) explains that:

> Such a relationship is individual, and individuating, in relation to convention, because it cancels or suspends the order of conventional reference in which men, for instance, and cockatoos are assumed to be distinct and nonoverlapping entities. The 'as if' of the name, so to speak, sets itself to the 'as if' of referential designation; the name defines for itself a possibility, excluded by convention, in which a man might be considered . . . a cockatoo. That possibility coincides rather uniquely with the name, and so [one] may conclude that the name 'stands for' the possibility that it elicits (and hence signifies its own relationship, or itself), and also that it self-references itself through that possibility.

It is at this point that Wagner (1986: 15) makes reference to Kripke's possible world arguments. I am incorporating Kripke's arguments here also because of the theoretical concerns with necessity discussed above.

Kripke on naming and necessity

When he delivered his account of 'naming and necessity', the audience that attended Kripke's three lectures had a general 'acquaintance' (1980: 28) with his analytical language and the kinds of examples that he summons to illustrate his argument. I am keeping the notion of 'acquaintance' in quotation marks in order to invoke an aspect of Kripke's argument: that the meaning of names may not necessarily derive from their descriptive content (as had been theorized by philosophers such as Frege and Russell) but from the fact that names are meaningful because people belong to a particular linguistic community which shares certain conventional understandings and acquaintances (1980: 28, 95). The audience that attended his lecture would have comprised largely people from various sub-disciplines such as philosophy of mind, and the history and philosophy of science. While the argument he makes developed from a concern with theories of referentiality and necessity, it has implications for other topical issues in philosophy such as the enduring problems of the mind–body dichotomy, the identity thesis, and the substances of natural kinds such as gold and water (1980: 34).

While employing a metaphysical notion of necessity, Kripke utilizes his critique against the descriptive theories of names to put forward a criticism against the Kantian view of necessity a priori by arguing that 'truths' can also be known after particular experiences. In Kripke's view, the Kantian view that necessary truths are only known a priori is problematic (1980: 59). Kripke summons a variety of examples to illustrate his view. For example, one concerns the stars Hesperus and Phosphorus and the planet Venus. When a star is sighted in the evening, it is named Hesperus. Another star is seen the following morning and is named Phosphorus. Soon after this, it was discovered that the stars are not different but refer to the planet Venus. After that discovery Hesperus and Phosphorus now have the same referent. These stars are identical since the star which was seen in the morning is also the one that was seen in the evening (1980: 28–9). Since it was discovered that the stars have the same referent, the truth about them is not known a priori but was known only after the discovery.

From such examples, Kripke argues that some necessary truths can also be known a posteriori. While aprioricity is, for Kripke, an epistemological concept, Kripke defines necessity in metaphysical terms (1980: 34, 35) to rethink the conceptual opposition between necessary and contingent truths in order to argue that there are also necessary a posteriori truths. In contrast to logical necessity, which locates truth in the province of the a priori, Kripke views metaphysical necessity as that which is discovered empirically and is therefore a posteriori truth. There are other examples that Kripke summons to illustrate his argument. One of them is that of water as H2O (1980: 128). His argument is that if a statement such as 'water is H2O' is true, then it follows that this must be true in every possible world in which water is found. But the proposition that water is H2O can only be known through empirical validation since there can also be 'fools' water'. The distinction between H2O and 'fools' water' is, and can only be, known through empirical validation.

Kripke employs the notion of possible worlds as a semantic device to evaluate the possibilities of truth in the context of counter-factual situations. Possible worlds are not places in a different country but are the 'total ways the world might have been, or state, or histories of the entire world' and they are stipulated by qualitative descriptions, not through telescopes (1980: 18, 44). A necessary truth is one that prevails in every possible world. With respect to naming, therefore, Kripke sees names such as Hesperus and Phosphorus as 'rigid designators' since, in every possible world, they refer to the planet Venus. Kripke therefore argues that proper names are rigid designators. As rigid designators, the proper names identify the same individual or referent in every possible world (1980: 48, 77–8). In light of this, the sense of 'possibility' that Wagner (1986: 15) refers to is mainly to do with the possible relationship that the name elicits—the possibility of how a man is 'as if' a sulphur-crested cockatoo. If Kripke's notion of metaphysical necessity provides a way of imagining the possibility of necessity a priori, then its epistemological promise resonates with Wagner's theory of meaning.

Rigid designators refer to a 'necessary existent'. Amidst his discussion of rigid designators are personal names of individual persons such as Aristotle and Nixon, as well as substances such as gold and water. Kripke introduces the notion of an 'initial baptism' (1980: 96). Initial baptism functions as a heuristic device deployed in the service of explaining why rigid designators should persist in every possible world. It does not refer to an act like the christening service in a Christian church, despite the implicit metaphoric associations. An initial baptism is not a ritualized event taking place in a particular place and time but it sustains a proper name as a necessity that transcends time and space. Initial baptism is based on a historically prior network of social relations (1980: 91, 96) and this causal network of relationships requires the bearers and recipients of names, such as the Iatmul, to keep the basic referential content of the name from age to age.

There is a basic agreement amongst the clan members as to what the names refer to. In the context of the Iatmul, the notion of an 'initial baptism' appears in the manner in which their names intimate the original act of cosmological creativity whose locus is the transcendent world of totemic mythology. The notion of transcendence, as used here, refers to eternal perpetuity or temporal continuity rather than to an overarching societal sphere. The link between an initial baptism and members of a community such as Kanganamun village is one that is maintained through the system of patrilineal clans and lineages by which names, myths, and songs are transmitted. Through this kinship system there is a common understanding by clan members about the referential content of a name. Kripke's notion of an initial baptism is appropriate for a kinship-based community such as in Iatmul, where clans observe particular practices of clan exogamy and there is a concomitant movement of women between clan groups in marriages (cf. Butler 1993: 211–18).

Kripke's notion of rigid designators is not synonymous or identical with descriptions that people can offer about a person who is known or has been given a particular name. However, Kripke concedes that through the act of the initial baptism there is a descriptive aspect to the act of naming. Therefore the persons who bear such names also bear elements which may be synonymous with such descriptions. But the descriptions do not function as rigid designators and this is a point which weakens Wagner's reference to Kripke. Wagner's descriptions of Daribi names are based on descriptive attributes such as skin colour. On this note, Butler (1993: 280) explains that the 'cluster of descriptions that constitute the person prior to the name do not guarantee the identity of the person across possible worlds; only the name in its function as a rigid designator, can provide a guarantee'. The descriptive quality of Daribi names is fluid and contingent, and is characteristically ephemeral in the sense that their meaning can disappear in so far as it is created. In making reference to Kripke, Wagner's description of Daribi naming practices weakens, because its descriptive content is based on the contingencies of social life and experiences, and not on a persistent necessity that is sustained in all possible worlds. It is with this in mind that we now turn once again to a comparison of the Iqwaye and Iatmul system of personal names. We open with Mimica's suggestion that sometimes metaphysical necessity can appear as contingency.

Iqwaye and Iatmul systems of names

'In the hindsight of their historicity, the Iqwaye and other Yagwoia have made their cosmogony, the very source of their necessity and being, appear as contingency' (Mimica 1991b: 97). The context of his discussion is about how incest—which he describes as a form of autocreation—reflects the structural configurations that are embedded in kinship relations, exchange, the naming system, and institutionalized male homosexuality (IMH) among the Iqwaye (Mimica 1991a, 1991b).

Mimica opens his discussion of the sensitive topic of IMH with a relationalist conception of the 'self' (cf. Battaglia 1995; Carrithers and Lukes 1985; Morris 1994; Taylor 1989) and assigns an ontological status to the body (Langer 1989; Merleau-Ponty 1962; A. Strathern 1996) by rendering it as a *causa sui* since it 'has the autopoietic significance of being the source of itself' (1991b: 81). He goes on to note that:

> every Iqwaye bodily fleshy envelope is the self-identity of other selves: the self of the sister/brother, mother, her sister and brother. Fundamentally, the Iqwaye bodily self does not possess itself as its own self but as a . . . body of another self. My sister is myself, and likewise for the mother, mother's sister and maternal uncle. My father and father's sister are also myself, but through the interiority of my bones. (1991b: 85)

As he showed, such a conception of self is linked to how incest passions (and ritualized homosexuality) are premised upon a particular view of autosexuality and self-copulation. The basis of such a view is rooted in the mythological understandings of Iqwaye cosmogony.

Existing originally as a self-generating being, the primal being called Omalyce had his fingers and toes interdigitated and his umbilical-penile organ was sucked into his mouth, indicative of self-copulation.[3] It was when Omalyce released his umbilical cord-penis organ from his mouth to breathe that the world was created. Celestial and terrestrial configurations, as well as myriad beings that dwell in the heavens and upon the earth, were also created from the ruptured fragments of the body of Omalyce. Omalyce then created five men out of the mud taken from the earth (which is his own body). These five men were imbued with life and then Omalyce orally inseminated them, making them men and his sons. The last of these five men, however, was not endowed with genitals. After being inseminated he became pregnant and, because he did not have the appropriate bodily passage to give birth, he laboured in pain. Subsequently that last man underwent a series of metamorphoses, by transforming initially into an eel, then a python, and eventually a cassowary. In his cassowary form, he was shot and killed by the four men who then cut open his womb and a red man emerged from the womb of the cassowary in the form of a marsupial.[4] The red man was shot and his body eaten as food.

The consumption of marsupials figures prominently in birth and death ceremonials among the Iqwaye. For example, when a mourning period

[3] See Gell (1999: 52) for an elaborate pictorial depiction of Omalyce.

[4] The bone from the leg of that cassowary was later used in male initiation rituals which involve nose-piercing (Mimica 1991b).

comes to an end, the deceased's maternal relatives eat a dead marsupial. The deceased's own mother does not eat such a marsupial because she had already incorporated one in her own body when the deceased was still a foetus. The deceased's maternal relatives often take back their identity embodied in their sister's children through various forms of reciprocal exchanges and prestations when the deceased was still alive. When the marsupial is eaten at the close of the mourning period, and when the deceased's maternal relatives receive mortuary payments from the deceased's paternal descent group, exchange with the deceased's matrifilial relatives is closed off. Mimica (1991b: 92) explains that:

> The progeny's flesh is reincorporated without residues into the stomachs of the mothers, the primordial locus in which the child came into being . . . The bones. . . [of the deceased are later] collected and interred in the deceased's own PDG [paternal descent group's] soil, which is their substantial equivalent . . . In death the dialectics of incest negation and affirmation, the interplay of auto and allo orientations merge in the final affirmation of the primordial passion for self-closure. Through bodily decomposition, a human being is . . . the ultimate self-fulfillment of the transcendent realm of the world which, being the cosmic man Omalyce, is also the source of himself. Death as the human loss of the self is by the same stroke, the human recovery of the self as the cosmos.

Since the cosmos is also the man and the man is also the cosmos in a different scale, death has the effect of reabsorbing the human into his or her primal origins which is the cosmos. Thus the transcendental cosmos is also simultaneously the world of immanent human sociality. Death in Iatmul has the effect of instituting eternal continuity through separation because it was through separation that the cosmos and the human world were initially established. The reader will recall one of the myths of origin narrated earlier. The primal crocodile had to open its mouth and his upper jaw became the heavens with all the celestial configurations and the lower jaw became the earth with its terrestrial configurations, including topographic features as well as flora and fauna. The separation of the body of this primal crocodile gave birth to the two totemic moieties. When a young teenager from Kanganamun village told me this story, I went to verify it with Keman Kaman from Yenjan village. When I asked Keman about this story, he replied to me in the following way. 'Yes it's true that such a story exists and we know it, it is true. However, the best way for you to understand it is this.' Using his right toes, he drew three circles (as in kinship diagrams) on the ground before me and said:

> This is your father [referring to the first circle], and this is your mother

> [referring the second circle]. When your parents came together, they had sex and you came up. And this is you [referring to the third circle]. This is how human beings in every part of this earth come up. When you get married, you will sleep with your wife and she will carry some children. We all human beings do this to make our population come up.

Keman explained the myth of origin by referring to Iatmul procreative understandings.[5]

The procreative idioms of the Iatmul resonate well with those of the Iqwaye. In both societies, it is believed that semen from one's father contributes to the making of a person's bones, whereas substances from the mother provides for one's flesh and blood. Both societies are patrilineal in cast. Names of males in both societies are taken from both sides of one's parents. However, while an Iatmul woman is given names from both sides, her Iqwaye counterpart is given names only from her father's side and not from her mother's side, and this is because of Iqwaye understandings of gender. Every Iqwaye is considered to be both androgynous in gender and phallic in body, except that females do not have an external phallus like males but an internal one which gives birth to children. The primary focus of Iqwaye matrinames is the external phallic genitalia and, since women do not have an external phallus, they are not given matrinames.

Matrinames amongst the Iatmul are not based on a gender understanding but recall the links to the mother and her clan. Each Iatmul patriname and matriname has suffixes that designate the gender of the name. As in Iqwaye, there is a close association between names and bodies. Patrinames in both societies are linked to the bones of a person, the interior aspects of a person's physical make-up, whereas men's matrinames in both societies are connected with a person's exterior bodily make-up, which includes flesh, blood, and nourishment.

Amongst the Iqwaye, the names of a particular descent group are also the names which are bestowed on their members. Thus, for instance, a man from the patrilineal descent group (PDG) A will have the same name as his sister and, if their mother is from PDG B, the man will also be called A-B while his sister is known by A only. The man and his sister are both A but

[5] Sometime later on, during a football match in the Sawos village of Nangusap, a dispute emerged among some players and the players were swearing at each other using vulgar languages such as 'eating your mother's vagina' and so forth. Kemen was offended with that abusive language and he said that these young men were really abusing the name 'vagina'. He said all of us come out of the vulva and the vulva is owned as a totem of his moiety, 'mother/earth people' (see also Bateson 1958: 241), while the penis is owned by the opposing totemic moiety, 'father/sun people'.

only the man is A-B. Iatmul men and women have separate names despite the fact that they are of the same PDG. Matrinames designate the clans (or groups) that a mother comes from. Whereas matrinames identify males who are agnatically related amongst the Iqwaye, matrinames differentiate both males and females who are of the same descent group or lineage amongst the Iatmul. Iqwaye names are also bestowed following birth order and there are two birth orders, one male and the other female. To reflect birth order amongst siblings, Iqwaye names have suffixes which are based on their fingers.[6]

In both societies then, names reflect the substantial parts of the 'corporeal person'. Excluding the females in Iqwaye, the matrinames in both bear a strong relationship with one's mother's group, and they recall and make references particularly to one's bodily exteriority of flesh, blood, and nourishment. The moment of death in both societies reveals perhaps a metaphysical aspect of their names. In the Iqwaye situation, it is believed that the deceased is reabsorbed into the body of his own mother as well as the earth, which is the body of the primal man Omalyce. The body of a woman is absorbed in her children. The bones of the deceased are later taken and buried in the soil in the land which is owned by the PDG of the deceased. With the Iatmul, however, at death the matriname returns to the deceased's mother's clan where it belongs. The deceased is said to dwell in the place of the dead by his or her matriname, whereas the patriname is reincorporated and used again for children of the clan or lineage, implying a process of perpetual reincarnation. Death amongst the Iqwaye has the effect of consuming or reabsorbing a man into the earth, which is part of the transcendental cosmos and body of the primal man. At death, the Iatmul bury the body of the deceased in his or her clan mound (wives are buried in their husband's clan mound). Days or weeks later after the burial, the spirit (*undumbu*) of the deceased is incorporated in an effigy erected on raft-platform, which is then sent out on the Sepik River by both maternal and paternal relatives of the deceased after the mourning period is over. The

[6] The suffixes of Iatmul names reveal not birth order but gender. The two birth-order series amongst the Iqwaye is based on the sex of the siblings. 'Thus, female names are say, "A-the thumb" (i.e., first born), "A-the index finger" (second born), "A-the middle finger" (third born), and so on. Male names "A-B-the thumb" (first born), "A-B-the index finger" (the second born), etc.' (Mimica 1991b: 84). In a situation such as this, a first-born male child will also have the same name as his sister, the second born, who will also be called 'A-the thumb', but the elder brother will also be known as 'A-B-the thumb' supposing that their mother comes from the PDG B. Iatmul, however, do not bestow names with respect to the birth order of their children.

spirit of the deceased then travels down the Sepik to the world of the dead (see also Bateson 1958: 47–8; Wassmann 1991: 91). Whereas the earth (and the heavens) is the body of the primal man Omalyce, for the Iatmul, the primal man is not earth but water (see Wassmann 1991: 91), as it was out of water that everything was first created, and so it is to water that one should return after death.

Iatmul names in Bumbu settlement

In light of the analytical concepts of necessity and contingency, as well as immanence and transcendence, that have been highlighted so far, I would like close this chapter with a story about how Iatmul names are used in everyday life to connect people who live in remotely distant places. During a sojourn in Lae in July 2001, I met a young man of Parimbe village named Joram Nambalimbange, who was working towards a degree in Development Studies at the university there. Joram was born of Iatmul parents; his father Andrew worked as a primary school teacher in the Southern Highlands Province where Joram grew up. Then aged 25 years, Joram recalls that the last time he had been in his village on the Sepik River was when he was 8 years of age. Joram was in the seminar I gave to the first-year students about issues of name ownership amongst the Iatmul. Joram was happy when I showed pictures of his village and men's houses, and could vaguely remember his father talking about disputes over names in their village some years back. After the lecture Joram met me and drew my attention to a death that has taken the life of a woman from his Parimbe village, and who had been living in the Bumbu squatter settlement. Since he was heading to the 'house-cry' (mourning place), I followed him in order to have a sense of the kind of life some of these Iatmul people lead in the fringes of a city away from their village.

When we arrived in the settlement, the people who knew Joram greeted him but enquired of me by asking '*Anda ngepma nien?*' to which Joram replied '*Ngepma nien*', which basically translates as 'What place man?' and 'Place man' respectively. They were curious about the place-name of my origin but Joram proudly replied I came from his place too. This startled many of his village people in the settlement into thinking about whose son I was or which clan I belonged to. One particular woman at whose house we stopped by on our way to the 'house-cry' was a classificatory mother of Joram. She took us in briefly when we exchanged with her some areca nuts for her lime, with which we chewed our areca nuts. Joram introduced me to his mother as a man from Kanganamun village. At that point, that woman was curious about whose son I was. When I mentioned the name of my adopted father, Yarme Mambingawi, she told Joram that I was an elder brother to her and that Joram could call me his *wau* (mother's brother). Because she knew who Yarme was, she said to me, 'Oh your mother, Marimbunjin [Yarme's wife] would be a sister to Joram, and therefore you could call Joram your *wau*.' At this, Joram broke out with laughter and then observed that we started out at the university, where we first met as simply '*ngepma nien*' (man of the same place), and we have now ended up being uncle (*wau*) and nephew (*laua*) to each other. It was the names of my adopted parents that drew us into the relationships that we did not previously realize that we already embodied.

Leaving Joram's mother behind, we made our way to the 'house-cry'. On arriving there, we found a handful of women and their children. It was early in the afternoon, and many others had yet to come. We sat on a platform under a temporary shelter erected with a canvas suspended on poles. After preliminary introductions, the eldest daughter of deceased came out of her house and discussed with Joram the details of the funeral arrangements. When the discussion finally shifted to me, the ladies appreciated my visit to them and told me that I must have been really enjoying my time on the Sepik River with sago, fish, and mosquitoes. Then one of the older ladies among them, who learnt that I was an adopted son of Yarme Mambingawi, figured that Yarme's own sister, Ndambiandawa, was living close by and so the lady went and informed my aunt (*iau*). Ndambiandawa was old and wan and was under the impression that I was one of Yarme's real sons. She came out of her house and as she approached me she started calling out my adopted father's name and other totemic clan names. She also cried for joy at seeing one her elder brother's sons.[7] Although I embraced her while she was crying, inside me I felt embarrassed for I was not really one of Yarme's sons. When Ndambiandawa finished crying, she asked about her elder brother and his children, in response to which I gave a brief report of their stay in Kanganamun. I then found a chance to squeeze in an explanation about myself as an anthropologist who has been adopted by her brother. She took in quietly what I told her. She then enquired which name my adopted father had given me. When I told her that I was given the name Walindanmeli, she was even happier because it was the most senior name of her clan and she thought it appropriate that

[7] Such an encounter could also provoke a *naven* ceremonial.

her brother has bestowed that name on me. Then she asked me about whether or not I had undergone men's initiation, to which I replied positively and she immediately asked me to remove my shirt so that she could see the scars. She was greatly impressed with what she saw and said, 'You are already one of us.'

I have recited this account in order to portray what I think are the most defining existential qualities of Iatmul names. Despite the spatial distance between Bumbu and Kanganamun village, despite the length of time that has separated Ndambiandawa from Yarme, the name Yarme was powerful enough to cause Joram's mother and Ndambiandawa to mentally see their relatives in that name. The names contain a kind of relational capacity that allows and causes people to establish connections between relatives of a kind. The example shows that Iatmul names mobilize identities and sentiments of affection based on relationships which are oriented by kinship. Iatmul names are always embodied by people and other aspects of their socio-cosmic universe, and these are kept in the memories of Iatmul clan leaders and knowledgeable women. These names are transcendental in the sense that they do not die. They are embodied in people's minds and borne by people as personal names whose use and appropriation anticipates the conduct of relationships between people in this immanent world of human sociality. Moreover, since Iatmul names are bound up with a notion of temporal continuity that is premised upon the ontology of brotherhood, and since the names epitomize the Iatmul version of 'fractal personhood', who is a but a 'unit with relationship integrally implied', I have thought it important to ponder the ontological status of such a notion of relationships.

Conclusion

Towards an Ontological Understanding of Relationships

What [Western anthropologists] are predisposed to call . . . 'social relationships' is for Papuans the very ground of being: it is not a distinct property of man, but rather, man's greatest resource.

(Wagner 1977: 397)

An experiential dimension invests conceptual categories with ontological status: to that extent they do not need thinking about; they are acted upon.

(Strathern 1988: 27)

We have seen how ownership manifests itself as an enveloping reality of Iatmul social life and experience. The language of personifying idioms has been used as a heuristic device to portray ownership—*nyait*—as a 'person' whose house is built upon relationships. The discussion in Chapter 2, which dwelt on the two distinct architectural forms: the men's (*ngeko*) and the residential houses (*ngeio*) not only portrayed these houses as 'spheres of interaction' but also as 'spheres of ownership'. There we saw how 'ownership' appears to have an individual and collective dimension, a dimension that is continuous with the nature of relationships in which an Iatmul person finds him/herself enmeshed. Ownership has been described mainly in terms of use-rights and the control over these use-rights, for instance, in the use and borrowing of canoes, personal possessions, tools, clan names, and the management of the men's house. The contrast between the two men's houses, based on totemic affiliation, has consequences which are bound up with access or the denial of access to resources such as forested areas and fishing lagoons. History plays a critically pivotal role in constituting ownership as an organizing institution of relationships between people with respect to the kinds of things they own. When the men of Wolimbi *ngeko* denied the clans of Minjimbit/Kosimbi *ngeko* access to the Takasep lagoon, they did so not only because the lagoon is located in their area of the village territory, but also because of the fact that it was their relatives who dug the trench to create the lagoon. The clans of Minjimbit/Kosimbi *haus boi* were using the same historical account to try to get access to the lagoon, but were denied it. In its collective face, ownership appears to be fraught with the perpetual tensions and differences that are so characteristic of Iatmul totemic affiliation. In its individual face, ownership becomes a matter of negotiation and there is a lot of borrowing and shared use of things between individuals who are related as kin or through other social connections. For instance, although a hair comb is owned by a particular girl and kept in her house, others of her family members use it frequently and friends may borrow it from her from time to time.

In both instances of its collective and individual life, through appropriating history, ownership momentarily gathers things to itself and, in controlling access and their use, it effects a particular kind of identity on the owner(s) (Strathern 1996). I would argue that this penchant to discriminate and divide people between those who own a thing and those who do not own that thing is the most significant behaviour of ownership. This discriminating behaviour stems from the fact that ownership is predicated upon relationships between people, and therefore its discriminating behaviour confers on ownership a moral and 'legal' character. Its moral and 'legal' quality privileges the owner with the liberty to enjoy and exercise dispositional control but, at the same time, ownership may render an owner susceptible to the liabilities and responsibilities that are necessarily connected to that which is owned. We have seen that although the Wolimbi *ngeko* is owned as part of Papua New Guinea's national cultural heritage, its use and maintenance, and the concomitant responsibilities that go along with it, rests with the clans of Wolimbi. The clans of Wolimbi have daily access to and use of the *ngeko*, and monies which are earned from tourists' visits go to the clans which make up the *ngeko*. At the same time, when the *ngeko* needs to be maintained, it is those clans which assume the responsibility of maintaining it. As far as the heritage legislation of PNG goes, there are also other heirlooms owned by the Iatmul which cannot be sold and exported overseas. In Chapter 2, we saw how the hour-glass drum, Kwarum, owned by the Nawa clan in Kanganamun, is entangled in complex web of ownership claims. While it is owned by the Nawa clan members, the government of PNG regulates the movement of artefacts such as this in the national interest through the heritage legislation, and therefore prevented it leaving the country. However, some Nawa members in need of money sold the drum to an international art dealer, a transaction deemed illegal by virtue of PNG's heritage legislation. Although the tussle of ownership over this drum has not yet been resolved, the example shows how ownership of these particular types of artefacts extends beyond the local social context of clan membership into national and international arenas by virtue of the heritage legislation.

The observations mentioned above stem from the discussions that centre around the men's and residential houses, as well as the two types of men's houses associated with the two totemic moieties in Kanganamun village. What needs to be said now concerns the ownership of ritual action and totemic names. I argue that the claim of owning ritual action, as compared to ownership of ritual prerogatives (Harrison 1992), derives its legitimacy from the fact that all the men are related to each other by virtue of their initiation. The mock display of the initiation ritual is an enactment of what makes initiated men of Kanganamun related to each other (cf. Houseman and Severi 1998). All the initiated men in an Iatmul village are members of the body of the primal crocodile. As discussed in Chapter 3, it is in initiation rituals that this crocodile becomes visible in the form of leading and opposing ritual moieties. The leading moiety is the 'head' and the opposing moiety is the 'tail' of this primal crocodile, the initiates being the children of this crocodile. When the 'ownership' claim to the ritual action was made, it took its persuasive force from the fact that the claimants are already initiated. A historically prior set of relationships legitimizes the present claim. A subtle aspect of this claim of ownership is its implicit reference to relationships and time which are the *vital soul* to any claim of ownership. With this in mind, let us now consider how relationships and time appear in the context of name ownership.

In the dispute over the name Tanginwuli, I described how Iatmul make claims of ownership by asserting themselves through the use of the first-person pronoun, for instance, when Saungombi asserted his claim that 'I am Tanginwuli'. I think that this Iatmul proclivity to assert their claim of 'ownership' through the use of the first-person pronoun couched in the language of the present tense reveals how time is *necessarily* involved in the intrinsic constitution of ownership (cf. Honoré 1961: 120). If that is true of ownership, the claim to owning an Iatmul name renders ownership as a concern about the future through the past. Wassmann (1990: 32) succinctly observes that such an Iatmul claimant finds himself being simultaneously in the past as well as in the present.

The name Tanginwuli is totemic in origin and, while it is associated with a mythical sphere of transcendence, ownership acts as a gravitational force which brings together or synthesizes mythical transcendence with the immanent world of human sociality. The Iatmul use of the present tense reveals two things: one is that, through the totemic relationship, it unifies a collectivity of clan ancestors and living members as being *one* and the same; and, second, it shows clearly that ownership is *always* a claim in the present-now. Ownership gathers not only persons and things and brings them into a sense of 'oneness' but it also synthesizes temporal 'moments', such as the past, present, and the future, into the existential concerns of 'now' in order to effect the kinds of identities that it carries for owners. I want to suggest that this behaviour of ownership in bringing things together or synthesizing temporal moments is akin to the synthetic behaviour of relationships. That is, in the same way that ownership synthesizes temporal moments and presents itself as a concern in the now, relationships can produce Iatmul people such as Saungombi—who presented himself as Tanginwuli, who is both a man described in myths and a man who belongs to Wanigo clan as does Saungombi himself.

Having suggested that the synthetic behaviour of ownership is akin to the synthetic behaviour of relationships, what remains, finally, is to enquire into the characteristics of relationships themselves. I have described vignettes which show how Iatmul names contain relationships. I have also argued that, due to the distribution of the same totemic system throughout the region, the Iatmul region can be best seen as an ensemble of names and beneath this is an intersecting network of relationships. Seen from such a perspective, I have argued that names contain relationships and the Iatmul have rights of ownership in such relationships. Thus we have now gone back to where we started: relationships are presumed and then become the object of anthropological analysis. But the critical question that Weiner posed is about the essence of relationships, much as Heidegger's question is about the essence of Being (Heidegger 1962). Since it was Weiner who imported this question into anthropology, I provide a commentary on his recent approach to a Heideggerian anthropology (Weiner 2001).

Weiner uses the term *irisae medobora* which is a kind of veiled speech (A. Strathern 1975) that the Foi call 'tree leaf talk', a manner of talking among the Foi that is loaded with metaphorical allusions. This kind of talk is used by men of high status who are skilled in the art of dreaming and magic. Dreams are revealed to men in solitary places, such as next to whirlpools along a river or beside trees that attract birds in the forest. Following appropriate ritual observations, ghosts appear to men and reveal secret names and other metaphors that men then use in magic. The German parallel to this Foi term is *Holzwege*, which means a firebreak or a path that is cut in the forest to stop the spread of fires. Weiner uses these techniques of concealment and revelation and the image of a firebreak to criticize the theory and method of social constructionism. Here I want to draw the attention of the reader to the manner in which Weiner describes Foi naming practices and the manner in which he discusses Melanesian ontology.

The Foi spatial world is envisioned through a system of place and personal names which serve not only as mnemonics of productive social history but also of how these names imbue the landscape with purpose and meaning. His general argument is that place 'emerges as a by-product of their focus on certain activities such as food getting, which demand movement and activity over and through a terrain' (Weiner 2001: 15). Weiner observes that the 'bestowing of place names constitutes Foi existential space out of a blank environment' (2001: 16). Such an observation might give the impression that the Foi territory is a kind of palimpsest that is subject to a constant process of inscription, and such an impression carries the risk of constructionism that Weiner criticizes. However, Weiner explains that it is through naming that place comes into being. These names are historically contingent in the sense that they are created out of people's activities carried out in their territorial landscape. The names have metaphoric qualities which may either reveal or conceal people's thought and the consequences of their actions.

Concealment and revelation also appear in the context of men showing their sons tracts of land, sago stumps, or bamboo stands while they are out hunting in the forest. Weiner compares this Foi notion of 'showing' (*mitina*) with Heidegger's rendition of the Greek concept of *aletheia* which means to 'unconceal'. This unconcealing of land between men is done furtively and sometimes reluctantly. The showing reveals something that has been previously hidden. Weiner (2001: 25) then inserts a gender dimension into his interpretation and observes that while men:

> . . . reveal hidden places . . . women . . . in poetry, reveal hidden names and bring these hidden names in relation to hidden places. And this nexus is only made possible through death. Women's poetic creations thus constitute in Heidegger's terms an authentic use of names and naming, because they situate the 'fundamental project' of death as the condition of placedness; men, by keeping the productive and inscriptive relations hidden, deny the existential fact that it is through death that places 'move' from person to person through time, just as it is through life that persons move from place to place.

The relations between men become an unending process of concealment and revelation, while in their use of poetry women 'reveal language's ontological status: they reveal the nexus of space and time that is encapsulated in personal and place-names and restore the movement of life activity to language and names' (2001: 27). To further illuminate this, Weiner invokes a Heideggerian distinction between speaking and saying which characterizes language. 'Speaking employs the power of language to represent things "as if" they were factical, "ontic", "in-themselves" . . . Saying on the other hand, is the domain of poetic language in its most comprehensive sense: it is any discourse that reveals the ontological dimensions of the world . . .'. Given that it is women who create poetic songs while men appropriate these songs, Weiner is courting the problem of ontological difference which Heidegger disavows (see also Howarth 2004: 241). Heidegger's notion of ontological difference is a methodological distinction between 'ontical' and 'ontological' investigations of phenomena. The ontical refers to the investigations undertaken by empirical sciences while the ontological is specifically a philosophical or a metaphysical enquiry. In aligning the ontological with the poetic and the ontical with the representational power of words, Weiner is inadvertently using gender as a device of asserting ontological difference. It therefore appears that gender among the Foi constitutes separate ontological worlds for men and women.

The problem of ontological difference appears in the manner in which Foi comport themselves towards death, and in the temporal dynamics of rest and motion. Men are associated with rest and stillness while women are connected with motion and movement. For instance, men would abstain from sexual intercourse and confine themselves to solitary places in the bush where they are able to dream and receive secret names from ghosts that are used in magic. Women on the other hand are not solitary; they associate with other women and, while they are working together such as in sago production, they compose poetic songs. These songs reveal the hidden names of deceased kinsmen or spouses and are later appropriated by men who sing them publicly in their longhouse. In procreative idioms, men are thought to halt or block the flow of menstrual blood with their semen while women's secretions are 'debilitating to men—nevertheless [women] are the true sources of life-sustaining motion' (Weiner 2001: 45). A central argument of the chapter is the suggestion 'that men and women in Foi have different ontological relations to death' (2001: 34). Weiner cautions that his description of the 'social and sexual categorization is not essential, determinate or structural, but rather interpretative, or analogical, encompassing simultaneously both a "model of" and "model for" the roles that the Foi see' (2001: 46). Yet he asserts that the discursive 'contrast is as *much a comment upon* or *interpretation* of as it is a *normative summation of* behavioural tendencies . . . [The Foi] *embody the contrast in the way discourse is situated with respect to the other temporal processes of the lifeworld*' (2001: 46, 48; original emphasis).

Such a hermeneutic position is nested in a conceptual framework of contingency and historicity that treats meaning and interpretation as an open-ended matter. To embody a discursive contrast is to live that contrast in discourse. This may serve to exemplify what Weiner means by the ontological status of language. Elsewhere, Heidegger describes language as the 'house of being' (see also Mimica 1993: 92), yet however apt this architectural imagery of language may be, the critical question is on what *ground* is such a house built (cf. Ingold 1995: 57–80)? I would insist that if ontology is an excavation of epistemological schemes, then a Heideggerian anthropology might want to excavate the ground on which language, as the house of Being, has its foundations. We shall return to the issue of 'ground' below. Now let us consider the manner in which Weiner outlined the discursive modalities in which the Foi comport themselves towards death. Weiner made it seem as though the discursive field and death are inseparable, but I believe it is appropriate to keep them separate. For me at least, the discursive is located in a domain of contingency which is variable and particular, while death is located in the province of metaphysical necessity; it is a necessary given. By this I mean that, despite all the uncertainties associated with the nature of death, one thing that humans can be assured of is the unavoidable certainty of the physical death that awaits us. Therefore, to conflate the analysis of discourses about death with death itself is to conceal and misplace the ontological gravity of death.

As we know from Heidegger, the inevitability of death is central to his hermeneutical conception of Being and, at the conceptual level, death serves as a function of individuation and totalization whereby the project of being human is liquidated and reconciled in the abyss of nothingness. However, while death is an ontological orientation towards finality as Heidegger (1962) contends, death seems to be serving a different kind of project among the Foi. And, as Weiner describes with admirable eloquence, the Foi discourse on death summons 'ontological relations' that carry a gendered inflection of the kind that is missing in Heidegger's conceptualization. In light of such an understanding of death, one wonders if Foi men and women are ontologically different? I say this in light of the Iatmul notion of *nyamun shambu*, which I have used to explicate an ontology of brotherhood. If life is the elder brother and death is the younger brother then it follows that, irrespective of life or death, we find an ontological process that is oriented towards becoming the other brother, much like Mimica's (1993: 88) notion of being-towards-the-beginning. As we have seen in the Iatmul case, it is in separation that the ontological process of the being-towards-the-beginning is brought forth. Let us now return to the issue concerning the 'ground of being'.

Weiner holds that it is the nature of human Being to conceal its own 'ground' of being. While Heidegger thinks of Earth as the ground of human existence (Weiner 2001: 163), Weiner discusses the notion of 'ground' both in the Leibnizian sense of cause and principle as well as the literal earth itself. Weiner carries through the Heideggerian notion of the Earth as the ground of being and argues that Papua New Guinean sociality cannot be alienated from the Earth because it is fundamentally the ground of their being as well 'as a spatial record of human life-span, a track consisting of a linked series of inhabited spaces' (2001: 166). This ground is often concealed and revealed momentarily through furtive encounters, such as when a father shows his son a plot of land to cultivate or a sago stand to harvest. Weiner appears to be inconsistent in what he credits as the 'ground of being' in Melanesia. For instance, at one stage he observes that the way in which pearl shells are displayed reveals a *mode of being* where 'people like the Melpa and the Foi affirm to themselves *relationship* as the ground upon which human action proceeds' (2001: 75, my emphasis). But at the end of his book we encounter the Earth as the ground of being. Initially we see Weiner describing the Foi spatial world as a blank environmental *tabula rasa* which is imbued with the human inscription of meaning and intentionality. While we see Foi people going about their hunting, gardening, dreaming, singing, etc., we do not see clearly how the Earth emerges with a causally generative capacity. Perhaps we require a rigorous demonstration of how one could ontologize the Earth as the ground of being: 'the non-historical, spontaneous, self-generating aspect of things against which the humanly-made World stood as figure, but which it did not precede ontologically' (2001: 163). Finally, Weiner finds Strathern's *Gender of the Gift* reveals contrastive modes of being. Despite its productionist bias, which Weiner criticizes implicitly, I find Strathern's conceptualization of 'relations' has a particular causally generative capacity so that 'relations' appears as a second-order trope, internally endowed with its own contours of figure–ground (Strathern 1988: 172–3, 2000: 24–5). This is also exemplified in the Iatmul notion of paired brothers. While Weiner raises important ontological questions about the relational premises of anthropology, his ontologization of the Earth as the fundament of being stems from a particular Heideggerian view of language that appears to misplace the ontological status of relations. This is the juncture at which I turn to the manner in which Strathern (2001b, 2005) has conceptualized the category of relationships as it is used amongst anthropologists.

In this vein it is worthwhile to quote at length the manner in which Strathern (2001b: 24–25) has defined the category of 'relation'.

> The notion of relation can be applied to any order of connection; this is its first property. Hence one can, seemingly, make connections anywhere. For in describing phenomena, the fact of relation instantiates connections in such a way as also to produce instances of itself. At whatever level or order, the demonstration of a relationship, whether through resemblance, cause and effect or contiguity, reinforces the understanding that through relational practices—classification, analysis, comparison—relations can be demonstrated. We could call the relation a self-similar or self-organising construct, a figure whose organisational power is not affected by scale.
>
> [Second], the relation . . . requires other elements to complete it—relations between what? This makes its connecting functions complex, for the relation always summons entities other than itself, whether the appearance is that these entities are pre-existing (the relation is 'between' them), or whether they are obviously brought into existence by the relationship (and thus 'within' it). One does not only see relations between things but things as relations. Yet insofar as 'things' (the terms bound by or containing the relation) are routinely conceptualised apart from the relation, we can call the relation an organising trope with the second order capacity to organise either the similar or dissimilar.

The theoretical thrust of Strathern's definition of the category of relationships is epistemological rather than ontological. In the vignettes I have provided of Sepik names in the Bumbu settlement in Lae, I described how names are able to draw people into establishing connections and relationships. When one name was mentioned, its mention provoked other names to be called as well. That is to say that one relationship brings into view other relationships. Strathern's notion of the second-order power of relationship can be explained in the following way. Supposing we spell out the category of 'relation' as 'R-E-L-A-T-I-O-N', then what we have is a collection of an arbitrary set of symbols (letters). None of these letters is able to convey any kind of meaning on its own individual accord. It is the power of relationships that lies at the back of these arbitrary symbols and brings these symbols together and bestows on them a semiotic sensibility.

In view of the fact that not only is ownership rooted in time and that Iatmul names contain relationships, but also that Iatmul names are totemic in origin, I have thought it necessary to compare the Iatmul system of names with those of the Daribi and the Iqwaye. In making this comparison, I have utilized the philosophical concepts of necessity and contingency, as well as transcendence and immanence, to give relationships an ontological character. Given the fact that Iatmul names are abundant in supply, as opposed to their Manambu (Harrison 1990a) neighbours, who have a finite supply of comparable names, I have thought it important to ponder analytically the question of the connection between 'relationships' and 'infinity', and that was the reason why I thought it analytically necessary to make a comparison between the Iqwaye and the Iatmul system of names.

Mimica (1988) provides a fascinating account of the 'intimation of infinity' in a PNG society based on the counting and number system of the Iqwaye. The Iqwaye system of counting is a totalizing process, based on the relationships between part and whole. The ultimate one is Omalyce, the cosmological hero, who embodies all number. But what is the point of citing this study by Mimica here? On analytical grounds, Mimica focuses on the category of number to articulate how the Iqwaye intimate infinity, whereas I am raising a question and seeking an analysis of infinity through the category of relation. While Mimica focuses on the counting system of the Iqwaye, I pursue this problematic through the ownership of personal names of the Iatmul. Ethnographically, the Iatmul do not count in the same vein as the Iqwaye, nor do the Iatmul have a single cosmological hero comparable to Iqwaye's Omalyce, nor do the Iqwaye have a system of names comparable to that of the Iatmul. But just as Omalyce is a name of the main cosmological hero of the Iqwaye, so the Iatmul system of names is based on the totemic activities of named cosmological heroes and totems, which are namesakes of all the past, present, and future Iatmul people.

The analytical vocabulary employed by Mimica is derived from phenomenological philosophy, and he presents the Iqwaye intimations of infinity in the totalizing language of part and whole relationships. The Iatmul intellectual cosmos is not conceptualized in terms of part–whole relationships but through the dynamics of paired relationships modelled on the two brothers. Mimica's account of the Iqwaye counting system dealt with several sorts of ontological contrasts, such as the abstract and concrete, part and whole, quantity and quality, immanence and transcendence, and finite and infinite. He showed how all these contrasts are mediated through the body. Analytically, Iatmul names work in a similar way to Iqwaye numbers. That is, in Iqwaye, human beings are numbers whereas in Iatmul human beings are names, embodying not number but relationships. Through the relationships they contain, names have a capacity to elicit the sense of oneness that underlies their totemic system. Whereas every Iqwaye number recursively returns to one, the sense of the one in Iatmul names is rooted in totemic cosmology. Because totemic clans are like the 'sprouts of a sago stump', ownership is the moment that reveals their common root of origin—ownership is the father of all that is one among the Iatmul.

The comparison between the Daribi and Iatmul system of names provided us with the ontological contrast between contingency and necessity. I have shown that the Daribi system of personal names is predicated on an array of contingencies which provide the context for Daribi to give names to their children and adults. The Iatmul, however, already have a system of personal names which they use in naming their children. Iatmul names contain relationships and these are names derived from a realm of transcendence which is embodied in immanent human sociality through the institution of ownership. Seen in this light, the question is: 'What constitutes an ontological theory of relationships?'

I argue that, despite her exhaustive and sophisticated understanding of Melanesian forms of relationality, Strathern much like her American colleague, Wagner, represents how anthropology has interested itself exclusively in an epistemological view of relationships. I am suggesting that the properties of relationships as delineated by Strathern be redefined in ontological terms, and this requires thinking in terms of the concepts of necessity and contingency and immanence and transcendence. Contra Strathern, I argue that what distinguishes 'relationships' ontologically from the epistemological forms of relational practices—such as connection, association, resemblance, comparison, etc.—is necessity and transcendence, which give 'relationships' the character of an infinite being. How has that been shown in Iatmul ethnography outlined in this book? The answer lies in the ontology of brotherhood. I have shown that the Iatmul person embodies a pair of brothers and is ontologically endowed with an internal relation that orients the process of one forever becoming the other brother. The other brother is not only an external other brother in a relational sense but also the self-same brother whose internal configurations resonate with the relation as a self-similar construct.

If an Iatmul person embodies a pair of brothers which are life and death, in whatever form of existence he (or she) assumes, the other brother (relation) is always implicit as ground is to a figure. In the *naven* pantomime that I have discussed briefly, we see how women such as a father's sister (*iau*), in ritually reversing the conventional ethos of how a woman behaves, not only represents her brother but also herself, that is, she is also the other brother. In the *bandi* ritual, we have seen how the colour symbolism of totemic moieties (pair of brothers) function as the ground on which ritual moieties (pair of brothers) figure in ritual action. The male initiate embodies simultaneously the contrasting modes of death (younger brother) and life (elder brother) when he undergoes initiation. The symbolic dimension of these rituals is an external mask of contingency that conceals an internal necessity that is oriented towards becoming the other brother. In short, the Iatmul ontology of brotherhood shows that a person is a brother to him/herself as well as to others who are internally related as members of a clan (*yaranga ndu*). The onto-logic of brotherhood appears in the system of names in which every pair in a list of names is considered as a pair of brothers, and the same applies to the kinship and marriage practices which I have explained above. Iatmul names are always already there as a matter of necessity and are not created in any way out of contingency as are Daribi names. In their transcendence, Iatmul *names are thicker than blood.* In their ownership, they pull together both transcendence and immanence, yet ownership is necessarily rooted in time and is predicated on relationships between persons. To extend Strathern's definition of 'relationships' in ontological terms is to say that relationships have the capacity to be their own figure and ground, in a manner reminiscent of the Iatmul ontology of brotherhood.

Appendix

Below are names of all the posts in Wolimbi *ngeko* in Kanganamun village owned by individual clans most of which are members of the *nyowi nimba* totemic moiety. Posts 1–5 are the king posts around which are assembled clan associations. Posts 6–16 and 41–52 are owned by clans which make up the *ndama ngeko* (front part) while posts 17–40 are owned by clans of the *ngumbu ngeko* (back part) of Wolimbi.

	Name	*Type of post*	*Clan*	*Clan association*
1.	Kanawimeli	King	Yabu	Walgem
2.	Maimndimi	King	Graken	Walgem
3.	Tuatmeli	King	Sui	Sui
4.	Sigasaku	King	Samiangwat	Nawa Masam
5.	Wobasui	King	Nawa Masam	Nawa Masam
6.	Tambiam	Poro	Mbei	Walgem
7.	Katjiki	Nana	Yabu	Walgem
8.	Yabuindjanmange	Poro	Yabu	Walgem
9.	Nyandimange	Poro	Yabu	Walgem
10.	Kolichanmange	Poro	Kembiam	Walgem
11.	Kambrimbau	Poro	Yabu	Walgem
12.	Mongrubandu	Nana	Kembiam	Walgem
13.	Biakut	Poro	Yabu	Walgem
14.	Ngambinjiki	Poro	Graken	Walgem
15.	Kouloumei	Nana	Graken	Walgem
16.	Tukopwi	Poro	Graken	Walgem
17.	Mambinjawa	Poro	Simal	Sui
18.	Mendangwopoi	Nana	Simal	Sui
19.	Wileimange	Poro	Sui	Sui
20.	Sirimbo	Poro	Simal	Sui
21.	Mendungapimange	Poro	Nawa	Nawa Masam
22.	Tchangunmbanjoi	Nana	Nawa	Nawa Masam
23.	Kundungapimange	Poro	Suaru	Nawa Masam
24.	Yumbunusmange	Poro	Suaru	Nawa Masam
25.	Angwabangrarakwa	Poro	Miembei	Nawa Masam
26.	Masamtagwa	Nana	Masam	Nawa Masam
27.	Masakumban	Nana	Masam	Nawa Masam
28.	Lumbai	Poro	Masam	Nawa Masam
29.	Kusamanapa	Poro	Masam	Nawa Masam
30.	Nawakumban	Nana	Samiangwat	Nawa Masam
31.	Samiangwattagwa	Poro	Samiangwat	Nawa Masam

32.	Mariwanmange	Poro	Mbei	Nawa Masam
33.	Lisauagwui	Poro	Samiangwat	Nawa Masam
34.	Meimbo	Poro	Samiangwat	Nawa Masam
35.	Yenjanwuru	Poro	Samiangwat	Nawa Masam
36.	Wendinganambit	Poro	Samiangwat	Nawa Masam
37.	Kangaimange	Poro	Prindu-Aimosa	Sui
38.	Kolopmauwi	Poro	Prindu-Aimosa	Sui
39.	Machukibangi	Nana	Prindu	Sui
40.	Djapmasumbia	Poro	Sui	Sui
41.	Apangunumbut	Poro	Sui	Sui
42.	Laiknawan	Nana	Sui	Sui
43.	Mailalagwa	Poro	Sui	Sui
44.	Akilamban	Poro	Sui	Sui
45.	Wanigotagwa	Poro	Wanigo	Walgem
46.	Krambandu	Poro	Wanigo	Walgem
47.	Kaisindawa	Poro	Kembiam	Walgem
48.	Maringundawa	Poro	Kembiam	Walgem
49.	Miembeinjawa	Poro	Mbei	Walgem
50.	Tipwuimbau	Poro	Kembiam	Walgem
51.	Bangameli	Poro	Wanigo	Walgem
52.	Kembiamtagwa	Poro	Wanigo	Walgem

Bibliography

Allen, B. 1987. *Into the crocodile's nest: a journey inside New Guinea*. London: Macmillan.

Barlow, K. 1990. The dynamics of siblingship: nurturance and authority in Murik society. In N. Lutkehaus, C. Kaufmann, W.E. Mitchell, D. Newton, L. Osmundsen and M. Schuster (eds) *Sepik heritage: tradition and change in PNG*. Durham, NC: Carolina Academic Press.

Barlow, K. and D. Lipset. 1997. Dialogics of material culture: male and female in Murik outrigger canoes. *American Ethnologist* 24(1): 4–36.

Barber, J.R. and F.R. Berdan. 1998. *The emperor's mirror: understanding cultures through primary sources*. Tucson: University of Arizona Press.

Bashkow, I. 2000. Confusion, native skepticism, and recurring questions about the year 2000: 'soft' bellies and preparations for the millennium in the Arapesh region, Papua New Guinea. *Ethnohistory* 47(1): 133–69.

Bashkow, I. 2006. 'Pigs for dance songs': Reo Fortune's emphatic understanding of the Araphesh roads. In R. Darnell and F.W. Gleach (eds) *Histories of anthropology annual*, vol. 2. Lincoln and London: University of Nebraska Press.

Bateson, G. 1932. Social structure of the Iatmul people of the Sepik River. *Oceania* 2: 245–91, 401–53.

Bateson, G. 1935. Culture contact and schismogenesis. *Man* 35: 178–83.

Bateson, G. 1936. Music in New Guinea. *The Eagle* 48(214): 158–70.

Bateson, G. 1946. Arts of the South Seas. *The Arts Bulletin* 2: 119–23.

Bateson, G. 1958. *Naven: a survey of the problems suggested by a composite picture of the culture of a New Guinea tribe drawn from three points of view*, 2nd edn. Stanford, CA: Stanford University Press. (First published 1936.)

Battaglia, D. 1990. *Bones of the serpent: person, memory and mortality in Sabarl Island society*. Chicago: University of Chicago Press.

Battaglia, D. 1995 (ed.). *Rhetorics of self-making*. Los Angeles: University of California Press.

Bowden, R. 1983. *Yena: art and ceremony in a Sepik society*. Oxford: Pitt Rivers Museum.

Bowden, R. 1990. The architecture and art of Kwoma ceremonial houses. In N. Lutkehaus, C. Kaufmann, W.E. Mitchell, D. Newton, L. Osmundsen and M. Schuster (eds) *Sepik heritage: tradition and change in PNG*. Durham, NC: Carolina Academic Press.

Busse, M. 2000. The National Cultural Property (Preservation) Act. In K. Whimp and M. Busse (eds) *Protection of intellectual, biological and cultural property in PNG*. Canberra: Asia Pacific Press.

Butler, J. 1993. *Bodies that matter: on the discursive limits of sex*. London: Routledge.

Carrithers, M., S. Collins and S. Lukes (eds). 1985. *The category of the person: anthropology, philosophy, history*. Cambridge: Cambridge University Press.

Carsten, J. and S. Hugh-Jones. 1995. Introduction. In J. Carsten and S. Hugh-Jones (eds) *About the house: Lévi-Strauss and beyond*. Cambridge: Cambridge University Press.

Christman, J. 1991. Self-ownership, equality, and the structure of property rights. *Political Theory* 19(1): 28–46.

Coiffier, C. 1990. Sepik River architecture: changes in cultural traditions. In N. Lutkehaus, C. Kaufmann, W.E. Mitchell, D. Newton, L. Osmundsen and M. Schuster (eds.) *Sepik heritage: tradition and change in PNG*. Durham, NC: Carolina Academic Press.

Dreyfus, H. 1997. *Being-in-the-world: a commentary on Heidegger's* Being and Time *Division I*. Cambridge, MA: MIT Press.

Duly, C. 1979. *The houses of mankind*. London: Thames and Hudson.

Eoe, S.M. 1990. The National Cultural Property (Preservation) Act and the art of Sepik. In N. Lutkehaus, C. Kaufmann, W.E. Mitchell, D. Newton, L. Osmundsen and M. Schuster (eds) *Sepik heritage: tradition and change in PNG*. Durham, NC: Carolina Academic Press.

Errington, F. and D. Gewertz. 1987. *Cultural alternatives and feminist anthropology: an analysis of culturally constructed gender interests in PNG*. Cambridge: Cambridge University Press.

Filer, C. 1997. Compensation, rent and power in PNG. In S. Toft (ed.) *Compensation and resource development*. Port Moresby: PNG Law Reform Commission and Canberra: Monograph 6/Canberra: Australian National University.

Forge, A. 1966. Art and environment in the Sepik. *Proceedings of the Royal Anthropological Institute of Great Britain and Ireland for 1965*, pp. 22–31.

Forge, A. 1971. Marriage and exchange in the Sepik: comments on Francis Korn's analysis of Iatmul society. In R. Needham (ed.) *Rethinking kinship and marriage*. London: Tavistock.

Gell, A. 1992. *Anthropology of time: cultural constructions of temporal maps and images*. Oxford: Berg.

Gell, A. 1998. *Art and agency: an anthropological theory*. Oxford: Oxford University Press.

Gell, A. 1999. *Art of anthropology: essays and diagrams*. London: Athlone Press.

Gellner, E. 1959. *Words and things: an examination of, and an attack on, linguistic philosophy*. London: Routledge and Kegan Paul.

Gellner, E. 1993. *Language and solitude: Wittgenstein, Malinowksi and the Habsburg dilemma*. Cambridge: Cambridge University Press.

Gewertz, D. 1983. *Sepik River societies: a historical ethnography of the Chambri and their neighbors*. New Haven, CT: Yale University Press.

Gewertz, D. and F. Errington. 1991. *Twisted histories, altered contexts: representing the Chambri in a world system*. Cambridge: Cambridge University Press.

Handelman, D. 1978. Is naven ludic? Paradox and communication of identity. *Social Analysis* 1: 177–91.

Hann, C. 1998. Introduction. In C.M. Hann (ed.) *Property relations: renewing the anthropological tradition*. Cambridge: Cambridge University Press.

Haraway, D. 1985. A manifesto for cyborgs: science, technology and socialist feminism in the 1980s. *Socialist Review* 80: 65–107.

Harrison, S. 1982. Yams and the symbolic representation of time in a Sepik River village. *Oceania* 53: 141–61.

Harrison, S. 1984. New Guinea Highlands social structure in a lowland totemic mythology. *Man* 19: 389–403.

Harrison, S. 1985. Names, ghosts and alliances in two Sepik River societies. *Oceania* 56: 138–46.

Harrison, S. 1989. Magical and material polities in Melanesia. *Man* 24: 1–20.

Harrison, S. 1990a. *Stealing people's names: history and politics in a Sepik River cosmology*. Cambridge: Cambridge University Press.

Harrison, S. 1990b. Concepts of the person in Aratip religious thought. In N. Lutkehaus, C. Kaufmann, W.E. Mitchell, D. Newton, L. Osmundsen and M. Schuster (eds) *Sepik heritage: tradition and change in PNG*. Durham, NC: Carolina Academic Press.

Harrison, S. 1992. Ritual as intellectual property. *Man* 27(2): 225–44.

Harrison, S. 1993. *The mask of war: violence, ritual and the self in Melanesia*. Manchester: Manchester University Press.

Harrison, S. 1995. Anthropological perspectives on the management of knowledge. *Anthropology Today* 11(5): 10–14.

Hauser-Schäublin, B. 1990. In the swamps and on the hills: traditional settlement patterns and house structures in the Middle Sepik. In N. Lutkehaus, C. Kaufmann, W.E. Mitchell, D. Newton, L. Osmundsen and M. Schuster (eds) *Sepik heritage: tradition and change in PNG*. Durham, NC: Carolina Academic Press.

Heidegger, M. 1962. *Being and Time*, trans. J. Macquarrie and E. Robinson. Oxford: Blackwell.

Herle, A and A. Moutu. 2004. *Paired brothers: revelation and concealment, Iatmul ritual art from the Sepik River, Papua New Guinea* (museum catalogue). Cambridge: Cambridge University Museum of Archaeology and Anthropology.

Hirschon, R. 1984. *Women and property, women as property*. London: Croom Helm.

Hoffman, P. 1993. Death, time, history: Division II of *Being and Time*. In C. Guignon (ed.) *The Cambridge companion to Heidegger*. Cambridge: Cambridge University Press.

Holbraad, M. 2002. Belief in necessity: Ifa divination and money in contemporary Havana. PhD Dissertation, Department of Social Anthropology, University of Cambridge.

Honoré, A.M. 1961. Ownership. In A.G. Guess (ed.) *Oxford essays in jurisprudence*. Oxford: Clarendon Press.

Houseman, M. 1998. Painful places: ritual encounters with one's homeland. *Journal of Royal Anthropological Institute* 4(3): 447–67.

Houseman, M. and C. Severi. 1998. *Naven or the other self: a relational approach to ritual action*. Leiden: Brill.

Howarth, D. 2004. Towards a Heideggerian social science: Heidegger, Kisiel and

Weiner on the limits of anthropological discourse. *Anthropological Theory* 4(2): 229–47.

Hugh-Jones, S. 1979. *The palm and the Pleiades: initiation and cosmology in northwest Amazonia.* Cambridge: Cambridge University Press.

Hugh-Jones, S. 1995. Inside out and back to front: the androgynous house in northwest Amazonia. In J. Carsten and S. Hugh-Jones (eds) *About the house: Lévi-Strauss and beyond.* Cambridge: Cambridge University Press.

Ingold, T. 1995. Building, dwelling, living: how animals and people make themselves in the world. In M. Strathern (ed.) *Shifting contexts: transformations in anthropological knowledge.* London and New York: Routledge.

Iteanu, A. 1998. Synchronisations among the Orokaiva. *Social Anthropology* 7: 265–78.

Jackson, A. 1986. *Anthropology at home.* London: Tavistock.

Kaberry, P. 1941. The Abelam tribe, Sepik District, New Guinea. *Oceania* 12: 331–63.

Kalinoe, L. 1999. *Water law and customary water rights in Papua New Guinea.* New Delhi: UBS Publishers' Distributors.

Kalinoe, L. 2001. The bases of ownership claims over natural resources by indigenous peoples in Papua New Guinea. In L. Kalinoe and J. Leach (eds) *Rationales of ownership.* New Delhi: UBS Publishers' Distributors.

Kirsch, S. 2006. *Reverse anthropology: indigenous analysis of social and environmental relations in Papua New Guinea.* Stanford, CA: Stanford University Press.

Korn, F. 1971. A question of preferences: the Iatmul case. In R. Needham (ed.) *Rethinking kinship and marriage.* London: Tavistock.

Kripke, S. 1980. *Naming and necessity.* Oxford: Blackwell.

Langer, M. 1989. *Merleau-Ponty's* Phenomenology of perception*: a guide and commentary.* London: Macmillan.

Laycock, D.C. 1965. *The Ndu language family (Sepik District, New Guinea).* Canberra: Australian National University.

Lea, D. 1997. *Melanesian land tenure in a contemporary and philosophical context.* Lanham, MD: University Press of America.

Leach, E. 1976. *Culture and communication: the logic by which symbols are connected.* Cambridge: Cambridge University Press.

Leach, J. 2001. Land, trees and history: disputes concerning boundaries and identities in the context of development. In L. Kalinoe and J. Leach (eds) *Rationales of ownership.* New Delhi: UBS Publisher's Distributors.

Leenhardt, M. 1979. *Do Kamo: myth and person in a Melanesian world,* trans. B.M. Gulati. Chicago: University of Chicago Press.

Lipset, D. 1982 [1980]. *Gregory Bateson: the legacy of a scientist.* Boston, MA: Beacon Press.

Lipset, D. 1990. Boar's tusk and flying foxes: symbolism and ritual of office in the Murik Lakes. In N. Lutkehaus, C. Kaufmann, W.E. Mitchell, D. Newton, L. Osmundsen and M. Schuster (eds) *Sepik heritage: tradition and change in PNG.* Durham, NC: Carolina Academic Press.

Lipset, D. 1997. *Mangrove man: dialogics of culture in the Sepik estuary*. Cambridge: Cambridge University Press.

MacCormack, C. and M. Strathern (eds). 1980. *Nature, culture, gender*. Cambridge: Cambridge University Press.

Mackenzie, M.A. 1991. *Androgynous objects: string bags and gender in Central New Guinea*. Chur: Harwood.

Mead, M. 1935. *Sex and temperament in three primitive societies*. London: George Routledge and Sons Ltd.

Merlan, F. and A. Rumsey. 1991. Ku Waru: *language and segmentary politics in the Western Nebilyer Valley*, Papua New Guinea. Cambridge: Cambridge University Press.

Merleau-Ponty, M. 1962. *Phenomenology of perception*, trans. C. Smith. London: Routledge and Kegan Paul.

Métraux, R. 1975. Eidos and change: continuity in process, discontinuity in product. *Ethos* 3(2): 293–308.

Métraux, R. 1978. Aristocracy and meritocracy: leadership among the Eastern Iatmul. *Anthropological Quarterly* 51(1): 46–58.

Mimica, J. 1988. *Intimations of infinity*. Oxford: Berg Publishers.

Mimica, J. 1991a, 1991b. The incest passions: an outline of the logic of Iqwaye social organisation. *Oceania* 62: 34–58, 81–113.

Mimica, J. 1993. The Foi and Heidegger. *Australian Journal of Anthropology* 4(2): 79–95.

Mimica, J. 2003. Out of the depths of saurian waters. *Anthropological Notebooks* 9(1): 5–46.

Morris, B. 1994. *Anthropology of the self*. London: Pluto Press.

Mosko, M. 1985. *Quadripartite structures: categories, relations and homologies in Bush Mekeo culture*. Cambridge: Cambridge University Press.

Moutu, A. 2003. Names are thicker than blood: concepts of ownership and person amongst the Iatmul. PhD dissertation, Department of Social Anthropology, University of Cambridge.

Munn, N. 1986. *Fame of Gawa: a symbolic study of value transformation in a Massim (Papua New Guinea) society*. Chicago: University of Chicago Press.

Narokobi, B. 1988. *Ownership*. Goroka: Melanesian Institute for Socio-economic and Pastoral Order.

Peirano, M.G.S. 1998. When anthropology is at home: the different contexts of a single discipline. *Annual Review of Anthropology* 27:105–28.

Reeve, A. 1986. *Property*. Basingstoke: Macmillan.

Rubel, P.G. and A. Rosman. 1978. *Your own pigs you may not eat: a comparative study of New Guinea societies*. Chicago: University of Chicago Press.

Ruff, W. 1981. *A compendium of drawings: settlement patterns, dwelling houses, ceremonial architecture of PNG*. Lae: PNG University of Technology and Port Moresby: National Cultural Council.

Ruff, W. and R. Ruff. 1990. The village studies project for the recording of traditional architecture. In N. Lutkehaus, C. Kaufmann, W.E. Mitchell, D. Newton,

L. Osmundsen and M. Schuster (eds) *Sepik heritage: tradition and change in PNG*. Durham, NC: Carolina Academic Press.

Rumsey, A. 2000. Agency, personhood and the 'I' of discourse in the Pacific and beyond. *Journal of the Royal Anthropological Institute* 6: 101–15.

Sahlins, M. 1976. *Culture and practical reason*. Chicago: University of Chicago Press.

Schindlebeck, M. 1990. Tradition and change in Kwanga villages. In N. Lutkehaus, C. Kaufmann, W.E. Mitchell, D. Newton, L. Osmundsen and M. Schuster (eds) *Sepik heritage: tradition and change in PNG*. Durham, NC: Carolina Academic Press.

Schmidt, J. 1990. Tourism in Yenjan village. In N. Lutkehaus, C. Kaufmann, W.E. Mitchell, D. Newton, L. Osmundsen and M. Schuster (eds) *Sepik heritage: tradition and change in PNG*. Durham, NC: Carolina Academic Press.

Schneider, D. 1984. *A critique of the study of kinship*. Ann Arbor: University of Michigan Press.

Schuster, G. 1990. Aibom genealogy as history. In N. Lukehaus, C. Kaufmann, W.E. Mitchell, D. Newton, L. Osmundsen and M. Schuster (eds) *Sepik heritage: tradition and change in PNG*. Durham, NC: Carolina Academic Press.

Schuster, M. 1990. Aspects of the Aibom concept of history. In N. Lutkehaus, C. Kaufmann, W.E. Mitchell, D. Newton, L. Osmundsen and M. Schuster (eds) *Sepik heritage: tradition and change in PNG*. Durham, NC: Carolina Academic Press.

Silverman, E. 1996. The gender of the cosmos: totemism, society and embodiment in the Sepik River. *Oceania* 67(1): 30–49.

Silverman, E. 2001. *Masculinity, motherhood and mockery: psychoanalyzing culture and the naven rite in New Guinea*. Ann Arbor: University of Michigan Press.

Stanek, M. 1990. Social structure of the Iatmul. In N. Lutkehaus, C. Kaufmann, W.E. Mitchell, D. Newton, L. Osmundsen and M. Schuster (eds) *Sepik heritage: tradition and change in PNG*. Durham, NC: Carolina Academic Press.

Strathern, A. 1972. *One father, one blood*. Canberra: Australian National University Press.

Strathern, A. 1975. Veiled speech in Mount Hagen. In M. Bloch (ed.) *Political language and oratory in traditional societies*. London: Academic Press Inc.

Strathern, A. 1996. *Body thoughts*. Ann Arbor: University of Michigan Press.

Strathern, M. 1984a. Subject or object? Women and the circulation of valuables in Highlands New Guinea. In R. Hirschon (ed.) *Women and property, women as property*. London: Croom Helm.

Strathern, M. 1984b. Marriage exchanges: a Melanesian comment. *Annual Review of Anthropology* 13: 41–73.

Strathern, M. 1988. *The gender of the gift: problems with women and problems with society*. Berkeley: University of California Press.

Strathern, M. 1991. *Partial connections*. Savage, MD: Rowman and Littlefield.

Strathern, M. 1996. Potential persons: intellectual rights and property in persons. *Social Anthropology* 4(1): 17–32.

Strathern, M. 1998. Divisions of interest and languages of ownership. In C.M. Hann (ed.) *Property relations: renewing the anthropological tradition*. Cambridge: Cambridge University Press.

Strathern, M. 1999. *Property, substance and effect: anthropological essays on persons and things*. London: Athlone Press.

Strathern, M. 2000. Environments within: an ethnographic commentary on scale. In K. Flint and H. Morphy (eds) *Culture, landscape and the environment: the Linacre lectures 1997*. Oxford: Oxford University Press.

Strathern, M. 2001a. The patent and the malanggan. *Theory, Culture & Society* 18(4): 1–26.

Strathern, M. 2001b. Emergent properties: Robert and Maurice Rothschild Distinguished Lecture, 18 April 2000, Department of the History of Science, Harvard University.

Strathern, M. 2005. *Kinship, Law and the unexpected: relatives are always a surprise*. Cambridge: Cambridge University Press.

Swadling, P., B. Hauser-Schäublin, P. Gorecki and F. Tiesler. 1988. *The Sepik-Ramu: an introduction*. Port Moresby: PNG National Museum and Art Gallery.

Swadling, P. 1990. Sepik prehistory. In N. Lutkehaus, C. Kaufmann, W.E. Mitchell, D. Newton, L. Osmundsen and M. Schuster (eds.) *Sepik heritage: tradition and change in PNG*. Durham, NC: Carolina Academic Press.

Taylor, C. 1989. *Senses of the self: the making of modern identity*. Cambridge, MA: Harvard University Press.

Telban, B. 1998. *Dancing through time: a Sepik cosmology*. Oxford: Oxford University Press.

Thomas, N. 1991. *Entangled objects*. Cambridge, MA: Harvard University Press.

Tresch, J. 1998. Heredity is an open system: Gregory Bateson as descendant and ancestor. *Anthropology Today* 14(6): 3–6.

Tuzin, D. 1980. *Voice of the Tambaran: truth and illusion in Ilahita Arapesh religion*. Berkeley: University of California Press.

Tuzin, D. 2001. *Social complexity in the making: a case study among the Arapesh of New Guinea*. London and New York: Routledge.

Tuzin, D. 1991. The cryptic brotherhood of big men and great men in Ilahita. In M. Godelier and M. Strathern (eds) *Big men and great men: personifications of power in Melanesia*. Cambridge: Cambridge University Press.

Wagner, R. 1972. *Habu: the innovation of meaning in Daribi religion*. Chicago: University of Chicago Press.

Wagner, R. 1975. *Invention of culture*. Englewood Cliffs, NJ: Prentice Hall.

Wagner, R. 1977. Scientific and indigenous Papuan conceptualizations of the innate: a semiotic critique of the ecological perspective. In T. Bayliss-Smith and R. Fechem (eds) *Subsistence and survival*. London: Academic Press.

Wagner, R. 1978. *Lethal speech: Daribi myth as symbolic obviation*. Ithaca, NY: Cornell University Press.

Wagner, R. 1986. *Symbols that stand for themselves*. Chicago: University of Chicago Press.

Wagner, R. 1987. Daribi and Barok images of public man: a comparison. In L.L. Langness and T. Hays (eds) *Anthropology in the high valleys.* Novato: Chandler and Sharp Publications Inc.

Wagner, R. 1991. The fractal person. In M. Godelier and M. Strathern (eds) *Big men great men: personifications of power in Melanesia.* Cambridge: Cambridge University Press.

Wagner, R. 2001. *Anthropology of the subject: holographic worldview in New Guinea and its meaning and significance for the world of anthropology.* Berkeley: University of California Press.

Wagner, R. 2006. Aesthetic technology and the golden moment: the pragmatic counteragency of the Massim canoe prow board. Unpublished lecture presented at the British Museum, London.

Wassmann, J. 1990. The Nyaura concepts of space and time. In N. Lutkehaus, C. Kaufmann, W.E. Mitchell, D. Newton, L. Osmundsen and M. Schuster (eds) *Sepik heritage: tradition and change in PNG.* Durham, NC: Carolina Academic Press.

Wassmann, J. 1991. *Song to the flying fox.* Port Moresby: National Research Institute.

Weiner, A. 1992. *Inalienable possessions: the paradox of keeping while giving.* Berkeley: University of California Press.

Weiner, J. 1988. *Heart of the pearl shell: mythological dimensions of Foi sociality.* Berkeley: University of California Press.

Weiner, J. 1991. *The empty place: poetry, space and being among the Foi of Papua New Guinea.* Bloomington: Indiana University Press.

Weiner, J. 1993. Anthropology contra Heidegger, II: the limit of relationship. *Critique of Anthropology* 13: 285–301.

Weiner, J. 1997. Televisualist anthropology: representation, aesthetics, politics [and comments and reply]. *Current Anthropology* 38(2): 199–235.

Weiner, J. 1999. Psychonanalysis and anthropology: on the temporality of analysis. In H. Moore (ed.) *Anthropological theory today.* London: Polity Press.

Weiner, J. 2001. *Tree leaf talk: a Heideggerian anthropology.* Oxford: Berg.

Wilden, A. 1971. *System and structure: essays in communication and exchange.* London: Tavistock Publication.

Index